PEOPLE'S SPACES

Who controls space? Powerful corporations, institutions, and individuals have great power to create physical and political space through income and influence. *People's Spaces* attempts to understand the struggle between people and institutions in the spaces they make.

Current literature on cities and planning often looks at popular resistance to institutional authority through open, mass-movement protest. These views overlook the fact that subaltern classes are not often afforded the luxury of open, organized political protest. *People's Spaces* investigates individuals' diverse approaches in reconciling the difference between their spatial needs and spatial availability. Through case studies in Southeast Asia, India, Nepal, and Central Asia, the book explores how people accommodate their spatial needs for everyday activities and cultural practices within a larger abstract spatial context produced by the power-holders.

Nihal Perera is Professor of Urban Planning at Ball State University and Director of CapAsia. He has taught in China, Germany, India, Italy, and Sri Lanka. The two-time Fulbright Scholar was also Senior Research Fellow at the National University of Singapore. His publications include *Decolonizing Ceylon* and *Transforming Asian Cities*.

"That the making of urban space and life is largely located in the systematic, impetuous, and equivocal efforts of the majority of a city's inhabitants, and which persist in spite of the impositions and destructions of both well-known and unfamiliar forces, remains an interminable reality and conundrum. For the ordinary contributions of this majority are undervalued to the extent of being rendered invisible or irrelevant. But by offering a sweeping historical account across varied Asian contexts and circumstances—particularly that of his war-torn homeland—Perera restores the breadth of the creation, adjustments and intersections at work in how such contributions confront all kinds of disasters, dispossessions, and potentials as a vital common sense. There is no book I know that so clearly renders apparently shrinking horizons into testaments of uneasy endurance".

AbdouMaliq Simone, *Research Professor, Max Planck Institute for the Study of Religious and Ethnic Diversity*

PEOPLE'S SPACES

Coping, Familiarizing, Creating

Nihal Perera

Routledge
Taylor & Francis Group

NEW YORK AND LONDON

First published 2016
by Routledge
711 Third Avenue, New York, NY 10017

and by Routledge
2 Park Square, Milton Park, Abingdon, Oxon OX14 4RN

Routledge is an imprint of the Taylor & Francis Group, an informa business

© 2016 Taylor & Francis

Library of Congress Cataloging in Publication Data
Perera, Nihal.
People's spaces : coping, familiarizing, creating / Nihal Perera.
   pages cm
   Includes index.
   1. Social ecology–Developing countries. 2. Spatial behavior–Developing countries. 3. Human settlements–Developing countries. 4. Cultural geography–Developing countries. I. Title.
   HM861.P47 2016
   304.2–dc23   2015019629

ISBN: 978-0-415-72028-1 (hbk)
ISBN: 978-0-415-72029-8 (pbk)
ISBN: 978-1-315-86706-9 (ebk)

Typeset in Bembo
by Wearset Ltd, Boldon, Tyne and Wear

Printed and bound in the United States of America by Publishers Graphics, LLC on sustainably sourced paper.

To
Nelanka, Sohith, Dharini
and
ordinary people whose stories contributed to the findings

CONTENTS

ILLUSTRATIONS

Figures

Table

ACKNOWLEDGMENTS

Nihal Perera

This was a large-scale, long-term project with many roots, originating at different times and places in my life, as well as the lives of co-authors of chapters. Unfortunately, they cannot all be acknowledged here. I wish to begin by thanking Lily Kong at whose invitation I wrote my first article from a "people's perspective" (Perera 2002). Kong's encouragement has been immense.

I must thank my closest collaborators who co-authored particular chapters in this volume: Sanjeewani Habarakada, Gaurab Kc, Nirmani Liyanage, Sweata Pradhan, and Hikoyat Salimova. They not only inspired me to continue this project from their school days, but also their close connections with the places we investigated enabled us to deeply connect with the people who shared aspects of their spatial stories in this volume. Their diverse interests, different insights, and the various localities they come from served well to broaden and diversify the scope of this work. I was fortunate to catch them before their unruliness was trimmed by mainstream education; they not only engaged with their hearts, but also never stopped questioning. Many discussions with them evoked a variety of concepts, languages, and perspectives. Without them, this book would not have this quality.

My Fulbright Scholar award in Hong Kong, during which time I focused on the precursor project: *Transforming Asian Cities* (Perera and Tang 2013), helped lay a framework for this volume and test some of the ideas and hypotheses. Many initial ideas were developed in the critical environment of Hong Kong Baptist University's human geography program led by Wing-Shing Tang. He helped me see a people's Hong Kong where people resist and negotiate redevelopment projects which largely define mainstream Hong Kong.

Being a senior visiting research fellow at the Asia Research Institute of the National University of Singapore immensely helped me to fine-tune my arguments for *Transforming Asian Cities* and this volume and to develop confidence to do this project. The Asia Research Institute led by Kong was the most grounded institution of scholarly exchange on topics pertaining to Asia that I have experienced. Although there is so much that we do not know about Asia, the environment of the Institute enabled me to discuss, test, and become comfortable with the arguments that I was developing. While discussions with Song Ping and Goh Beng-Lan contributed to the development of many ideas, brief meetings with Prasenjit Duara gave me self-assurance. The wide range of scholars and practitioners who attended conferences organized by Tim Bunnell helped me further ground myself in Asia.

The CapAsia (CapAsia.iweb.bsu.edu) immersive semester in Asia that I created and direct was a major help in many ways. First, it enabled me to immerse myself in communities for a semester every other year and live with different people, sharing time and space, and getting a sense of how ordinary people create space. Second, its learning-by-doing method enabled me to complement the inquiry driven by the critical question "why?" with the creative question, "why not?" Third, the students always deeply connected with local people and made observations that I would not have been able to make by myself. The field studies were the point of departure for the Kalametiya and Dharavi chapters and for many ideas I further developed in this volume.

Many of the research questions and ideas which connected theory and practice were developed over multiple cups of coffee and various field trips with Wes Janz and Olon Dotson. Amit Baishya, Jeff Brackett, Jennifer Erickson, Melinda Messineo, and Eva Zygmunt inspired many questions and thoughts. Ball State's ASPiRE grant enabled me to devote the last summer to the book. I thank Guillermo Vasquez de Velasco, Dean of the College of Architecture and Planning, and Michael Burayidi, Chair of the Department of Urban Planning, for their best possible support.

I also wish to thank Jamal Ansari, James Duncan, Kristi Koriath, Paul Mitchell, Lawrence Vale, and Immanuel Wallerstein, who have been in the background supporting my scholarly work and/or grant applications in various forms. Intellectually, it largely boils down to the doors that Anthony King opened for me.

When I was very young and scientific as I should be, it was Padmakumara Navaratne who asked me the simple question of whether I believe in objective truth. Charles Small used to brush aside some of my points by simply calling them my interpretations. I am glad they asked these questions and that my scientific mind did not dispose of them. The brilliance of contemporary scholars like Will Golver, Jyoti Hosagrahar, Jane Jacobs, Tariq Jazeel, Abidin Kusno, Anoma Pieris, Sasanka Perera, Libby Porter, Sanjeev Vidyarthi, Wang Di, Brenda Yeoh, and Oren Yiftachel has been intimidating, challenging, and enormously encouraging. I thank the anonymous reviewers who commented on earlier versions of particular chapters.

My thinking was grounded and inspired by very ordinary people like local residents and community leaders of Styakali, a self-built community in Bhubaneswar; Soyam Prava Sahoo, who fights for the rights of the community; and Dakxin Chhara and Roxy Gagdekar, who fight against discrimination for social acceptance and dignity of the Chharas. These activists are complemented by the grounded intellectuals I met. Ganesh Devy not only gave up his professorship to work with the men and women who are labelled tribal people in India, but he also listened to them for three years before teaching them.

Countless local residents helped our field research, and it is ironic that we cannot acknowledge all in this volume about them. This itself highlights the issue that we (including the co-authors of chapters) deal with in this volume. Although the number may be too high, we thank everyone who featured in this volume, who tirelessly exposed their spaces for us to make sense of, and who shared their stories. We want to acknowledge at least a few key people who helped: Praneeth Amaratunga, Professor Balasubramanium, Shanthini Balasubramanium, Gopalakishnan Kalaeswaran, and Mohamed Yehiya.

The production of the final manuscript was a grind. Pradeep Dissanayake made a few suggestions, including the idea of a cartoon; Hasantha Wijenayake drew a cartoon characterization of Moratumulla Handiya (Chapter 10). In the middle of all other responsibilities, Jeffrey Lauer and Christine Rhine tirelessly edited, proofread, and made valuable comments. I appreciate the help of Kaushalya Herath who prepared the maps and the index at the last moment. It was Nirmani Liyanage who filled all other gaps, including the preparation of illustrations and the bibliography to complete the book. They treated the manuscript like their own. I am very grateful to them.

I wish to acknowledge the support of my wife Karuna, who has been patiently tolerating my devotion to this project, taking care of other aspects of life.

I dedicate this volume to Nelanka, Sohith, and Dharini, who constantly reminded me of people's spaces, particularly of hidden transcripts, the use of the weapons of the weak, and negotiations, right at home. They made me live what I write. I am so grateful to them.

References

Perera, N. (2002) "Indigenising the Colonial City: Late 19th-century Colombo and its landscape," in L. Kong and L. Law (eds.) *Urban Studies* 39: 1703–21.

Perera, N. and Tang W.S. (2013) *Transforming Asian Cities: Intellectual impasse, Asianizing space, and emerging translocalities*, New York: Routledge.

INTRODUCTION

Seeing and Engaging People's Spaces: Deprivations and Challenges

Development, policy, planning, and governance are all directed at the public and claim to serve the public health, safety, and welfare. Yet, in these discourses, people largely appear in the form of bodies and abstract categories such as populations, publics, and the civil society represented through impersonal means such as statistics, maps, and ideologies. Questioning top-down approaches to housing, planning, and development, scholars and professionals have argued for grounded, bottom-up, community-based, and advocacy approaches. Yet our knowledge of the spaces ordinary people produce for and through their everyday activities and cultural practices is minimal. In Abdou Maliq Simone's (2010a: 285) words, there has been a lack of attention paid to "the continued small and medium-level developments of residential and commercial districts ... within cities for a long time." This volume focuses on the spaces of ordinary people.

Leading scholars of social space such as Henri Lefebvre (1991) and David Harvey (1973) have introduced us to a whole range of social spaces. Still the scholarly attention is almost exclusively devoted to absolute and abstract spaces: the "raw" physical space that is "out there" and the spatial structures produced by dominant social actors. A large majority of urban and spatial scholars—many implicitly—base their work on the belief that they have direct cognitive access to absolute space, i.e., "raw" physical space prior to definition, classification, and categorization into rivers, valleys, and built elements. In regard to socially produced spaces, literature largely focuses on abstract spaces, particularly the forms, structures, and processes established by dominant actors such as the state, corporations (companies), and the wealthy who hold power to both shape and erase spaces and histories of others.

As the holder of formal political power to regulate activities and the physical environment, the state is the main producer of abstract space. Through programs, plans, laws, policies, and policing, states create, restructure, define, and organize space at neighborhood, urban, regional, and national scales. Standardization is a key feature of statecraft (Scott 1998). According to Richard Sennett (1992), the ordered and standardized urban-form is mainly constituted of business-enterprise ideology, particularly the commodification of land and buildings. One of the main instruments,

> [the] grid iron creates regular lots and blocks that are ideal for buying and selling.... They are abstract units detached from any ecological or topographical reality. They resemble a kind of currency which is endlessly amenable to aggregation and fragmentation.
>
> *(Scott 1998: 58)*

Anthony King (1976, 1990) has convincingly argued that the vehicle for shaping such abstract environments outside of Western Europe was colonialism. In regard to White settler colonies such as the USA and Australia, Libby Porter (2010: 52) confirms that the "modern form of controlling and regulating space and population—the production of . . . 'abstract space'—[is] influenced by colonial processes." I shall use "Modern" for Western Modern.

In the process, "man's mastery over nature" is established by removing inconvenient parts of the urban form to create a workable landscape (Sennett 1992: 55). The commodification of land created the biggest abstract space. It separated nature and people: "'nature' is . . . where people are not . . . [; the] raw, untouched, primeval nature that the colonists and their descendants see outside the lands that are settled and 'in use'." (Porter 2010: 77). Donna Haraway (1991) demonstrates that nature known through (Western) science is a cultural artifact constituted through both the practices and technologies of scientific research and the language used to describe and explain scientific findings. Projecting the idea of absolute space on "nature" and making it "pure," the colonial/Modern ideology erases the human intervention. Abstract space is thus alienated from nature and people, making both invisible, and creating an "objective" place for abstract space between these. This is further reinforced by the separation of nature and culture (see Haraway 1991; Rose 1993). Moreover, in the process, the (Western) culture and politics of this construction are also rendered invisible.

This power of the state is not total: Powerful and wealthy corporations, institutions, and individuals also have substantial discretion in making locational decisions. They acquire the most desirable locations for their living and activities mainly through market mechanisms, but also use both formal mechanisms including zoning variations and litigation and informal mechanisms such as lobbying (see Birch 2005). When exerted, their decisions restrict the choices of others, creating spatial structures organized through wealth and class (Harvey 1973). Those with less economic and social power are thus deprived of otherwise more suitable and desirable locations for habitation and are obliged to inhabit not-so-suitable to high-risk areas. In this spatial structure, the least powerful—or the leftover people, in Wes Janz's (2013) words—settle in "leftover" areas such as unsupervised government land and/or canal, road, and railway reservations.

Post-Katrina New Orleans presented a compelling representation of this spatial structure. While the Ninth and Lower-Ninth wards were devastated, the Garden District was hardly touched by the hurricane of 2005. The upper classes had reduced their vulnerability to natural disasters by locating themselves on the high ground of the Garden District. When the levees breached, the poorer people who located themselves right below the levee were washed away. The post-hurricane landscape thus looked as if nature discriminated against the African-Americans and the poor.

Despite the stronger control they enjoy, capital and the state are not the sole producers of space nor are the abstract spaces total and complete. In Africa, as Simone (2008: 103) highlights, state administrations and civil institutions have lacked the political and economic power to assign buying, selling, exchanging, collecting, disassembling, stalling, importing, fabricating, and residing to specific bounded spaces of deployment, codes of articulation, or the purview of designated actors. As I have demonstrated elsewhere, the Chandigarh, Kotte, and Mahaweli projects are neither ideal nor successful in producing complete abstract spaces (Perera 2005a; 2005b; 2010). Moreover, the occupation of (abstract) space itself disrupts the imposed order. Internal contradictions and the incompleteness of abstract space are largely overlooked in academic work.

This volume delves into the realm of "people's spaces": the production of lived spaces by those who do not have the power to produce abstract spaces and erase other spaces. As demonstrated in the following chapters, ordinary people do not passively submit themselves to abstract spaces and constituent social orders. As people use their own imaginations in occupying space, the subjects transform the provided and/or assigned spaces—and their subjectivities—into something meaningful to them.

The creation of lived spaces is evident in self-established settlements inhabited by a majority of people in most cities of the "global south" (Neuwirth 2005; Roy 2005; Sharma 2000). Informality is usually equated with poverty and poor housing conditions (see Mukhija and Loukaitou-Sideris 2014). Rahul Mehrotra (2008), who views the city in terms of static and kinetic physicalities, sees the latter carrying local wisdom into the contemporary world without the fear of the Modern represented in the static environment (i.e., architecture for him). The formal authorities and communities also use temporary structures to modify the static environment to support various religious festivities and national day celebrations.

The influence of particular individuals, social groups, and cultural and/or business institutions on space goes far beyond the immediate environment; they have varying impacts on the spatial organization of their neighborhoods and the larger society, even the nation (Chapters 7–10). The political authoritarianism of China is often considered national, total, and comprehensive. Yet Sonia Schoon (2013) provides meticulous accounts of how local leaders, especially the ones with charisma, create niche authorities for themselves; through negotiation with the governments and the local populace, they use this power to direct aspects of urban renewal.

Culture is as important as power and the economy to understand resistance and the spaces of the weak. While the British ruled Kowloon, Hong Kong, its inhabitants lived in Jiulong, defined by the nine dragons who came from the mountains. The British could never familiarize the local space because it is still illegible. This not only highlights the separation between the British and the Hongkongnese, but also the fact that the area was a distinct place for each group precisely because of the cultural difference. Space is largely cultural. Culture is an enormous resource for the weak that the powerful and the scholars and professional whose studies are validated by their significance for the power, policy making, and market activity have neither been able to read nor penetrate (Chapter 7).

The cultural complexity of contemporary space is well highlighted in Huey-Jiun Wang's (2013) account of the transformation of the 406 Plaza in Taipei from a Japanese Hongwanji (Buddhist) temple to a self-built settlement and, recently, to a multicultural plaza. The approach of government and business leaders to redevelop the district—and surrounding districts—was urban renewal: i.e., to remove the poor from the site and use it for "economic growth." The inhabitants, however, displaced this neoliberal attempt. During protests against the gentrification of the site and the district, the inhabitants turned the media coverage into a platform to convey their stories, emotionally relating themselves to, and effectively drawing the audience to, people and memories, displacing the centrality of land value and capital accumulation. The city finally built a cultural plaza, highlighting the diverse histories of those who inhabited the site since its Japanese appropriation.

Yet we know very little about these basic and widespread space-making processes and spaces produced by ordinary people (Perera 2009a). There is very little attention paid in literature to spaces which the majority of people aspire to create, the paths people take, and the strategies and tactics they employ to get there. As argued by Perera and Tang (2013) in regard to Asian cities, the knowledge produced in Western academia is largely limited to the high-end, low-end, and traditional, the reference of which is the modern and developed Western city. This leaves out most of the city occupied and used by ordinary people, including a large segment of the middle class.

The focus on abstract space is not limited to its admirers. A large majority of opponents share a common ground: They focus on the spaces of power, wealth, and their creators, but (critically) view these as oppressive and exploitative. In this oppositional structure, the "system" is seen as total and its subjects as victims. How the subjects react and respond to imposed spaces falls off the intellectual radar.[1] These subjects are the focus of this volume.

People's Spaces is an exploration into the realm of ordinary people to explore spatial stories revealed beside, between, and in the interstices of the hegemonic social and spatial structures. Instead of docile bodies, or *victims* of abstract space, it views the subjects as *survivors* of war, tsunami, colonialism, and patriarchy. Following the spatial stories of *survivors*, the volume investigates how they continue their journeys from the point of victimization, through coping, recovery, and resisting social and spatial impositions. It looks beyond survival strategies adopted by victims into the negotiation of space for daily activities and cultural practices carried out by survivors, somewhat on their own terms.

This book highlights people's ways of becoming persons through negotiating subjectivities and spaces for better lives, using ordinary weapons and the spaces they produce, beginning from the particular predicaments and spaces in which they live. Negotiation refers to people trying to change the social and spatial assignments they are obliged to inhabit, beginning with finding basic ways to occupy the same.

The Knowledge Gap

Seeing and understanding urbanisms, particularly residual and emerging spaces and the transformative practices of ordinary people, is a dramatically different exercise than collecting new data within existing intellectual or theoretical paradigms. The latter does not contribute to theoretical or methodological breakthroughs. It is clear that we cannot capture the complexity of people's spaces, nor their production processes, within existing vocabularies and frameworks.

Mainstream research on social space falls short on two important counts: first, to develop a substantive knowledge about the spaces of ordinary people and, second, to interrogate researchers' own culturally influenced positions. Ordinary people's views, particularly their aspirations and the spaces they produce, cannot be substantively understood through Westernized and/or middle-class frameworks and perspectives. Local knowledge is different and more diverse than the formal. There is hardly any evidence to say that ordinary people see the world in terms of pure and complete categories, opposites, hierarchies, revolutions, and similar intellectual tools employed by academics and professionals. Lea Jellinek (in Dick 2003) observes that *kampung* (urban village) dwellers in Indonesia do not see poverty and prosperity as opposites, but as alternating conditions, nor do they see globalization as inevitable or desirable. In a broader sense, they have a tendency to see multiple realities.

Yet the perceptions, perspectives, and worldviews of the weak are hardly accepted by academics and professionals as tools for understanding, analyzing, explaining, and interpreting the spaces created by the very same people. They are subalterns: people without voice who are subjected to domination without hegemony (see Guha 1998).

When observers make sense of ordinary spaces by contorting observations to fit within mainstream frameworks, such interpretations marginalize and transform the spaces and activities of the producers and users. As spaces are simplified, abstracted, and adapted within bureaucrats' and professionals' categories, technical language, and worldviews, they become data within planners', policy makers', and urban scholars' intellectual frameworks. Most crucially, lived spaces enter mainstream literature as the low-end, as the spatial other, under categories such as the slum, the informal, the organic, and/or vernacular that are largely viewed as the "other" of Western(ized) middle-class spaces (Perera and Tang 2013; Simone 2010a). The recently reinvigorated discourses have not posed any substantive challenge to this positioning (Roy and AlSayad 2004; Robinson 2006; Roy 2005).

Second, while most leading scholars of social space are explicit about their intellectual frameworks, they have failed to turn the critical lens on their own work and interrogate researchers' own culturally influenced positions. Social space is central to the ordering of society, whether it is colonial, modern, or traditional (Lefebvre 1991; Harvey 1973; Holston 1989). Lefebvre stresses that social transformations are less substantive, less effective and, in many instances, impossible without corresponding spatial transformations. Harvey (1990: 419) argues that "the assignment of place within a socio-spatial structure indicates distinctive roles, capacities for action, and access to power within the social order." The designation of subject positions is evident in the molding of the subjected body with regard to race, class, gender, and other socially constructed categories. Despite the great contribution they make, these discourses and the recent critiques of neoliberalism refer to abstract spaces of the powerful. They further victimize the subjects.

To be fair, cultural practices developed outside of the Western and Westernized middle-class domains are hardly self-evident to scholars trained in the Western academy, whether in the West or elsewhere. This bias is built into our research. The most acceptable validation of a research project is its contribution to state policy. The recent globalization discourses, as Ravi Sundaram (2010: 97) observes, tend to focus on the state and its regulatory regime as a major reference point. Despite great progress shown in the past few decades, mainstream analytical tools do not provide much access to the realities of lower classes, marginalized communities, and Others.

This structural condition became evident to me when scholars and educators kept telling me that (1) everyone knows individuals change given spaces and (2) talking about these spatial changes does not contribute to policy. Hence, why bother to conduct research? The highly reputed scholars hardly said the same about the circuits of capital, the production and distribution of goods and services, or the real-estate markets, which are much better known. Not only the statist and the capital-centered scholarship is unable to see significance in people's spaces; this taken-for-granted view of people's spatial processes is both ignorant and oppressive. This reminds me of Anthony Giddens' (1986: xxii) observation: "The comfort of established views can easily be a cover for intellectual sloth." They miss an opportunity to validate and engage the experience of ordinary people.

Postcoloniality combines both colonial and local knowledges and blurs much of the West/non-West separation; similarly, local actors combine formal and local knowledges. These do not dissolve the difference contained in distinct ways of understanding. In Andreas Huyssen's (2008: 2) words: "as citizens of the Western academy and critics of the neoliberal triumphalism of globalization, we often do not know enough about deep histories and current developments of urban areas elsewhere in the world."

This (inadvertent) ignorance is much stronger among academics and professionals in the non-West (Perera and Tang 2013; Simone 2008; 2010a; 2010b). An architect or a policy maker in Colombo—about 150 km away—can be as far from Hambantota as one in Chicago (Chapter 6). Many professors in leading schools of planning in Asia hardly know the most discriminated people in their own cities, like the Chharas in Ahmedabad (India) or the inhabitants of Wedding Card (Li Tung) Street in Hong Kong.

The West- and upper-class centeredness and the othering of the rest continue to linger in scholarship. De Certeau (1984) observes that social theory often replicates the epistemological vision of the powerful. This contextualization, what Gayatri Chakravorty Spivak (1999) calls the "worlding," within the dominant (colonial) world, subjects the powerless to the episteme of the power-holders. Besides being marginalized, the weak are thus subjected to formal (bourgeois) views of acceptability, progress, and development through the acts of abstraction, categorization, and assimilation. Instead of acknowledging people's practices on their own terms, the people are largely met with epistemic, cultural, and institutional violence. Even when the Others are appreciated, they belong in museums, festivals, and restaurants. It is highly significant that we examine the subjective investments of Western and Westernized scholars in the narratives they produce and the historical institutionalization of their own subject positions (Spivak 1994; Jacobs 1996; Porter 2010; Said 2004).

Main Impediments

An inquiry into people's spaces calls for intellectual frameworks that enable us to see people's spaces from the spaces of their production and interpret the observations in ways that acknowledge and engage the producers' and users' perspectives (Perera, 2009a). Even to see local practices for what they are, we need a language, i.e., an instrument of mediation, between the consciousness and the world that consciousness inhabits. The acknowledgment of people's spaces requires the "validation" of such spaces within the researcher's discourse, neither marginalizing nor fully absorbing the observations into the researcher's framework.

Scholars' own approaches may be the biggest impediment. Hayden White (1987: 125–6, in Spivak 1999: 203) makes the following observation in regard to historians:

> [The message] has not yet reached the historians buried in the archives hoping, by what they call a "sifting of the facts" or "the manipulation of data," to find the form of the reality that will serve the object of representation in the account that they will write "when all the facts are known" and they have finally "got the story straight."

That the "proper" method will bring correct results and that the real world can be known this way is a faith shared among theory-driven, data-hungry, serial-thinking social scientists, planners, and policy makers (see Hamdi 2004). The intellectual engagement with people's spaces makes us question our own approaches, frameworks, and worldviews (see Porter 2010; Sandercock 2005; Spivak 1999). Learning about people's spaces is a careful project of unlearning, considering our privilege as our loss (see Spivak 1999: 9), and paying attention to interpretation in knowledge production.

Although there is only so much we can know about others' spaces and processes, four tools are vital: the scope/focus, the analytical frameworks, the vantage point/s of inquiry, and the methodology. Attending to these factors may not be sufficient, but it is necessary to establish an effective intellectual framework as a point of departure.[2]

The *scope and focus* of scholarly investigations contribute to the lack of understanding about how ordinary people create their spaces. Ordinary place-making is not easily detected. As scholars and professionals explore and investigate cities and neighborhoods, they focus their attention on the most pertinent areas, objects, and/ or issues from the standpoint of the project. The drawing of these boundaries creates an inside and an outside, centralizes, privileges, and valorizes select actors, structures, and processes, and marginalizes others, constructing social power and producing political implications.

A large majority of research projects on social space adopt a problem-oriented (Western-scientific) approach in which the problem and the hypothesis guide the confines and the direction of research. The research focus and the scope guarantee that the well-disciplined and focused researcher will not find something outside of these; any such finding has to go back through the same assembly line of hypothesis testing which will sanitize, discipline, and contextualize the outcomes. In this, the world is thoroughly known and reconstituted within the Western Enlightenment worldview.

The data source is an issue: Ordinary people prefer to stay out of the police station, government offices, archives, revenue department, and other formal institutions. They have agency; they evaluate the purpose of data before volunteering to any researcher, including myself. James Scott (in Holtzman and Hughes 2010: np) observes, in regard to peasants, that there is a "collective conspiracy" of silence that relies on tacit cooperation and shared norms and values:

> [W]hen you find the peasants in the archives, it means that something has gone terribly wrong.... Their resistance is more like a desertion than a mutiny, which is a public confrontation with political power. It's the difference between squatting and a public land invasion with banners.

How most people struggle over property, work, the day, and space lies beyond the realm of formal politics.

Observing how people struggle over and create their own spaces requires us to pay attention to people's politics, or what Scott (1985; 1990) calls infrapolitics. Based on his studies in Sedaka village in Malaysia, Scott (2005: 71–2) defines infrapolitics as the strategic form of resistance that "subjects must assume under conditions of great peril." In this, "all political action takes forms that are designed to obscure their intentions or to take cover behind an apparent meaning" (ibid.). Explained through the metaphor of a drama and public and hidden transcripts, he employs stage and backstage activities to reveal that the subordinates in large structures of domination have a fairly extensive social existence outside the immediate control of the dominant. The interactions between these two transcripts explain how domination shapes the form and content of what is hidden and how the hidden transcript occasionally insinuates itself—disguised—into the public transcript (ibid.). This resistance carried out through tactics more than strategies (De Certeau 1984) is not clearly evident to the dominant; it has a sense of moving away.

The problems legible to academics and professionals, such as lack of housing (Chapter 5) and living in a slum (Chapter 7), are developed within mainstream understandings and require formal solutions. The absence of solutions is precisely why some problems persist. Addressing problems for which there are no formal solutions requires different conceptualizations. As evident in the following chapters, the disadvantaged create discourses and solutions that are different than mainstream understandings. They lay outside of mainstream intellectual boundaries, and we need to make an effort to see and acknowledge them.

Excluding, marginalizing, and/or trivializing people's spaces is an ordinary act built into "ordinary" research. It is so hegemonic, it seems natural. Focusing on the high-end, low-end, and the traditional, as argued by Perera and Tang (2013), the researchers have left a gaping hole in our understanding of contemporary Asian cities. What is missing is the ordinary city. In Israel, Scott Bollens (2005) demonstrates how planners and policy makers largely dismiss "low-politics" of subjects as unimportant compared to "high-politics" of authorities that is about power and economics. Policy makers, development practitioners, and planners have a way of focusing on growth and being silent about important tensions emanating from ethnic, religious, and other cultural differences by portraying these as "low-politics."

The planners and policy makers thus hop back into their technically rational pods which are safe from such social and cultural issues, convictions, and emotions. This creates a power structure, separating mainstream policy, planning, and scholarship from volatile issues central to everyday life. The official story of planning, argues Leonie Sandercock (2005), portrays the profession as a heroic pursuit leaving out gender, class, race, and cultural biases, and by implication, serving as an agent of social control that regulates bodies in space. The mainstream story—similar across most professions—is partial, has huge gaps, and marginalizes the spaces and space-making processes of ordinary people.

The issue of exclusion through scoping is not new: Cultural-studies scholars have highlighted aspects of it. To find people's spaces, the researcher should include these within the scope of research and make an effort to look for them. In regard to planning, this is precisely what Sandercock (1998) attempts in her *Making the Invisible Visible*. The notions such as third culture (King 1976), hybridity (Bhabha 1994; Haraway 1991), and third space (Bhabha 1994; Soja 1996) represent scholarly attempts to acknowledge spaces that lay outside formal dualities. Transcending extant intellectual limitations requires scholars to pay attention to the complex and dynamic space-making activities carried out by ordinary people.

There is a danger of predetermining, or falling prey, to the same processes questioned here: the researcher simply finding what s/he is looking for, overlooking and marginalizing others. Success may also encourage the researcher to romanticize the other, aestheticize poverty, and/or to disregard power structures (voluntarism, in structuralist vocabulary). Such exoticizing of people's spaces strips away the agency of the subjects and blocks our ability to view their social and cultural processes as serious and sophisticated versions of human experience. In short, finding people's spaces requires the researcher to exercise some freedom and search below, beside, beyond, between, and in the margins and cracks of these abstract spaces.

As evident in all chapters, most of the spaces produced by weaker subjects are illegible for authorities, professionals, and academics. Place-making at the margins remains, according to Nabil Kamel (2014: 133), "ad hoc, disjointed, and with limited linkages to other practices," i.e., according a formal view. This makes "it difficult [for the scholar and practitioner] to perceive their production as a collective social movement in the conventional sense" (ibid.). This relates to the second tool: the *intellectual frameworks* which include concepts, theories, and heuristic tools. It is the researchers' frameworks that defy them the ability to recognize people's spaces. These have escaped the intellectual detection of scholars of social space at large, including Lefebvre and Harvey, who focus on abstract spaces.[3]

It is not the lack of theories that has transformed the weak into the Other and subjected them to epistemic violence, but the particular theories themselves. Urban and spatial studies have undergone many changes from the Chicago School to New York to Los Angeles; influenced by urban political-economy, colonial urbanism, and landscape interpretation; and taken various turns such as the statistical turn and the cultural turn. Leading scholars in this rich field are intellectually well equipped: They use sophisticated theories, concepts, methodologies, question significant aspects of globalization, neoliberalism, and social (spatial) justice, use Marxist, feminist, and other sophisticated theories, and reveal much about class, gender, and other social structures and issues. This volume critically builds on these intellectual developments.

Although related, people's spaces is a different story. Perera and Tang (2013) point to the absence of knowledge of ordinary spaces in Asian cities. In regard to Africa and Southeast Asia, Simone (2010b) highlights that the realities of cities have largely been peripheral to the process in which theories about cities and urban policies are made. Theories and approaches both stereotype, condition, and transform spaces (ground conditions): Sometimes entire districts are stigmatized, based on the form of housing, the particular kind of inhabitants, the ways they earn their living, and the lack of high-tech facilities (Simone 2010b). Garth Myers (2011) confirms the lack of understanding of African cities.

Abstraction is a crucial step in conventional theorization, but it removes local realities. Theories, according to James Roseneau and Mary Durfee (1999: 3), impel us "to treat any observation ... as partly a product of our premises about the way things work." In regard to understanding the Asian city, Perera and Tang (2013) question the use of abstract categories applicable to any city. Such "Theories" become useless to understanding local realities. In regard to East-Asian geo-graphy, Wing Shing Tang and Fujio Mizuoka (2010: 3) are frustrated that theoretical frames discard local realities as peculiarities undeserving of attention.

Despite all authenticity, reveals Ranajit Guha (2000: 37), a document (evidence) needs to fulfill an important condition: the contextuality. The production of meaning is carried out by scholars selecting observations (overlooking others), locating these within larger instances, experiences, and contexts, and explaining the observations in relation to these contexts, especially structures, processes, and conjunctures. In regard to space, the renowned Jane Jacobs (1972) notes how the instincts of the planner she met made him feel that the North End of Boston is a good place to live, but his professional training informed him that it is a bad place in need of urban renewal. He was unable to see the North End for what it is, instead projecting his abstraction and transforming it into a "slum."

The questioning of contextualization of evidence within larger structures and processes is at the base of Guha's (1998) work and the subsequent development of subaltern studies. He brilliantly demonstrates how mainstream historiographies of India conveniently suppressed, marginalized, and/or ignored peasant struggles. The meanings of historical struggles are largely predetermined, and, within Indian historiography, the peasant struggles had been classified as "petty struggles" and "prepolitical" because these did not have the potential to be explained as part of already mapped-out historical social movements such as nationalist struggles or proletarian revolutions. Scholars of social space, too, employ their own contexts such as city, urban, and rural. Planners make comprehensive plans. It is hard to acknowledge local contexts which are more sensitive to small changes in time and space than these large narratives.

These larger constellations of meanings provide two main options for local and current (here and now) information: Either get appropriated, or get marginalized. Local knowledge is both appropriated and expropriated in the production of mainstream knowledge. According to Roseneau and Durfee (1999: 6), "A thoroughgoing paradigm closes off the anomalies by resorting to deeper explanations that bring the exceptions within the scope of its central tendencies." The data with the potential to be compatible within the analytical framework are appropriated, and anomalies are turned redundant. In both cases, the "theoretical" possibilities of evidence, events, and instances are expropriated and turned into data within "larger instances." In this, localities are abstracted into data within larger theories and structures.

Yet theories are also time and space specific; they are largely universalized versions of Western experience or the West's interpretation of the world. In this, even non-Western worldviews such as Confucianism, astrology, and Ayurveda have become data. The universalization and application of theories built in the West have locked, blocked, and framed out other specificities (see Laclau and Mouffe 2001). Robert Beauregard (2011: 199) questions such universal claims in urban theory:

> I am skeptical of [Chicago, Los Angeles, and New York] city-based urban theories. . . . They are theoretically problematic: flirting with a fictional radical uniqueness, embracing an unreflective naturalism, undermining inclusivity, distorting space and place, and abetting an uncritical theoretical pluralism

even as they resist it. Too many different types of cities are omitted from such formulations.... These theories have emerged from the largest cities [of the USA] and some of the country's major academic institutions. [They] reinforce ... hierarchical and elitist tendencies. Like theories of globalization that draw knowledge and perspective from the global north, such theories narrow rather than expand our vision.

The result is the lack of grounded theoretical understanding of local transformations. Despite their pretensions to comprehensiveness and universality, the extant theories have largely failed to observe the production, reproduction, negotiation, and transformation of space by ordinary citizens and institutions. Diganta Das (2013) observes the documentation and analysis of various urban aspects from the development of megaprojects to issues of political economy, urban aspiration, inequality, fragmentation, livability, and sustainability (Bunnell and Miller 2011; Gillen 2010; Moser 2010; Douglass *et al.* 2008; Shatkin 2007, 2008; Dittrich, 2007). Yet the large majority of literature—he observes—has given very little attention to human subjects and their everyday experiences. When locals are acknowledged, the focus is on the body, hardly the self.

The "Other-ing" of particular peoples has been discussed in a number of disciplines. Johannes Fabian's (1983, 1990, 2006) brilliant critique reveals how anthropologists have traditionally produced their subjects by locating people in different times: in some primitive world in the past. While scholars are more sensitive to this refusal to share the same time, what Fabian calls coevalness, the location of people in other spaces such as the "slum" or the "underdeveloped" world—now the "global south"—is still prevalent in spatial studies.

Despite their abstractness, theories are produced in real places, within specific cultures, to understand specific phenomena through theorizing these. Social theory has different meanings in different contexts. When imposed from outside, the theories transform local realities, suppressing and devaluing intellectual tools that are more pertinent to understand specific locales. Robert Neuwirth (2005), for example, lived in what he calls *shadow cities* and observed that more brickwork and concrete is laid by the inhabitants of these than all the formal contractors combined. If true, shadow cities are the future which contradicts the assumption that drives much of urban development, i.e., one day the cities will be Modernized (Chapter 7). Yet Neuwirth's observation is hardly debated by planners, policy makers, politicians, or scholars of space. The realities that are incompatible with their larger beliefs become anomalies that could be overcome in the global convergence of the market economy, or those need to be corrected through law, policies, planning regulations, and/or other state intervention.

Beauregard (2011: 199–200) insists on acknowledging both specificity and complexity:

> any urban theory has to specify the space to which it refers; it has to be grounded ... while a single city can be quite real ... it is no more natural. All

concepts and categories are deficient in this way. One solution is to retreat to ordinary cities as do Ash Amin, Stephen Graham, and Jennifer Robinson. For them, urban theory should be about, and be derived from, what cities have in common ... this approach ... too easily drifts into the realm of general theory in which all cities are the same ... or retreats to an implicit debunked urban–rural dichotomy.

Guha (2000) reasons the lack: The fact that specificity of the South Asian experience has not been thematized thoroughly or thoughtfully enough is the notoriously statist disposition of academic work. The study of people's spaces cannot be statist either: The recognition of the tension between the state and the civil society is central to subaltern studies. So is the conflict between abstract space and lived space for the study of people's spaces. Simone (2010b: 288) observes that "Cities are full of discrepant eligibilities and statuses, codes and requirements for accessing particular experiences, places, and opportunities, ... [and] there are many people and stories we would like to become part of ... but feel that we have no basis or point of entry." This point of entry is the main quest of this volume, and this lay between ordinary people and the institutions with power to create abstract spaces: i.e., the state and the market.

The implications of standardized analyses are much harsher; they are used as strategies of power. Gustavo Esteva and Madhu Suri Prakash (1997: 279) highlight that "You can never know the Earth except reducing it statistically, by some reductionist science." Such appropriation within the hegemonic knowledge system reduces people, events, and their environments into abstract maps, statistics, and other forms of data, neutralizing any emotion or meaning that these may associate.

Statistics, maps, and other data by themselves have no meaning, but they acquire meaning within the web of other spatial practices, larger discourses, and authority to represent the world truth claims. Arjun Appadurai (1998: 133) elaborates the role of numbers and statistics:

> number, by ... nature, flattens idiosyncrasies and creates boundaries around these homogeneous bodies as it performatively limits their extent.... Statistics are to bodies and social types what maps are to territories: they flatten and enclose.... The language of numbers ... allows these [unruly] bodies to be brought back ... counted and accounted for ... taxation, sanitation, education, welfare, and loyalty.

Libby Porter (2010: 71) explains the role of the map in the context of European colonialism:

> Exploration and surveying produced colonial space by rendering it intelligible to the colonial gaze through what Jackson (1998) terms "exploration epistemologies." Geographical knowledge, implemented through the scientific

technologies of surveying and cartographic mapping, and the discursive strategy of naming (see Carter 1987) rendered places known, ordered, rational, and ultimately "settled." Exploration rested on the assumption of being the "first" to discover hitherto "unknown country," the racial assumption upon which the legal fiction of *terra nullius* ultimately came to rest.

In short, more empirical information is not the solution to the lack of knowledge of people's spaces. There is an overabundance of empirical information; the vast empirical presence of ordinary people and their spaces in the form of census, maps, and other narratives are simply transformed into data within mainstream theories. What is sorely lacking in literature is an intellectual presence, the presence of selves with agency rather than docile bodies. For this, information needs to be interpreted in ways that acknowledge the worldviews and practices of the producers, transformers, and users of ordinary spaces as serious and sophisticated ways of understanding the world. This requires the displacement of the dominant views, the provincialization and critical use of mainstream scholarship, and the acknowledgment of people's approaches to and their agency in space making.

The intellectual presence of ordinary people can be facilitated by the acknowledgment of the subjects' *vantage point of inquiry*, i.e., the third helpful tool. Distancing from human emotions with the intention of being "objective," mainstream studies largely adopt outside-in approaches. "The outsider here is the observer who does not inhabit the conceptual or theoretical framework of the actor whom he or she observes" (Chakrabarty 2002: 69). The intellectual presence of ordinary people demands an inside-out approach.

In his work on Lahore, William Glover (2008: xvi) exposes the European (colonial) practice of assessing objects to determine the cultural orientation of their producers and/or users. While the same process may result in the same product, there is no guarantee that other similar objects were produced through the same process, or they have the same meaning for their producers and users. This type of inquiry assumes that the meanings of objects are self-evident and thereby discounts producers' and users' meanings. As the producers, the investigators also operate within intellectual contexts. When an object (or space) is separated from its producers and the socio-cultural processes of production (and use), the investigators rely on their own familiar contexts for meaning. This produces a gap between the meaning of the object (space) for its producers and the investigators (i.e., between the product builders and the knowledge builders).

There is no lack of interest among scholars to represent weaker actors, whether the working class, the colonized, or the slum dwellers. While these self-appointed attempts acknowledge the subjects, they are mostly filled with sympathy. They hardly adopt a viewpoint empathic toward the perceptions, worldviews, and practices of these people (Perera 2009a).

Explicitly accepting social responsibility, the large majority of hardline critics of capitalism directly oppose powerful agents (the state, capital, and, recently, neoliberalism) and argue for people's rights. However, they spend most of their time and energy defining and constructing their opponents and objects of analysis. While useful, this focus on political and/or economic power-holders reinvigorates their power (Chapter 3). These studies are strongly characterized by "oppositional politics" which, according to Terry Eagleton (1990: 26), move under the sign of irony, following "a terrain already mapped out by [their] antagonists." They hardly offer an alternative to state- and capital-centered knowledge production and research; in fact, the state and capital centricity is reinforced. They pay little attention to how ordinary and less powerful people and institutions, which are not in direct collusion or confrontation with power or capital, adapt themselves within the extant political economy and transform the abstract spaces of power-holders.

The focus on power-holders turns the subjects into victims. Intellectually, such work—inadvertently—occupies the historical spaces of those places and people the critics claim to represent. In contrast, Karl Marx—who inspires most of these critics—attempted to make factory workers think of themselves not as victims of capitalism, but as agents of production and change (see Spivak 1999). As opposed to outside-in perspectives—or voyeurism in de Certeau's (1984) words—which largely overlooks the people involved, people's spaces are more visible when observed from the spaces of production (Perera 2009b) with an empathy for people's perceptions of space.

Research *methodology* also affects the outcome. While the method is considered a crucial determinant of credibility of a project and its findings, it also limits the scope of findings. Seeing people's spaces requires the researcher to bridge the gap with the subjects. As Sandercock (2005: 310) highlights: "community actors have great stories to tell, but no means of telling them, except to each other." People's stories cannot be substantively heard unless the researcher develops empathy toward the story-teller. This requires the researcher to not only see physical spaces, but also to understand how and why the spaces and their meanings are produced and negotiated from the producers' and users' worldviews and perspectives.

The methodological challenge is to find ways to acknowledge people's spaces in our own discourses, to open up room for the voices of their producers and users, and to figure out ways to talk about and question them (see Lassiter 2005). Methods such as observation, ethnography, and participant observation are central to such research (see Duneier 1999). Pushing this boundary, Nadasena Ratnapala (1999: xxvii–xxix) argues that in "participant observation ... you become a participant and an observer without forgetting the fact that you are a researcher and an observer ... you chose your problem and have a ... structure of observation that is like the one in the script." "Lived experience," claims Ratnapala (1999), helps researchers to observe more than what they expect to see in the field and branch off in new directions.

Ganesh Devy (2006), the creator of the *adivasi* ("tribal") academy in southern Gujarat, India, challenged himself to understand the local *adivasis* by first listening to them for three years, before teaching anything substantive. In this he became socialized in their culture before beginning to interpret what he was hearing. Building on these methods, this study uses the inside outside threshold to look out, to find the way the "people" perceive externally imposed structures and respond, resist, find accommodation, and negotiate their own spaces within and without provided and/or imposed spaces.

People's Spaces

"People" in this volume are those with no explicit power to create space as the state and capital. From a mainstream standpoint, they are subjects of abstract space. This category is almost identical with "civil society" but acknowledges individual agency and initiatives. Also, "people" is neither a homogeneous category, nor a group with a particular essence; they defy homogeneity assumed in abstract spaces and larger categories. People are similar by virtue of thinking of themselves as other than a self-identical example of the species (Spivak 1999).

It is crucial that the researcher acknowledges the person (self), and not simply the body and body-categories such as male/female and Black/White. As E.P. Thompson (1963) brilliantly highlights, the "objective" category working class does not materialize in a body so-classified until s/he thinks that s/he is a working-class person. The consciousness, particularly how they self-identify, their relationship to place, and their life goals, are central to the identity of subjects. This identity affects the spaces they need, desire, and aspire. As a strategy of differentiating these simply for the purpose of this project, I shall use the terms body and self, and focus on the latter.

As any concept, "people" and "people's spaces" are fuzzy around the edges. I draw on the rich scholarship of subaltern studies and also employ the term to provide some solidity to the core group of people with little or no voice. People here are largely subalterns but also include categories such as laborers and women. In this sense, people in this volume are closer to Scott's (1985) subordinates than Guha's (1999) subalterns.

Although not autonomous, people also move across social categories. The opening chapter discusses spaces of the burgeoning elite in Sri Lanka, who were subjects of the colonial state, and focuses on their early transformation. The volume thus focuses on the process and the role of actors at given stages rather than of structural time, *longue durée*, or the work of individuals or groups over a lifetime. The volume also pays attention to multiple identities: While being a part of the dominant society, White women in Colombo are also subjected to colonial controls (Chapter 2).

Moreover, I wish to maintain the contested and uncooperative nature of people. "People" is, therefore, a bit loose, but more specific for the project at hand, a working definition of sorts. Hence people have agency. They are not simply bodies—or categories—in space susceptible to social and cultural stereotypes and the manipulations of formal power-actors.

As the studies in this volume demonstrate, the occupation of a space and becoming a voluntary subject itself disrupt the dominant mapping of that space, structured according to the worldviews of the provider. People's responses to provided and/ or imposed spaces may begin simply as coping mechanisms, but a large proportion of subjects actively create or negotiate spaces for their own activities. Whether coping with abstract space, familiarizing the same, or producing their own, the ordinary people do develop their own perceptions of extant—abstract and absolute—spaces, respond to these, and negotiate spaces for living.

Key to the production of lived spaces is the incongruence between available spaces, whether provided and/or imposed, and the people's needs and desires. Lived spaces emerge through the people's process of reconciliation of this conflict. This takes place as negotiation between the needs and aspirations of the subjects and the context of constraints and potential that accommodates, resists, contests, and modifies the context. Here the contexts refer to political, ideological, economic, historical, sexual, and linguistic. In this complex process of negotiating space, subjects simultaneously adapt themselves to assigned and/or extant subject positions and (abstract) spaces and adjust and restructure these to accommodate their daily activities and socio-cultural practices (see Perera 2009a).

Yet "the subaltern does not take a step toward the theorist in the hope of a 'cure'" (Spivak 1999: 107). Although not always deliberately planned to avoid detection, people's spatial processes are complex and occur below the radar of the mainstream in the cracks, margins, and interstices, and outside of the formal spatial systems. In his critique of native knowledge, John Briggs (2005) asserts that the conceptualization of local knowledge, even as unitary in development practice, ignores the uneven, often fragmentary, and mediated nature of indigenous knowledge. It also ignores how such knowledge can become quite differentiated across the community.

Hence there is a mismatch between ground conditions and analytical frameworks. The development of locally-friendly interpretations directs us to theorize ground conditions, rather than apply theories which will transform ground conditions. This is no easy task. As Nabeel Hamdi (2004: xxii) highlights, the kind of knowing we need "is less normative, less easy to standardize in its routines and procedures, less tolerant of data-hungry study, and less reliant on statistics and systems analysis." To draw on Spivak (1999: 147), from a different context, people's spaces must be "understood" as unlike (not identical with) them and yet with reference to them. Hence this volume does not talk for ordinary people or subalterns; it is about them and their representation in scholarly and professional work.

People's Spaces aims to investigate, find, make visible, acknowledge, and critique the spaces produced and negotiated by ordinary people for their daily activities and socio-cultural practices. People's spaces are widespread but looking at the right places is a prerequisite to finding these. We opt to look below the cloud cover of mainstream theories; reinterpret the high end, the low end, and traditional, the meanings of which are derived in relation to the Western city (Perera and Tang 2013); look beside and between these for leftover spaces; observe beyond the empirical evidence that fits within dominant theories; pay special attention to interpretation instead of simply collecting empirical data for theories that have defined (and appropriated) the extant world; and adopt a critical approach to existing material and an investigative approach to new material.

Yet there is no pretension that we in this Western academy and the professional world can fully know people's spaces, especially subaltern spaces, and how they are produced. As Spivak (1999) insists, knowledge of the other subject is theoretically impossible. I do not situate myself as a knowledge keeper, rather as a facilitator of this investigative process. The role of this volume is to help create entry points for local knowledge to come through and to view local spaces from these perspectives (see Kovach 2009).

People's Spaces is, therefore, an incomplete project that works with the recalcitrant presence of diverse "ordinary people" for whom we are unable to be informants (see Spivak 1999). Nevertheless, it tries to speak as closely and sensitively as it can to subjects in ways that can evoke subjects' perspectives and cause us to question our own assumptions.

The Book

The chapters in this volume investigate communities, processes, and places with which I am most familiar, complemented by a few communities with which I opted to familiarize myself for the purpose of this research. The book is based on my own studies in select locations in Sri Lanka: nineteenth century Colombo, the war-torn Jaffna area, and the post-tsunami south. This base is diversified by studies carried out with my students in Daanchi (Nepal), Galle (Sri Lanka), Gangtok (India), Moratumulla (Sri Lanka), and Tashkent (Uzbekistan) (Figure I.1).

The first chapters on Colombo establish the fact that people make larger transformations that match or surpass formal changes. The next few chapters investigate how subjects resist the deprivation of spatial freedom due to disasters, prevailing

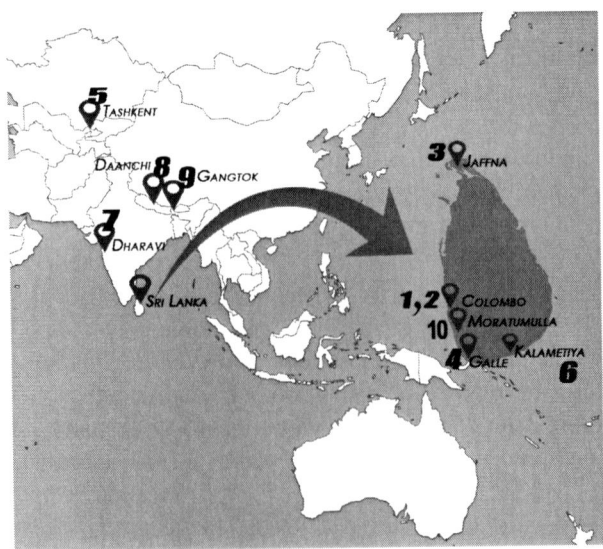

FIGURE I.1 Locations of Studies (credit: Nirmani Liyanage).

conditions, or the surveillance by authorities, and use extant conditions as a platform and "raw material" to build their lives. The chapter on Gangtok demonstrates how people shape neighborhoods, and even cities, through formal structures. The studies of Dharavi, Daanchi, and *handiya* reveal that people's creation of lived spaces preceded the spaces of power and capital, making the authorities and capital negotiate for their spaces.

Notes

1 Lived space for Edward Soja (1996) is the space of life story, space that encapsulates the everyday lived experience and expression of the social in space. My definition is closer to that of Lefebvre (1991) and would focus on people and their production of space.
2 These factors—the first three—were first mapped out in an earlier article on people's spaces (Perera 2009a), then adapted and elaborated for the understanding of Asian urban transformations (Perera and Tang 2013). Here I further develop and relate them to the subject.
3 These critiques by no means undermine the great work of these scholars upon whose work I build my own.

References

Appadurai, A. (1998) *Modernity at Large: Cultural dimensions of globalization*, Minneapolis, MN: University of Minnesota Press.

Beauregard, R.A. (2011) "Radical Uniqueness and the Flight from Urban Theory" in D.R. Judd and D. Simpson (eds.) *The City Revisited: Urban theory from Chicago, Los Angeles, and New York*, Minneapolis, MN: University of Minnesota Press, 186–202.

Bhabha, H.K. (1994) *The Location of Culture*, London and New York: Routledge.

Birch, E. (2005) "U.S. Planning Culture Under Pressure: Major elements endure and flourish in the face of crisis" in B. Sanyal (ed.) *Comparative Planning Cultures*, New York: Routledge, 331–58.

Bollens, S.A. (2005) "Urban Planning and Intergroup Conflict: Confronting a fractured public interest" in I.B. Stiftel and V. Watson (eds.) *Dialogues in Urban and Regional Planning*, New York: Routledge, 209–46.

Briggs, J. (2005) "The Use of Indigenous Knowledge in Development: Problems and challenges," *Progress in Development Studies* 5, 2: 99–114.

Bunnell, T. and Miller, M.A. (2011) "Jakarta in Post-Suharto Indonesia: Decentralization, neoliberalism and global city aspiration," *Space and Polity* 15, 1: 35–48.

Chakrabarty, D. (2002) *The Habitations of Modernity: Essays in the wake of subaltern studies*, Chicago, IL: University of Chicago Press.

Das, D. (2013) "Ordinary Lives in Extraordinary Cyberabad" in N. Perera and W.S. Tang (eds.) *The Transforming Asian Cities: Intellectual impasse, Asianizing space, and emerging translocalities*, New York: Routledge, 112–22.

De Certeau, M. (1984) *The Practice of Everyday Life*, Trans. S.F. Rendell, Berkeley, CA: University of California Press.

Devy, G. (2006) *A Nomad Called a Thief: Reflections on Adivasi silence*, Delhi: Orient Longman.

Dick, H.W. (2003) *Surabaya: City of work, a socioeconomic history 1900–2000*, Singapore: Singapore University Press.

Dittirich, C. (2007) "Bangalore: Globalisation and fragmentation in India's hightech-capital," *ASIEN* 103: 45–58.

Douglas, M., Ho, K.C. and Ooi, G.L. (eds.) (2008) *Globalization, the City and Civil Society in Pacific Asia*, New York: Routledge.

Duneier, M. (1999) *Sidewalk*, New York: Farrar, Straus and Giroux.

Eagleton, T. (1990) "Nationalism: Irony and commitment" in T. Eagleton, F. Jameson and E. Said (eds.) *Nationalism, Colonialism, and Literature*, Minneapolis, MN: University of Minnesota Press, 23–42.

Esteva, G. and Prakash, M.S. (1997) "From Global Thinking to Local Thinking" in R. Majid, and V. Bawtree (eds.) *The Post-Development Reader*, London: Zed Books, 277–89.

Fabian, J. (1983) *Time and the Other: How anthropology makes its object*, New York: Columbia University Press.

Fabian, J. (1990) "Presence and Representation: The other and anthropological writing," *Critical Inquiry* 16: 753–72.

Fabian, J. (2006) "The Other Revisited: Critical afterthoughts," *Anthropological Theory* 6, 2: 139–52.

Giddens, A. (1986 [1984]) *The Constitution of Society: Outline of the theory of structuration*, Berkeley. CA: University of California Press.

Gillen, J. (2010) "Tourism and Entrepreneurialism in Southeast Asian Cities," *Geography Compass* 4: 370–82.

Glover, W. (2008) *Making Lahore Modern: Constructing and imagining a colonial city*, Minneapolis: MN: University of Minnesota Press.

Guha, R. (1998) *Domination without Hegemony: History and power in colonial India*, Cambridge, MA: Harvard University Press.

Guha, R. (1999) *Elementary Aspects of Peasant Insurgency in Colonial India*, Durham, NC: Duke University Press.

Guha, R. (2000) "Chandra's Death" in R. Guha (ed.) *Subaltern Studies Reader 1986–1995*, New Delhi: Oxford University Press, 34–62.

Hamdi, N. (2004) *Small Change: About the art of practice and the limits of planning in cities*, Sterling, VA: Earthscan.

Haraway, D.J. (1991) *Simians, Cyborgs, and Women: The reinvention of nature*, New York: Routledge.

Harvey, D. (1973) *Social Justice and the City*, London: Edward Arnold.

Holston, J. (1989) *The Modernist City: An anthropological critique of Brasilia*, Chicago, IL: University of Chicago Press.

Holtzman, B. and Hughes, C. (2010) "Points of Resistance and Departure: An interview with James C. Scott," *Upping the Anti* 11. Online. Available: http://uppingtheanti.org/journal/article/11-points-of-resistance-and-departure-an-interview-with-james-c.-scott (accessed February 2, 2015).

Huyssen, A. (2008) "Introduction: World Cultures, World Cities" in A. Huyssen (ed.) *Other Cities, Other Worlds: Urban imagineries in a globalizing age*, Durham, NC: Duke University Press, 1–26.

Jacobs, J. (1972 [1961]) *The Death and Life of Great American Cities*, 2nd edn, Harmondsworth: Penguin.

Jacobs, J.M. (1996) *Edge of Empire: Postcolonialism and the city*, London and New York: Routledge.

Janz, W. (2013) *Leftover Rightunder: Finding architectural potential in found materials*, Chicago, IL: Half Letter Press.

Kamel, N. (2014) "Learning from the Margin: Placemaking tactics" in V. Mukhija and A. Loukaitou-Sideris (eds.) *The Informal American City: Beyond Taco trucks and day labor*, Cambridge, MA: MIT Press, 119–36.

King, A.D. (1976) *Colonial Urban Development: Culture, social power and environment*, London: Routledge.

King, A.D. (1990) *Urbanism, Colonialism and the World-Economy: Cultural and spatial foundations of the world urban system*, London and New York: Routledge.

Kovach, M. (2009) *Indigenous Methodologies: Characteristics, conversations, and contexts*, Toronto: University of Toronto Press.

Laclau, E. and Mouffe, C. (2001) *Hegemony and Socialist Strategy: Towards a radical democratic politics*, London: Verso.

Lassiter, L.E. (2005) *The Chicago Guide to Collaborative Ethnography*, Chicago, IL: University of Chicago Press.

Lefebvre, H. (1991 [1974]) *The Production of Space*, Trans. D. Nicholson-Smith, Cornwall: Blackwell Publishing.

Mehrotra, R. (2008) "Negotiating the Static and Kinetic Cities: The emergent urbanism of Mumbai" in A. Huyssen (ed.) *Other Cities, Other Worlds: Urban imagineries in a globalizing age*, Durham, NC: Duke University Press, 205–18.

Moser, S. (2010) "Putrajaya: Malaysia's New Federal Administrative Capital Cities," *The International Journal of Urban Policy and Planning* 27, 3: 285–97.

Mukhija, V. and Loukaitou-Sideris, A. (2014) *The Informal American City: Beyond taco trucks and day labor*, Cambridge, MA: MIT Press.

Myers, G. (2011) *African Cities: Alternative visions of urban theory and practice*, London: Zed books.

Neuwirth, R. (2005) *Shadow Cities: A billion squatters, a new urban world*, New York: Routledge.

Perera, N. (2005a) "Importing Problems: The impact of a housing ordinance on Colombo," *Arab World Geographer* 8, 1–2: 61–76.

Perera, N. (2005b) "Competing Imaginations: The authorship of the Chandigarh plan," *A+D Architecture + Design: A Journal of Indian Architecture* 22, 1: 38–48.

Perera, N. (2009a) "People's Spaces: Familiarization, subject formation, and emergent spaces in Colombo," *Planning Theory* 8, 3: 50–74.

Perera, N. (2009b) "Asian Urbanization and Planning: Viewing the production of space from the spaces of production," *Bhumi* 1, 2: 1–24.

Perera, N. (2010) "When Planning Ideas Land: Mahaweli's people-centered approach" in P. Healey and R. Upton (eds.) *Crossing Borders: International exchanges and planning practices*, New York: Routledge, 141–72.

Perera, N. and Tang W.S. (2013) *Transforming Asian Cities: Intellectual impasse, Asianizing space, and emerging translocalities*, New York: Routledge.

Porter, L. (2010) *Unlearning the Colonial Cultures of Planning*, Burlington: Ashgate.

Ratnapala, N. (1999) *The Beggar in Sri Lanka*, Colombo: Sarvodaya Vishva Lekha Publications.

Robinson, J. (2006) *Ordinary Cities: Between modernity and development*, London: Routledge.

Rose, G. (1993) *Feminism and Geography: The limits of geographical knowledge*, Minneapolis, MN: University of Minnesota Press.

Roseneau, J.N., and Durfee, M. (1999) *Thinking Theory Thoroughly: Coherent approaches to an incoherent world*, Boulder, CO: Westview Press.

Roy, A. (2005) "Urban Informality: Toward an epistemology of planning," *Journal of the American Planning Association* 71, 2: 147–58.

Roy, A. and AlSayad, N. (eds.) (2004) *Urban Informality: Transnational perspectives from the Middle East, Latin America and South Asia*, Lanham, MD and London: Lexington Books.

Said, E.W. (2004 [1978]) *Orientalism*, New York: Vintage Books.

Sandercock, L. (1998) "Framing Insurgent Historiographies for Planning" in L. Sandercock (ed.) *Making the Invisible Visible: A multicultural planning history*, Los Angeles, CA: University of California Press, 1–30.

Sandercock, L. (2005) "Out of the Closet: The importance of stories and storytelling" in B. Stiftel and V. Watson (eds.) *Planning Practice: Dialogues in urban and regional planning*, London: Routledge, 299–321.

Schoon, S. (2013) "Niche Authority in Urbanized Villages: Bottom-up codetermination in megacity developments in China" in N. Perera and W.S. Tang (eds.) *The transforming Asian city: Intellectual impasse, Asianizing space, and emerging translocalities*, New York: Routledge, 222–42.

Scott, J.C. (1985) *Weapons of the Weak: Everyday forms of peasant resistance*, New Haven, CT: Yale University Press.

Scott, J.C. (1990) *Domination and the Arts of Resistance: Hidden transcripts*, New Haven, CT: Yale University Press.

Scott, J.C. (1998) *Seeing Like a State: How certain schemes to improve the human condition have failed*, New Haven, CT: Yale University Press.

Scott, J.C. (2005) "Beyond the war of words: cautious resistance and calculated conformity" in L. Amoore (ed.) *The Global Resistance Reader*, London and New York: Routledge, 71–2.

Sennett, R. (1992) *The Conscience of the Eye: The design and social life of cities*, New York: W.W. Norton & Company, 46–62.

Sharma, K. (2000) *Rediscovering Dharavi: Stories from Asia's largest slum*, New Delhi: Penguin Books.

Shatkin, G. (2007) "Global Cities of the South: Emerging perspectives on growth and inequality," *Cities* 24, 1: 1–15.

Shatkin, G. (2008) "The City and the Bottom Line: urban megaprojects and the privatization of planning in Southeast Asia," *Environment and Planning A* 40: 383–401.

Simone, A. (2008) "The Last Shall be First" in A. Huyssen (ed.) *Other Cities, Other Worlds: Urban imaginaries in a globalizing age*, Durham, NC: Duke University Press, 119.

Simone, A. (2010a) *City Life from Jakarta to Dakar: Movements at the crossroads*, New York: Routledge.

Simone, A. (2010b) "On Intersections, Anticipations, and Provisional Publics: Remaking district life of Jakarta," *Urban Geography* 31, 3: 285–308.

Soja, E. (1996) *Thirdspace: Journeys to Los Angeles and other real and imagined places*, Oxford: Basil Blackwell.

Spivak, G.C. (1994) "Can the Subaltern Speak?" in P. Williams and L. Chrisman (eds.) *Colonial Discourse and Postcolonial Theory*, New York: Columbia University Press.

Spivak, G.C. (1999) *A Critique of Postcolonial Reason: Toward a history of the vanishing present*, Cambridge, MA: Harvard University Press.

Sundaram, R. (2010) *Pirate Modernity: Delhi's media urbanism*, Oxford and New York: Routledge.

Tang, W.S. and Mizuoka, F. (2010) "Thinking East Asia Geographically" in W.S. Tang and F. Mizuoka (eds.) *East Asia: A critical geography perspective*, Tokyo: Kokon Shoin, 1–16.

Thompson, E.P. (1963) *The Making of the English Working Class*, New York: Vintage Books.

Wang, H.J. (2013) "An Unexpected Urban Renewal Practice: The emergence of a multicultural historic plaza in Taipei" in N. Perera and W.S. Tang (eds.) *The Transforming Asian City: Intellectual impasse, Asianizing space, and emerging translocalities*, New York: Routledge, 65–77.

1

INDIGENIZING THE COLONIAL CITY

The Ceylonese Transformation of
Nineteenth-Century Colombo

Colombo, the former capital of Sri Lanka (Ceylon until 1972), was subjected to a massive transformation in the 1860s–1880s. The transformation is well known (Hulugalle 1965; Malalgoda 1976; Dharmasena 1980; Peebles 1981; Gombrich and Obeyesekere 1988; de Silva 1989; Brohier 2000; Jayawardena 2002), but the Ceylonese are missing from this story. Opening the volume, this chapter asks: What were the local people doing during such a major transformation? What were their responses? What spaces did the responses produce? This chapter will examine the magnitude and the character of the transformation caused by the Ceylonese.[1]

Contemporary Colombo is a colonial product. R.L. Brohier (2000: 2) asserts that "Colombo is a city forced on the peoples of Ceylon in spite of themselves. It was never a creation of their own choice or making." First established as a Portuguese outpost in the early sixteenth century, colonial Colombo was governed by the Portuguese (1517–1656), the Dutch (1656–1796), and the British (1796–1948). As I have argued elsewhere (Perera 1998), Ceylon did not produce modern Colombo, but Colombo produced Ceylon.[2] It is a foreign implant with neither a history of "organic evolution," nor a hinterland that produced it. Instead, Colombo produced its hinterland and Ceylon around it. Since then, it has been the prime organizer of Ceylon's (Sri Lanka's after 1972) "national" geography.

The existence and meaning of colonial Colombo had intimately depended on European metropolises. First established as a colonial military outpost and an instrument of colonization, it was developed into the administrative, economic, and cultural center of the colony (ibid.). In order to create their own city in what had been a "sea junction" in the Indian Ocean trade network, the Portuguese first expelled the Muslim traders. Keeping the indigenous inhabitants and Muslim population out, they established a White, male Christian city (ibid.). The Dutch East India Company also managed to preserve a "white face" in Colombo, especially in the fort (Knapp 1981).

The core of the divided city, i.e., the fort, was occupied by the colonial authorities. The outside was largely characterized as the "Black City," which was principally a market (Figure 1.1). Despite the changes in its size and shape, the fort served as the locus of political power with no comparable social and cultural institutions outside it (see King 1976). The British authorities further transformed the fort into their own ethnic enclave. They kept the people of Portuguese and Dutch descent, later known as Burghers, out of the fort and in intermediate positions in their administration.

The Burghers developed their neighborhood in the area immediately outside the fort, called the pettah. It held about 500 such families at the beginning of the twentieth century (Brohier 2000). The Black City was thus relocated further away in the late eighteenth century (Denham 1912). The address of the Black City, "Outer Pettah," clearly indicated for the colonial community that the native area was well outside the city. The Ceylonese called it *aluth kade* (the new market) (Figure 1.2). This chapter examines the Ceylonese reactions to the larger restructuring of the city in the late nineteenth century. It highlights the process through which the natives began to indigenize the colonial city.

FIGURE 1.1 Representations of the Black City (credit: Cave 1908).

FIGURE 1.2 Zones of British Colombo (credit: Perera 2009).

Massive Transformation: The Hegemonic Narrative

The late nineteenth-century transformation of Colombo was massive. By the end of the century, the city was known as "the Clapham Junction of the East" (Turner 1927: 152). Henry Cave (1908: 1) described it as "a spot on which converge the steamships of all nations for coal and the exchange of freight and passengers." Mainstream historiography explains this transformation in terms of the success of coffee plantations (de Silva 1989). This economy-centered explanation misses a larger transformation.

If we are to take clues from the spaces and landscape of Colombo, the changes indicate that British authorities had become comfortable living in Colombo and ruling Ceylon. This is evident by the demolition of fortifications in 1869 and the establishment of a residential district in Cinnamon Gardens, about four kilometers from the fort. After seven decades of keeping the natives out, the British expanded their own domain and moved select social institutions and administrative functions outside the fort.

Combining administrative functions with new socio-cultural institutions, the British built a cultural space in Cinnamon Gardens (Figure 1.3). The institutions included an Anglican church, cricket pitch, the Havelock Race Course, Ridgeway Golf Links, art galleries, and Garden and Prince's Club (Ferguson 1903; Hulugalle 1965; Cave 1908). In 1859, the large open area (the esplanade) adjacent to the fort,

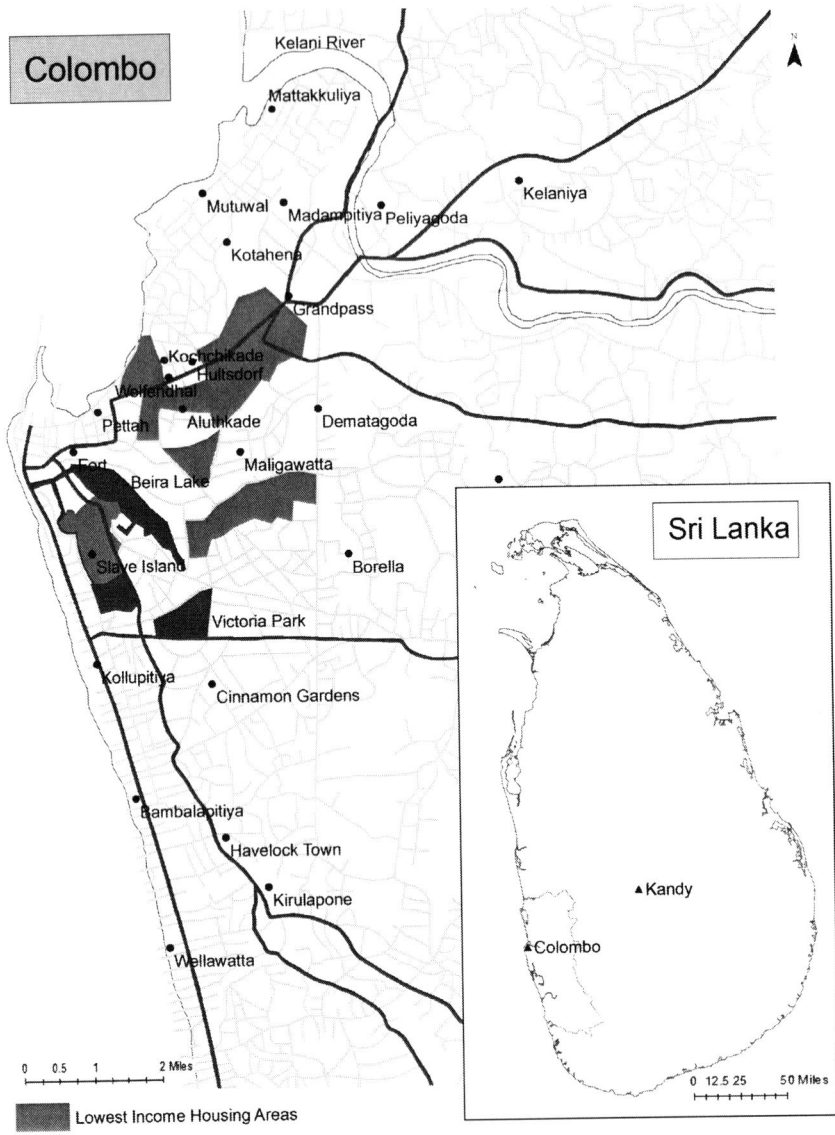

FIGURE 1.3 Places Referred to in the Text (credit: Kaushalya Herath).

the purpose of which had been to protect the fort from enemies, was transformed into a seafront promenade: the Galle Face. The disbandment of the Ceylon Rifles Regiments between 1869 and 1871 opened up Slave Island, where the British stationed mostly Malay regiments.

The municipal area was also expanded, incorporating these areas. In the 1880s, the municipal area was about ten times as large as the fort area (Hulugalle 1965). Moreover, a municipal council was established in 1865 to administer the city.

Relating the city to the larger world, the harbor was expanded in 1874. A mere four years after the laying of a telegraph connection between Calcutta and Bombay, the line was extended to Ceylon in 1858. From 1887, the English cricket team played a test match on their tours to Australia at Galle Face (Cave 1908). The large 400-foot Cave book store, which could not have been supported by the island and its culture, represents the magnitude of change. Colombo was a significant international coaling station and sea junction used by those who traveled between distant places.

The plantation economy survived the European economic downturn and established itself as the economic base of the colony in the 1840s (Perera 1998). While the economic success supported the massive change, it is insufficient to explain how the colonial rulers and the community became secure and comfortable in the city. This function was political.

Crushing the revolt of 1848, I argue, was the necessary condition to establish comfort for British rulers. As Arjuna Parakrama (1990) fluently demonstrates, the subjects saw British taxes, rule, and the authority as "jokes." Yet the British were confident they had eliminated all substantial threats to their rule. The key was the destruction in the Kandyan imagination of any hope of restoring political power back to the former kingdom of Kandy. According to K.M. de Silva (1997), by the 1870s the "traditional nationalism" guided by the Kandy-based aristocratic leadership had ceased to be a serious threat to the stability of British rule. It is in this political context that the expansion of the plantation economy supported the transformation of Colombo.

Most telling is the construction of Colombo Museum in 1877 (Ferguson 1903; Cave 1908) (Figure 1.4), to store the "dead Lankan culture" for the consumption of Europeans and Ceylonese.[3] This was the most prominent building in Cinnamon Gardens until the grand Town Hall was built in the 1920s. Behind the Georgian façade is a central hall displaying brass and ivory, galleries for Ceylonese products; natural history; rocks, minerals, and gems; indigenous birds, fishes, and insects; and

FIGURE 1.4 Colombo Museum (credit: Cave 1908).

archaeological rooms. This symbolical framing within a Georgian building, with a bronze statue of Governor William Henry Gregory, highlights the appropriation of one history and culture by a dominant other (Perera 1998). In so doing, the authorities Orientalized Lankan history and familiarized Ceylon for the British, simultaneously both dehistoricizing and defamiliarizing Ceylon and its own history.

The domination was complemented and facilitated by the hegemonic situation. During the early stages of colonialism, most Lankans rejected unfamiliar and disorienting colonial social structures with a view to returning to earlier ways of life (Perera 1998). As Frantz Fanon (1968) points out, where confrontation with the colonial order at first disoriented the natives, the colonial system became a point of envy. This transition from hostility to envy indicates the hegemony achieved by the colonial culture. By the 1860s, the British had not only created a plantation economy and incorporated the colony into the larger world economy, but had also established a high degree of cultural hegemony for their worldviews in Ceylon (Perera 1998).

Within the new and expanded Colombo, the former fort and pettah areas became simply "Fort" and "Pettah" for the Ceylonese. These politically neutral terms not only conceal colonial power relations, but also naturalize colonial perceptions among the Ceylonese. Unlike attitudes toward the fort in the early part of the nineteenth century, British officials did not fully prevent non-British inhabitants from moving into the vicinity of Cinnamon Gardens. The separation was largely maintained through the real-estate market and the restrictions to British cultural clubs (Roberts 1984).

In sum, defeating the Lankan revolt, extinguishing the Kandyan hope for restoring the kingdom, and expanding the colonial economy, the British established themselves in the late nineteenth century as the supreme power in Ceylon. In the process, Colombo moved from being a colonial port city located in the margins of the colony to the powerful capital of Ceylon (Perera 2002). The Ceylonese largely followed the call of the authorities to become subjects of the new and invigorated colonial system, but they were not passive recipients of this change.

Voluntary Subjugation, Adaptation of Space

Until 1815, the last kingdom of Kandy challenged the British authority in Colombo. Even after its fall, the Kandy of memories and dreams continued to provide inspiration for riots and rebellions against the colonial regime. While the mockery of colonial rule continued (Parakrama 1990), the "defeat" of the 1848 revolt led most Ceylonese to seek accommodation within the restructured colonial system.

Since then, the Ceylonese increasingly focused on making a livelihood or strengthening their positions within the colonial society. Many individuals and groups thus moved to Colombo, which had the most opportunities. They built homes and institutions, but negotiated daily for their activities and cultural practices. The process, as elaborated below, caused the displacement, redefinition, and appropriation of select colonial structures, spaces, and symbols. The familiarization became spatially evident in Colombo during the same decades: the 1860s–1880s.

This chapter focuses on the people who came from various places and engaged in a welter of quiet and anonymous action, eventually developing themselves into identifiable groups in colonial Colombo. The familiarization process was uneven: Some actors had better access to resources and ended up more powerful than others. Also, social groups identified in this chapter—which may appear to be cohesive— had large variations within them. In the following pages, I will examine the spaces produced in Colombo as part of the rise of a Ceylonese élite, migration, naturaliza- tion, and the Buddhist revival between the 1860s and the 1880s.

The Élite Formation

The Low-Country of Ceylon was subject to colonialism for the longest time, since the early sixteenth century. The British subjugation of Kandy, the last kingdom in the central highlands, in 1815 and their suspicion of the Kandyan élite changed the balance of power within Ceylon in favor of the Low-Country. In this context, select Ceylonese "entrepreneurs" progressed within the colonial society to form an élite group (Roberts 1982; Peebles 1995; Jayawardena 2002). By the 1880s, the Low-Country élite, consisting mainly of majority Sinhalese and of the largest minority Tamils, had surpassed the Kandyan aristocrats and established privileged places for themselves in economic, administrative, and political realms in Ceylon. The rise of the Low-Country élite, largely belonging to the three main non- Goyigama castes—Karava, Durava, and Salagama—is well addressed by Michael Roberts (1982), Patrick Peebles (1995), and Kumari Jayawardena (2002). This study concentrates on how Colombo became their center.

The capitalists, or the economic élite, became rich through alcohol- and transportation-related businesses (Jayawardena 2002). Toward the mid-nineteenth century, they had not only penetrated into the plantation economy dominated by the British, but had also created a significant share for themselves within it (Bandarage 1983; Perera 1998; Jayawardena 2002). In Colombo, they were penetrating into the colonial business district, especially Fort and Pettah areas, which had been exclusive European domains. According to H.A.J. Hulugalle (1965), apart from jewelers, there were many other Ceylonese businesses in the Fort, including C. Matthew & Co. ship-handlers and stevedores.[4] Colombo also attracted already established businesses from large cities such as Kandy and Galle. The oldest jeweler in town, Othaman Lebbe Makan Markar, who began his business in Galle in 1860, moved it to Colombo within a few years (Hulugalle 1965).

The Ceylonese administrators, who served in the lower ranks of the colonial administration, also advanced themselves into a new administrative élite. The role of traditional administrators was becoming less important than attributes of educa- tion, proficiency in English, lifestyle, profession, and landholding (Peebles 1995). By the nineteenth century, the Ceylonese administrators had changed from "bare- foot chieftains" in coats patterned after seventeenth-century Portuguese uniforms to Victorian lawyers with Oxbridge degrees and fashionable suits (Peebles 1995). Concurrently, the political élite—known as constitutionalists—also progressed within the colonial political system, but with no intention to radically change it.

By the 1880s, the Low-Country élite had established itself as the dominant strata of the formal Ceylonese society, and their family alliances made it a strong group (Jayawardena 2002). According to Roberts (1982), the foundation for the emergence of a Karava élite was laid earlier, during Portuguese and Dutch periods when the primary capital invested in the early nineteenth century was generated. They were prepared and did not hesitate when the opportunity arose. The Low-Country had also undergone commercialization, monetization, Westernization, and Christianization for almost three centuries before the fall of Kandy. The Low-Country people had the means to support the much-needed Western education and Westernization, and the Tamils were also outpaced by the Karavas with respect to the education of women (Roberts 1982). The Low-Country "entrepreneurs" also moved to Kandyan districts as laborers, businessmen, and teachers (Roberts 1982).

The British colonial culture achieved a high degree of hegemony among the owners of plantations and mines, political leaders, and administrators, particularly with their sons educated in England and families being Christian in faith. The English education and the acculturation that came with it differentiated the élite from the rest. They did not question the appropriateness of the colonial organization of Ceylon or the centrality of Colombo, but followed the British lead. Brought up within the colonial system, the élite depended on it for their identity. Many of the sons of the entrepreneurs and professionals emulated the British aristocracy in its penchant for dog-breeding and horse-racing, considered to be the sport of kings (Jayawardena 2002).

Despite race-based discrimination, the Burghers, Tamils, Muslims, and Low-Country Sinhalese, none of whom belonged to the upper strata of "traditional society," used the mobility within the colonial system to advance their positions (Roberts 1982). Higher education added an element of achievement, particularly useful within a system based on merit as opposed to inheritance. This education included manners and values, including punctuality, polite modes of address, and the importance of truthfulness (Tampoe 2013). The élite not only used the Westernized culture to symbolize their privileged position among the Ceylonese, they also jealously guarded it from further diffusion, perhaps increasingly exaggerating the aspects of metropolitan culture as a buttress to maintain their social and cultural difference (Duncan 1990).

Simultaneously, the Low-Country élite also challenged the supremacy of the Kandyan aristocracy and the Goyigamas, who were viewed as upper-caste people. As part of this struggle, they tended to pursue social prestige in a style that had been formulated by the Goyigama aristocracy, favoring the lifestyle of the *walauwa hamu* (lord of the manor house) (Roberts 1982).

The familiarization within the colonial system was thus influenced by Low-Country, Kandyan, and colonial values, ideals, and models. The élite third culture (see King 1976) was a Ceylonese culture constructed in a way that represented their power to the average Ceylonese and their worthiness to the colonial community. In addition to adaption, the élite also invented new traditions: Ponnambalam Ramanathan took to wearing the long-coat and turban of the Indian aristocracy (Jayawardena 2002).

As part of this culture, the élite also constructed their physical environments. The élite's adaptation to the colonial environment in Colombo caused radical changes in it. In addition to adopting Fort and Pettah, the Ceylonese entrepreneurs also mimicked colonial residential locations, house forms, and styles. Along with emulation, the élite began appropriating colonial structures, spaces, and symbols. After mid-century, the new élite adopted palatial houses in Colombo as symbols of their newfound affluence (Tampoe 2013).

Even under Dutch rule, the opulent and top bracket Sinhalese gentry, particularly the Chief Mudliars, whose seat of power was distinctly rural, established townhouses in Colombo. The four Maha-Mudliars had *walawwa*s (manor houses) with extensive groves of trees in the Wolvendal area (Roberts *et al.* 1989; Brohier 2000).[5] With the departure of their Dutch patrons, the administrators congregated around Wolvendal and lived with the ladies of rank, *lama etens*, in spacious *walawwas* off Green Street, Kuruwa Street, and Silversmith Street (Brohier 2000). The colonial residential trend, which was toward the north of the fort, especially to Mutuwal and Grandpass during early colonial periods, turned toward the south, particularly Kollupitiya and Cinnamon Gardens, in the 1860s (Hulugalle 1965). C.H. de Soyza, easily the richest Ceylonese in the late nineteenth century, moved to Alfred House Gardens, Kollupitiya, where he lived in a mansion on 40 acres (Tampoe 2013). By building new mansions adjacent to colonial residential areas, the Ceylonese élite were both expanding the colonial residential zones and indigenizing them.

The neighborhoods of the élite were patterned after the colonial model, and they followed the latest European architectural styles. Yet these were hybrids: In Colonial Secretary James Tennent's (1999: 161) words, these houses exhibited "European taste engrafted on Sinhalese customs." They projected their wealth and competitive spirit: "much money was spent [from the 1860s] on conspicuous housing; palatial residences ... with mock-Italian decor, large gardens and wedding cake architecture" (Jayawardena 2002: 258). Many of the houses had imposing names such as Oliver Castle and Deyn Court (Jayawardena 2002). For Homi Bhabha (1994: 86), "mimicry emerges as the representation of a difference that is itself a process of disavowal." This mimicry, which repeats rather than re-presents, leads to mockery and ambivalence (ibid.).

Yet the older Lankan values remained persistent, resilient, and relevant. The élite also followed Kandyan *walawwa* architecture. This hybrid is most evident in the interior organization of houses and their local names which followed the colonial pattern: Sukhastan (Abode of Happiness), Ponklaar (Golden Garden), and Sirimethipaya (Abode of Prosperity) (Jayawardena 2002). Drawing on both colonial and (Kandyan) aristocratic models, the élite produced particular residential areas that represented their worthiness to the colonial community and power to the average Ceylonese.

Providing English education to the subjects and recruiting them to the administration as the interface between the British and the locals did not mean they were accepted into British society or the colonial community (see Devy 2006). The access to British residential areas was regulated through the market, and admission to prime cultural clubs was restricted. The "colored" and "blacks" were barred from membership (Roberts 1984).

The élites were not pleased with this segregation but, instead of questioning such discrimination, struggled to be on the privileged (White) side of the divided city. They adopted areas of the city with superior services, the maintenance of which required disproportionate amounts of resources. They created their own exclusive Oriental Club in the vicinity of Cinnamon Gardens (Roberts 1974). Establishing their presence in Colombo, they also began publishing their own newspaper, the *Ceylon Standard* in 1898 (ibid.). Tamil and Sinhala journals and newspapers were also well established by the 1870s: *Utaya Tarakai* in 1841 and *Lankalokaya* in 1860 (de Silva 1987).

Following colonial locational preferences and emulating their building forms and lifestyles, the élite were expanding the commercial and residential zones conceived by the authorities. In so doing, they provided legitimacy for Colombo as the seat of power and the principal site of political negotiation in Ceylon, a mandate it had not enjoyed from its inception (Perera 1996). At the same time, they created and expanded room for Ceylonese within colonial Colombo. Those who became élite thus made use of the cracks in the system to establish themselves within the mainstream society, but as subordinates. They would make yet another move to replace the colonials at independence, a story that needs to be addressed separately.

Migration and Naturalization

Along with the élite, the residents and migrants were also familiarizing their locales, but in different ways. The population of Colombo grew from a meager 28,000 in 1800, to 150,000 in 1900, mostly occurring in the latter part of the century. By the 1870s, the Colombo municipal area held twice as many people as Galle and Kandy, the next-largest cities (Ferguson 1903; Turner 1927). The expansion of the city limits also incorporated indigenous and migrant neighborhoods. In addition, the "immigrants" in Colombo had also naturalized by the end of the nineteenth century, indigenizing both colonial spaces and their own cultural practices.

Prior to European colonization, Muslims had settled in Colombo for trading and related activities. According to Lorna Dewaraja (1995), the Muslims adopted the outward appearance, dress, and manners of the Sinhalese. By the late nineteenth century, they had adopted Tamil as the daily language (Arabic for prayers), and caste stratification had also seeped into their communities (Azeez 1986). Ismeth Rahim (1986) highlights that contemporary Muslim houses in Ceylon are similar to those of the Sinhalese and Tamils.

The European and Eurasian groups in Colombo consolidated into what became the Burgher community; it was created by generations of adaptation to local culture, environment, and mixed marriages. Clinging to the Dutch heritage and British leanings of the core group, and within a Ceylonese patriotism forged in opposition to British subjection, the Burghers had developed a comradery with Sinhalese and Tamil middle classes, creating a distinctly Ceylonese middle-class community (Roberts *et al.* 1989). Although the people of Portuguese and Dutch origin were privileged by the British at the beginning of their rule, about one-third of the Burghers, in 1871, were in the regular labor pool (Ibid.). As some moved out of Colombo, the main domain of the Burghers, the Pettah, became naturalized.

The Dutch élite houses were more akin to bungalows, freestanding houses with open verandahs, some with internal courtyards. Most Dutch people lived in houses built in rows. However, as they (later, Burghers) had indigenized over a long period of time, like the Muslims and other immigrant groups, their indigenization is not marked by radical changes in the physical landscape. The change was largely in the meanings of their spaces. Most significantly, the spaces the Burghers shared with the British became contested. In cricket fields, the Burghers were the first to represent Ceylon against the English.

The indigenization of various immigrant communities and their familiarization of the city were not even. The different origins, lengths of stay, speeds of naturalization, cultural perceptions, and spaces familiar to them transformed Colombo into culturally and spatially the most diverse city in Ceylon. The stevedores recruited labor from south India, thus adding a new immigrant population, especially in the docklands (Dharmasena 1980). The Dutch adaptation of verandas and courtyards in their houses inspired the local élite and the middle classes to develop their own hybrid versions, referring to both Dutch and Lankan-élite dwellings. Naturalization was, therefore, multidirectional and cut across lines that separated cultures, destabilizing pure categorization of cultures in many ways.

Migration from within the country naturalized the city as well. The introduction and expansion of communication networks, which began with the advent of the railways in the 1860s, facilitated the rural to urban migration, increasing Colombo's population by over 300 percent between 1824 and 1891. This also changed its ethnic, religious, and class composition. By 1921, 47 percent of Colombo's population was already Sinhalese (Hulugalle 1965). The Low-Country Sinhalese replaced the Europeans as the main ethnic group four centuries after they had acquired the city from the Muslims. The Tamil neighborhood of Wellawatta, then right outside the municipal boundary, had also been established by the 1880s (Roberts 1984). By then, demographically and spatially, Colombo had largely become a Ceylonese city. Yet, Colombo continued to be diverse, with the Sinhalese constituting only about 40 percent of the population in the early twentieth century (Roberts *et al.* 1989).

The expansion in the 1860s and 1870s, particularly the incorporation of indigenous and migrant areas, had also caused the colonial city to naturalize in Ceylon. In the 1880s, the municipality was about 13 times larger than the Fort and already included areas that had a large majority of Ceylonese. The population of Colombo in 1881 was about 20 times that of the Fort and Pettah (Hulugalle 1965). This made the previously large "White City" a small part of it. The outskirts of the city were also transformed; the early twentieth-century expansion of Colombo turned the outskirts of Wolvendal into low-income housing—called huts and tenements—of the Malays and the Javanese. After emancipation, the former slaves also settled in what used to be Slave Island, across the Beira Lake off the southern bank of Fort (Brohier 2000).

The expansion of the port and its associated industries in 1883 instigated the clustering of working-class tenements and small businesses, converting large areas such as Kochchikade and Gintupitiya into dockland areas (Roberts 1984) (Figure 1.5). The neighborhoods that spread across Maradana, New Bazaar, Kotahena, and Slave Island housed a large proportion of laborers. The dwellings in low-income areas represented the burgeoning working class and the increasing definition of the city by capitalism, overlaying colonialism. Most of these dwellings were produced as part of "industrialization," particularly the expansion of the harbor and the building of railway workshops, warehouses, and printing presses.

There were two main types of working-class dwellings: upper-class leftovers and self-built houses. The large houses were left behind by middle- and upper-class people who had lived north of Fort and Pettah. These were adopted between the 1860s and the 1910s as lodging houses, each occupied by 80–100 single men (Dharmasena 1980; Roberts et al. 1989). These were sometimes used as "multifamily" quarters shared by co-tenants (ibid.). One such residence in Slave Island had 32 dwelling rooms (Jayawardena 1972). Lodging houses, known among Indian immigrants as *kiddangies*, were sustained by small shops and other marginal services that were part of the informal economy (Roberts et al. 1989). These dwellings did not transform the larger physical landscape, but radically redefined its function and meaning.

FIGURE 1.5 Colombo Harbor and Kochchikade Area (credit: Nihal Perera).

The second type of dwelling, self-built housing, added a new dimension to the physical landscape of Colombo. A common solution to the lack of affordable dwellings had been the construction of single-storied, mostly detached, small housing units using less durable material found in the urban environment. Neither the Dutch nor the British allowed thatch houses in Colombo (Correa 1988; Percival 1990). In the late nineteenth century, the Ceylonese brought back to Colombo what Percival (1990) called "huts."

Building their own houses with materials available in the vicinity and using self-help methods to do so represents the migration of rural housing methods to the city. With regard to "Third World cities," Terence McGee (1971) argues that characteristics such as high fertility and the persistence of the "extended family" are aspects of "ruralness." As the migrants used familiar self-building to house themselves in the city, they also ruralized parts of it. Being between urban and rural, these houses represent a liminal space. Simultaneously, these are hybrids that combine urban living and building materials with rural building methods and dwelling forms. The city, marked by clock towers and Georgian buildings at its center, was thus infiltrated by self-built housing and subjected to ruralization and Ceylonization.

The housing of the lower-income population thus transformed both the overall landscape of the city and its meaning for the Ceylonese. The dwellings of ordinary Ceylonese were not built in high architectural styles, nor were they large in size. Nonetheless, by the 1880s the Ceylonese occupied a very large area of the city. They did not overpower the formal landscape in any formal way, but they both annexed a large indigenous component and infiltrated the foreign city.

Most significantly, the Black City gradually moved back to Pettah. It once again become a very diverse zone in regard to both people and activities (Figure 1.1). In 1893, Cave (1893: 10–11) described the colorful Pettah area as:

> an ever fascinating kaleidoscope ... [where] ... the handicraftsman works serenely in his open shed [*sic*] sometimes even in the open street; women are occupied in their most domestic affairs unveiled from the glance of the curious passer-by, and ... tiny children, clothed only in rich tints of their own complexions, sport amongst the traffic.

Cave (1908: 47) also highlights Pettah's character:

> Moormen or Indo-Arab traders occupy [the] Main Street, with well-stocked stores containing every description of goods.... in the vicinity of the Town Hall we notice the great diversity of races represented: Sinhalese, Moors, Tamils, Parsees, Dutch, Portuguese, Malays and Afghans; the variety of costumes worn by each race in accordance with caste or social position.... This mixed and motley crowd live their life and carry on their labours almost entirely in public. Neither doors, windows, nor shutters interfere with a complete view of the interior of their houses and stalls.

The "jabbering and jestication" that the British talked about highlight how the city had become unfamiliar to them. Yet others made Colombo their home, the place where they belonged. This transformation was not the result of an organized movement, but of the coming together of diverse types of familiarizations carried out by a range of diverse peoples including the Ceylonese, Sinhalese, Tamils, Muslims, Burghers, migrants, and naturalized citizens.

Buddhist Revival

Reinforcing the larger process of familiarization, the Buddhist revival brought a power institution to the indigenous side of Colombo, causing the city to become more directly contested from within. The late nineteenth century was a period of cultural and religious regeneration in Ceylon (Bastin 1997; Samaraweera 1997). A generation after the Hindu revival, Buddhism revived strongly in the late nineteenth century (Obeyesekere 1970; Malalgoda 1976; Gombrich and Obeyesekere 1988). In this process, Colombo was developed into the center of Buddhist institutions, with Kandy—particularly, the *Dalada Maligawa* (Temple of the Tooth)—continuing the role of the spiritual center. Colonial Colombo was characterized by the location of all power institutions in the colonial zone, or the White City (King 1976). Breaching this model of colonial city, in the late nineteenth century, the Buddhist institutions provided the "Black City" with a cultural institution capable of contesting the supremacy of colonial power institutions located in Fort.

The late nineteenth century saw cultural and religious revivals in Ceylon (Bastin 1997; Samaraweera 1997). The Hindu revival took place a generation before the Buddhist revival. The Catholic establishment that had been discriminated against under the Dutch and the British also recovered. This section focuses on the spatial impact of the Buddhist revival on Colombo. The broad-based transformation of Buddhism in the late nineteenth century is addressed by scholars such as Gombrich and Obeyesekere (1988), Obeyesekere (1970), and Malalgoda (1976), and will not be repeated here.

The Buddhist revival was marked by the creation of new key institutions, the adaption of old ones within the colonial system, and protests against colonialism and Christianity. These were largely organized in and around Colombo. The transformation was strongly characterized by "oppositional politics" which followed a terrain already mapped out by the opponents. Gombrich and Obeyesekere (1988) argue that, as part of its protest against British colonialism in general and Protestant missionaries in particular, Ceylonese Buddhism transformed in the late nineteenth century (1860–1885) into what they call "Protestant Buddhism." In this, Buddhist institutions acquired many Protestant missionary attributes. The formation of a Buddhist Theosophical Society, the invention of the international Buddhist flag, the incorporation of songs modeled after Christmas carols, and the use of English, among others, represent this change. The new missionary schools sponsored by the Buddhist Theosophical Society and the Mahabodhi Society adopted the model of Christian missionary public schools, whether in regard to the curriculum or cricket (Obeyesekere 1970; Gombrich and Obeyesekere 1988).

For the greater part of the nineteenth century, Protestant Buddhism was limited to a small emerging middle class in coastal cities. However, the changes were far reaching; in a broader sense, Buddhism became more socialized. The revival had a profound effect on smaller cities like Galle (Gombrich and Obeyesekere 1988), which was the leading center of Buddhism in the Low-Country in the late nineteenth century (Malalgoda 1976). The struggle against colonialism was paralleled by a struggle against the upper-caste hold on the Buddhist establishment. Five separate delegations of Salagama, Durava, and Karava traveled to Burma in the early nineteenth century to seek ordination. The result was the establishment of Amarapura Nikaya, open to all castes, perhaps encouraging a large number of Calvinists to return to the faith of their forefathers (de Silva 1987). With the collapse of the Goyigama (caste) monopoly on religious life, not only more non-Goyigamas entered religious activity, but the religious sphere also expanded, increasing the number of fraternities, monks, and temples. Laity became increasingly involved in religious activities and, from the 1880s, displaced monks from some of their traditional positions of religious leadership (Gombrich and Obeyesekere 1988; Malalgoda 1976; de Silva 1989). These developments socialized, reorganized, and strengthened the Buddhist establishment and caused Buddhist activities to spread rapidly across rural villages.

As part of this process, Colombo was transformed into the locus of the most important temples after Kandy, providing a strong Buddhist presence in the city. First, the temples at Kelaniya and Kotte, former Lankan seats of power in the vicinity of Colombo, were reinvigorated. Second, these historical temples were supplemented with new ones (Figure 1.6).[6] Third, the dominance of Colombo with regard to monastic educational institutions (*piriven*) was firmly established.[7] Therefore, the most visible symbols were located in the periphery of the city.

The temples and *piriven*s were supplemented with new organizations such as the Society for the Propagation of Buddhism and the Mahabodhi Society. Moreover, missionary-type institutions and schools such as the Young Men's Buddhist Association and Ananda College (1889), which involved more lay participation, were established in the city. These were supplemented by *daham pasala* (school for

FIGURE 1.6 Elements of the Buddhist Landscape (credit: Nihal Perera)

Buddhist education), the main one established at Dipaduttamaramaya (Figure 1.6). It was also in Colombo that the Buddhists established their main printing presses and publishing houses (the main one being the Lankopakara Press in 1862) (Malalgoda 1976; de Silva 1987). In this, a score of institutions, buildings, and related activities were developed, adapting Colombo as the center.

In regard to peasant struggles in India, Ranajit Guha (1983) stresses the importance of the violation of hegemonic signs and symbols as a process of identification that would otherwise be subjected to the ones assigned by the authorities. This is precisely what the Buddhist activists and institutions did in Colombo; the activists staged public debates and speeches against colonialism and Christianity, especially between 1865 and 1873. In so doing, the leaders gradually occupied the colonial public spaces, creating an alternative public sphere.

In regard to the built environment, the Buddhist revival created a clandestine landscape that was surreptitiously penetrating and infiltrating into colonial Colombo. The spread of Buddhism was represented in a relatively low visual profile in the middle of the city. For the most part, the Buddhists adapted existing buildings. The Buddhist Theosophical Society, for example, was located in a house in Slave Island (Amarasuriya 1981). The exception was Pettah: The Buddhist Educational Movement and its Sunday school were located on Maliban Street (Amarasuriya 1981). In contrast, temples were more visible on the outskirts of the city. In this, the Buddhist presence became more prominent as it spread outwards from the city center, giving the impression that Buddhist institutions were gradually encroaching the colonial city.

Most crucially, a principal Lankan institution capable of challenging the colonial authority was located, for the first time, on the indigenous side of Colombo, and the leaders began occupying the public sphere and public space. As Buddhism provided strength to the Ceylonese, Buddhist organizations spread like a web in Colombo but were differentiated by function and level of activity rather than by physical location and form. The very meaning of the colonial city in which all the power institutions were located in the White City was violated.

A Radical Transformation

As highlighted in the gap between the spaces of the authorities and the needs of the subjects, the city conceived by its authorities was neither complete nor stable. The authorities had little control over the familiarization process, which was a "necessary evil." The inhabitants contested the abstract space; the process invigorated immediately after the city was established as the colonial capital. Exceptions were, therefore, as important as the rules for this urban system to function and for us to understand.

The necessary condition for subjects' reactions was the loss of the 1848 revolt. In result, they looked for accommodation within the colonial society. The corresponding physical transformations neither showed up until the 1860s–1880s nor directly corresponded with the political transformation or the economic growth.

Although society and space operate together, the transformation of these were neither isomorphic nor isotemporal.

Indigenization was not a goal of any struggle, but the effect of a variety of local responses to colonialism. This transformation was much greater than that of the authorities. The people and institutions were highly imaginative, creative, and entrepreneurial to cause such profound transformation in Colombo under strong constraints and with limited resources.

The study also reveals that everyday familiarization of space could accumulate to cause radical change. Indigenizing Colombo was neither a direct challenge nor an escape from the colonial society: It was caused by a messy collection of efforts by a diverse group of subjects and institutions who, at first, opted to survive in the city. Becoming subjects, they strengthened and expanded the colonial city; simultaneously, they also engaged in building better living conditions for themselves. In the process, the subjects radically transformed the contents and meanings of the abstract space, producing a different city than what the authorities had conceived.

The subject positions and spaces in the colonial city belonged to a different culture and were unfamiliar to the Ceylonese. Occupying these required them to reconcile the differences. They did so through the familiarization of subject positions and spaces, from their own perceptual frameworks and languages, both literally and metaphorically. When employed, Ceylonese frameworks reinterpreted colonial structures and subject positions. The complex and interactive process of subject formation modified both the abstract spaces of the authorities and the frameworks and languages of the subjects.

The resultant landscape was multivalent. The colonial zones of Fort and cultural institutions in Cinnamon Gardens, built in high-style colonial architecture, continued to dominate the formal landscape of the city. Yet beyond the intermediate élite residential areas was the vast hybrid and ambivalent "indigenous" city in which the Buddhist presence was more apparent toward the outskirts of the city. As it moved toward the center, the Buddhist landscape blended with the environment, but its activities contested those of the authorities. In contrast, the élite lived next to the colonial residential area in grandiose houses built in styles that matched the same, and migrants lived near the harbor and other industries in houses and housing they newly introduced to the city.

This reveals a paradox: The colonial city would have failed without the subjects' compliance, but they came with their own perceptions and worldviews. As colonialism peaked and penetrated deeper into the lives of the indigenes, disrupting their subsistence living, the Ceylonese were compelled to engage the colonial system. Those who were in and migrated to Colombo constructed their subjectivities the way they saw restrictions and opportunities, employing their own beliefs and fulfilling needs to the degree possible. In this, the colonial city failed to achieve its creators' goals, but succeeded in building a compromised colonial city which lasted until 1948.

In this sense, colonization and indigenization are reciprocal: They are both complicit and in conflict. These processes were neither separate nor oppositional:

indigenization did not begin where colonization ended, it operated along with colonialism. The reinterpretation of subject positions and spaces provides new meanings for these. Most crucially, subjectivity provided access and opportunity for the indigenes to appropriate, re-inscribe, and restructure the very same structures from within. The subjects capitalized on it.

The power-holders were not in total control of space-making processes in Colombo. Small-scale space-making of the weak made utter shambles of the abstract spaces dreamt by their power-holders. The changes taking place at the bottom, the margins, the cracks and the interstices of the authority's city reveal that the colonial society and the city were not as systematic and structured the way the subjects were made to believe, and as the mainstream scholarship presents.

The spaces so "leftover" by the authorities were well deployed by resident groups and institutions to develop their own practices, spaces, and domains, staging a multitude of (uneven) negotiations, including indigenization, naturalization, and ruralization. Although the authorities controlled the public stage, the weak transformed the city from inside, or the back-stage. This study reveals the power of ordinary people to effect changes in urban social spaces and the impact that indigenous consciousness, intentionality, everyday practices, and collective action has had on shaping social space.

In another sense, what the Ceylonese produced was a "city of cities." The cities of the colonial community, the élite, the immigrants, the migrants, women, and the Buddhists had their own centers, frontiers, boundaries, and other recognized and unrecognized spatial elements. Yet these were not congruent; there were gaps between the authorities' and inhabitants' cities. Different (sub)groups of citizens and migrants also made different cities, generating huge gaps between absolute, abstract, and lived cities, and their representations.

Most crucially, the subjects usurped the colonial city. Ironically, as soon as the authorities were able to establish Colombo as the "uncontested" capital of colonial Ceylon, the inhabitants transformed it into a contested city, grounding within Colombo the former conflict between Kandy and Colombo. Also, the locals added a power institution, the Buddhist establishment, to the Ceylonese city. In this, they defied the fundamental definition of the colonial city in which all power institutions such as the military and the governor are located in the White City (King 1976; 1990). The Ceylonese also began to occupy the public sphere and space, bringing the contest back to the authorities, a subject further discussed in the next chapter.

Notes

1 For earlier versions of this study in different contexts, see Perera (2002, 2009).
2 Colombo is not unique; Mary Karasch (1985) makes a similar argument in regard to Rio de Janeiro.
3 The terms Lanka and Lankan are employed strategically to refer loosely to the island and its indigenous societies prior to European colonization, as well as to acknowledge the agency of "not fully colonized" indigenous subjects.

4 Ceylonese businesses in Pettah included H. Don Carolis & Sons (founded in 1860), N.S. Fernando (1875), Don Davit & Sons (1875), A.S.F. Wijegoonaratna (1876), W.D. Carolis (1879), S.L. Naina Marrikar (1888), and Arthur J. Fernando & Co. (1891).
5 Although commonly used for large mansions, *walawwa* is a Kandyan élite house form.
6 The most important of these were the residences of the founder of Amarapura Nikaya, Lankagoda Dhirananda—the Jayasekararamaya at Dematagoda—and of the leading anti-Christian polemicist of the 1860s and 1870s, Mohottivatte Gunananda—the Deepaduttaramaya at Kotahena built by a Thai prince in 1785 (Malalgoda 1976).
7 I refer to the founding of Parama Dhamma Cetiya Pirivena at Ratmalana (1845), Vidyodaya Pirivena in Maligakanda (1873), and Vidyalankara Pirivena at Peliyagoda (1875) (Malalgoda 1976).

References

Amarasuriya, M.P. (1981) "Colonel Olcott and the Buddhist Revival in Sri Lanka" in B.P. Kirthisinghe and M.P. Amarasuriya (eds.) *Colonel Olcott and His Service to Buddhism*, Kandy: Buddhist Publication Society, 21–33.

Azeez, M. (1986) "The Muslims of Sri Lanka" in M.M.M. Mahroof and Sir Razik Fareed Foundation (eds.) *An Ethnological Survey of Muslims of Sri Lanka: From earliest times to independence*, Colombo: Sir Razik Fareed Foundation, 3–16.

Bandarage, A. (1983) *Colonialism in Sri Lanka: The political economy of the Kandyan highlands 1833–1886*, Berlin: Walter de Gruyter.

Bastin, R. (1997) "The Authentic Inner Life: Complicity and resistance in the Tamil Hindu revival" in M. Roberts (ed.) *Sri Lanka: Collective Identities Revisited*, Colombo: Marga Institute, 385–438.

Bhabha, H.K. (1994) *The Location of Culture*, London and New York: Routledge.

Brohier, R.L. (2000 [1984]) *Changing Face of Colombo (1501–1972): Covering the Portuguese, Dutch and British periods*, Colombo: Lake House.

Cave, H.W. (1893) *Picturesque Ceylon: Colombo and the Kelany valley*, Colombo: Cave.

Cave, H.W. (1908) *The Book of Ceylon: Being a guide to its railway system and an account of its various attractions for the visitor and tourist*, London: Cassell.

Correa, I. (1988) *Colombo Municipal Council*, Colombo: Colombo Municipal Council.

de Silva, C.R. (1987) *Sri Lanka: A history*, London: Sangam.

de Silva, K.M. (1989) *A History of Sri Lanka*, London: C. Hurst and Co.

de Silva, K.M. (1997) "Resistance movements in nineteenth century Sri Lanka" in M. Roberts (ed.) *Sri Lanka: Collective identities revisited*, Colombo: Marga Institute, 145–164.

Denham, E.B. (1912) *Ceylon at the Census of 1911: Being a review of the results of the census of 1911*, Colombo: H.R. Cottle-Government Printer.

Devy, G. (2006) *A Nomad Called a Thief: Reflections on Adivasi silence*, Delhi: Orient Longman.

Dewaraja, L. (1995) "Indigenization of the Muslims in Sri Lanka" in G.P.S.H. de Silva and C.G. Uragoda (eds.) *Sesquicentennial Commemorative Volume of the Royal Asiatic Society of Sri Lanka*, Colombo: Royal Asiatic Society, 427–40.

Dharmasena, K. (1980) *The Port of Colombo 1860–1939*, Colombo: Lake House Publishers.

Duncan, J.S. (1990) *The City as Text: The politics of landscape interpretation in the Kandyan kingdom*, Cambridge: Cambridge University Press.

Fanon, F. (1968) *The Wretched of the Earth: The handbook for the black revolution that is changing the shape of the world*, trans. C. Farrington, New York: Grove Press.

Ferguson, J. (1903) *Ceylon in 1903: Describing the progress of the island since 1803, its present agricultural and commercial enterprises, and its unequalled attractions to visitors, with useful statistical information; a map of the island, and upwards of one hundred illustrations*, Colombo: A.M. and J. Ferguson.

Gombrich, R. and Obeyesekere, G. (1988) *Buddhism Transformed: Religious change in Sri Lanka*, Princeton, NJ: Princeton University Press.

Guha, R. (1983) *Elementary Aspects of Peasant Insurgency in Colonial India*, Delhi: Oxford University Press.

Hulugalle, H.A.J. (1965) *Centenary Volume of the Colombo Municipal Council 1865–1965*, Colombo: Colombo Municipal Council.

Jayawardena, K. (1972) *The Rise of the Labor Movement in Ceylon*, Durham, NC: Duke University Press.

Jayawardena, K. (2002 [2000]) *Nobodies to Somebodies: The rise of the colonial bourgeoisie in Sri Lanka*, Colombo: Social Scientists Association and Sanjeeva Books.

Karasch, M. (1985) "Rio de Janeiro: From colonial port town to imperial capital" in R. Ross and G.J. Telkamp (eds.) *Colonial Cities: Essays on urbanism in a colonial context*, Dordrecht: Martinus Nijhoff Publishers, 123–54.

King, A.D. (1976) *Colonial Urban Development: Culture, social power and environment*, London: Routledge.

King, A.D. (1990) *Urbanism, Colonialism and the World-Economy: Cultural and spatial foundations of the world urban system*, London and New York: Routledge.

Knapp, G. (1981) "Europeans, Mestizos and Slaves: The population of Colombo at the End of the seventeenth century," *Itinerario* 5: 84–101.

Malalgoda, K. (1976) *Buddhism in Singhalese Society 1750–1900: A study of religious revival and change*, Berkeley, CA: University of California Press.

McGee, T.G. (1971) *The Urbanization Process in the Third World: Explorations in search of a theory*, London: Bell.

Obeyesekere, G. (1970) "Religious Symbolism and Political Change in Ceylon," *Modern Ceylon Studies* 1: 43–63.

Parakrama, A. (1990) *Language and Rebellion: Discursive unities and the possibility of protest*, London: Katha Parks.

Peebles, P. (1981) "Governor Arthur Gordon of Sri Lanka, 1883–1890" in R.J. Crane and N.G. Barrier (eds.) *British Imperial Policy in India and Sri Lanka 1858–1912: A reassessment*, New Delhi: Heritage Publishers, 84–106.

Peebles, P. (1995) *Social Change in Nineteenth Century Ceylon*, New Delhi: Navrang.

Percival, R. (1990 [1803]) *An Account of the Island of Ceylon Containing its History, Geography, Natural History, with the Manners and Customs of its Various Inhabitants to which is Added the Journal of an Embassy to the Court of Candy*, New Delhi: Asian Education Service.

Perera, N. (1996) "Exploring Colombo: The relevance of a knowledge of New York" in A.D. King (ed.) *Representing the City: Ethnicity, capital, and culture in the 21st century metropolis*, London: Macmillan, 137–57.

Perera, N. (1998) *Society and Space: Colonialism, nationalism, and postcolonial identity in Sri Lanka*, Boulder, CO: Westview Press.

Perera, N. (2002) "Indigenising the Colonial City: Late 19th-century Colombo and its landscape," *Contested Landscapes, Asian Cities* 39: 1703–21.

Perera, N. (2009) "People's Spaces: Familiarization, subject formation, and emergent spaces in Colombo," *Planning Theory* 8, 3: 50–74.

Rahim, M.J.A. (1986) "Muslim Architecture" in M.M.M. Mahroof and Sir Razik Fareed Foundation (eds.) *An Ethnological Survey of Muslims of Sri Lanka: From earliest times to independence*, Colombo: Sir Razik Fareed Foundation, 224–30.

Roberts, M. (1974) "Problems of Social Stratification and the Demarcation of National and Local Elites in British Ceylon," *Journal of Asian Studies* 33: 549–77.

Roberts, M. (1982) *Caste Conflict and Elite Formation: The rise of the Karava elite in Sri Lanka, 1500–1931*, Cambridge: Cambridge University Press.

Roberts, M. (1984) "Colombo in the Round: Outlines of its growth in modern times," Paper presented at the *Second International Conference on Indian Ocean Studies* held at Perth, Western Australia, December, 5–12.

Roberts, M., Rahim, I., and Colin-Thome, P. (1989) *People in Between: The Burghers and the middle class in the transition within Sri Lanka 1790s–1960s*, vol. 1, Colombo: Sarvodaya.

Samaraweera, V. (1997) "The Muslim Revivalist Movement, 1880–1915" in M. Roberts (ed.) *Sri Lanka: Collective identities revisited*, Colombo: Marga Institute, 293–322.

Tampoe, M. (2013) *The Story of Selestina Rodrigo (Mrs Jeremias Dias): Pioneer in Buddhist girls education*, Colombo: Social Scientists Association.

Tennent, J.E. (1999 [1859]) *Ceylon: an account of the island*, New Delhi: Asian Educational Services.

Turner, L.J.B. (1927) *Handbook of Commercial and General Information for Ceylon*, Colombo: Government Printer.

2
FEMINIZING THE WHITE MALE CITY
Women Gaining Access to Colonial Colombo

Chapter 1 maps out how ordinary actors who were not powerful enough to create abstract spaces created lived spaces in late nineteenth-century Colombo. It demonstrates how the Ceylonese, who became subjects of Colombo, gradually nibbled into the city, first transforming it into a contested city and eventually undermining the very structure of the colonial city itself. The story is incomplete; however, without a knowledge of women in the city. Focusing on gender and social power, this chapter examines how women created spaces for their everyday practices in Colombo.[1]

Anthony King (1990) emphasizes that a distinctive demographic characteristic of the European colonial community was the relative absence of women. Colombo was literally established as a White male Christian city by the Portuguese authorities in the early sixteenth century. It was not only European and Catholic, but also a young male domain by design. The gender relations they established were largely based on their imperial objectives, but were compelled to accommodate the local colonial community.

Although the possibility cannot be erased, there is no indication of women in the fort. The fort, which housed the Portuguese *soldados* (soldiers), was later expanded to provide security to the residences of married settlers. Married Portuguese men, *casados*, lived in the extended area, outside of the core, but within the outer wall. They also lived to the north of the fort, between it and the Kelani River. The fort area was reduced by its Dutch rulers in the seventeenth century. Although women were present, it remained a male domain until the demolition of the fortifications by the British in 1869. This area then became a part of Colombo, which also expanded in the late-nineteenth century (Chapter 1).

Even as late as 1921, 61 percent of Colombo's population was male (Roberts 1984). This characteristic was accentuated by the fact that the early migrants were largely single men who came in search of urban fortunes. It would be four and a half centuries, until the 1960s, before the number of women was proportional to that of the "nation." In 1960, however, Ceylon became the first nation in the modern world to have a woman head of state.

The relative absence of women in the colonial city was intensified by the relative absence of literature on women. Studies on the colonial era hardly consider women or their agency to be a significant topic. They focus on activities such as seafaring, exploring new worlds, proselytizing, and empire-building, from which women were excluded. Charles Boxer (1975: 9) observes this lack: "if women are mentioned at all ... [it] is usually restricted to famous characters." The roles played by women in and around military and trading complexes ... were hardly documented. In Western urban history, women in urban environments are not only silenced, but those in public spaces were considered threats to urban order (Garber and Turner 1995). There are only a few recent works on women in Colombo and Ceylon during this period (Boxer 1975; Grossholtz 1984; Roberts *et al.* 1989; Jayawardena 1992, 1995). With few exceptions, literature hardly brings out the contested aspects of space and gender.

European colonialism goes far beyond simple political and economic subjugation. Under colonialism, nature, animals, men, and women were objectified, owned, consumed, and forced to yield and produce (Nandy 1994). As with colonization, the process of objectification and sexualization was never complete. It was flawed by the internal contradictions and convolutions of socio-spatial maps. The everyday practices of women and female groups progressively undermined the colonial structures of gender control. The process, which I call the feminization of Colombo, constituted the transformations of institutions and spaces, especially their meanings, representations, and power relations, enhancing the little power women had in the city (Perera 2002). The term "feminization" employed here is radically different from what is in common circulation; for example, in the "feminization of poverty," feminizing is viewed as a negative process that worsens the predicament of women. In this chapter, the term refers to the advancement in gender relations for certain groups of women within extant social structures. Instead of being passive recipients of its effects (as discussed below), women were involved in empowering themselves and transforming their environments into more friendly ones.

This chapter investigates gender relationships, the rules that govern their enactment, and the patriarchal power structures that maintain inequalities between women and men. Issues of gender are directly related to those of race, class, and ethnicity, and each of these groups has its own story about feminizing Colombo. This study is, therefore, informed by postcolonial and feminist theories, but focuses on social space and geography (Stansell 1987; Jayawardena 1992, 1993, 1995; Spain 1992; Blunt and Rose 1994; Garber and Turner 1995).

Highlighting the contested aspect of gendered spaces, this investigation exposes the official policies of spatial control and the power relations that marginalized women in colonial Colombo. It demonstrates how both European and Lankan women used physical and social-symbolic mobility to subvert these policies. By crossing assigned spatial boundaries and building coalitions across categorical divisions, these "trans-status subjects" (Sarker and De 2002) defied the socio-spatial order built upon separated, but synchronic, relationships between public and private spheres. In so doing, these women changed the values and meanings attached to their gender, race, and status.

In the following sections, I demonstrate how colonial places and spaces, constructed as part of systems of gender, race, class, and ethnic control, were open to deconstruction and redefinition by subordinate groups through their everyday practices. I also explore how they transform the same through the production of space for their daily activities and cultural practices. This gendered subversion led to the gradual increase in number and prominence of women in colonial Colombo through the creation of "women's third spaces." First nestled within the domestic sphere, this space was later extended into the public sphere by missionary and socialist women.

Establishing a White Male Christian City

The establishment of a young White male city involved several important strategies and steps, including the settling of young, single Portuguese *soldados*. The significance of being single was made clear to the *soldados* from the beginning. Any *soldado* who got married was immediately discharged from service (Brohier 2000). The Portuguese Crown actively discouraged women from going out to Asian and African colonies (Boxer 1969a; Russell-Wood 1998). Only a few women immigrated to Asia during the sixteenth and seventeenth centuries, and there were hardly any Portuguese women in colonies and outposts: One lived in Muscat in 1553 and one in Macao in 1636 (Boxer 1969b). This environment developed negative perceptions of women which culminated in the "witchification" of the few European women who immigrated. It is highly probable that any woman who stepped into the core of the fort area was seen as a prostitute or someone similar.

The exceptions were the "orphans of the king" and reformed prostitutes. The former were orphan girls of sometimes barely marriageable age who were sent out to "India" from orphanages in Lisbon and Oporto at the expense of the Crown. From the mid-sixteenth century to early eighteenth century, the orphans, who were intended as wives for public officials and garrison officers, were provided with dowries, largely in the form of minor government posts for their husbands (Boxer 1969b, 1975; Russell-Wood 1998).

As they did with male prisoners from the *Limoeiro*,[2] the Portuguese authorities did not hesitate to make use of the bodies of reformed prostitutes and orphan girls in Lisbon and Oporto to achieve their imperial objectives overseas. Hence, they transformed orphans in Portugal to prospective White wives in the colonies, and a problem at home into an asset of the empire.

The project was never successful; not more than 30 girls ever went out in a single year, and the average was about ten. Even those who went to the East did not impress the men, the cash bonuses were unappealing, and the official posts earmarked for prospective husbands were largely promises and not immediately effective. Also these positions were poorly paid and did not constitute significant financial attraction (Boxer 1969b; 1975).

Concurrently, the colonial authorities implemented policies of miscegenation. According to Roberts *et al.* (1989), the fact that the Portuguese who came East were mostly men was a conscious design of the Portuguese authorities to discourage women from venturing to the colonial outposts, so as to encourage miscegenation as a bulwark of colonial control. Nevertheless, these strategies and controls were flawed. The men created their own spaces. They responded to the situation by engaging prostitutes and drinking. These developments further degraded women.

The separation of unequal public and private spaces is significant to the establishment of spatial control (Garber and Turner 1995). Despite their presence outside the core of the fort, women in Colombo were largely prisoners of the husband or the *amigo* (friend), and their lives were perceived as cheap. The sexual license accorded to *soldados* and *casados* was not extended to women unless they were prostitutes. Yet "Portuguese prostitute" was an oxymoron; an Iberian woman who was the mistress of a man was expected to remain as faithful to him as an actual spouse would be.

Whether authorities or priests, nearly everyone who addressed issues of women and marriage was united in the view that adultery and unchaste behavior by a woman was a much more serious crime than the same committed by a man (Boxer 1975). Moreover, the chastity of women was not trusted (Pieris 1983). A cuckold was never blamed for killing an "erring" spouse, and the men who slew their innocent wives on mere suspicion were seldom punished (Boxer 1969b). The double standard of chastity for men and women was spatially mapped out in such a way that the women's domestic sociality would be subsumed by the men's public sociality, enabling the men to control the public world in which women became the devalued Other (Rosaldo 1974; Blunt and Rose 1994).

The Dutch, too, continued to control the mobility, identity, space, and place of women, but they faced different circumstances and outcomes. They had more deliberate policies of settler colonization, miscegenation, and the creation of a new Eurasian race. The celebrated founder of Dutch commercial supremacy in the East Indies, Jan Pietersz Coen, conceived a flourishing society of *vrij burgers* (free citizens) in Dutch stations in the East, trading side by side with the East India Company (Arasaratnam 1988). Yet the European Enlightenment-based belief of racial segregation, that "the White man, whether merchant, mariner or settler, should stand 'above and apart' from the coloured races" implied that White women should emigrate to colonies in adequate numbers with their men (Boxer 1990: 241).

In contrast to the Portuguese, more Dutch women were willing to go East. Yet the authorities were not satisfied with the kind of women who chose to emigrate. In the 1760s, Stavorinus (1798: 195) observed that a woman

> had disguised herself in men's clothes ... [and] enlisted as a soldier on board
> of the ship *Schoonzicht*; she had long kept her sex concealed, but being at last

discovered, she was put on the shore at the *Cape of Good Hope*, and kept there, in order to be sent back to Holland [Italics in original].

The authorities soon learned that it was hopeless to expect "respectable" women to emigrate in sufficient numbers to the tropics which were regarded as lands where life was short, especially for those bred in northern climates. Also, the acute discomforts of shipboard life on long voyages proved to be a powerful deterrent. For the East India Company, the women who went to the colonies were largely "light women," more conspicuous for their "adventurousness than their morals," who led "scandalous" and "unedifying" lives "to the great shame of the nation" (Boxer 1990: 241–2, 254–5). This language suggests that these women were seen as less controllable, less abiding, more willing to take risks, and, therefore, dangerous. As early as 1612, the Governor-General advised *Heeren* XVII not to allow these women to emigrate.

Incorporating Ceylonese Women

Ceylonese women, too, were incorporated into the colonial project, including its social and spatial order. This is evident in the Portuguese "protection" for the families of Sinhalese auxiliaries called *lascarins*, and the Portuguese and Dutch projects to create a Eurasian race. The usual garrison in Portuguese Ceylon comprised 700 soldiers supported by a standing force of about 15,000 local – *lascarins* (Boxer 1969b). Contrary to the policy governing *soldados*, Portuguese authorities allowed the *lascarins* to have families, but desired to locate them within fortified settlements near the (core) fort to protect them during war (de Silva 1972). The women and children were thus located in a knowable and controllable space, under the surveillance of the authority constructing the power to command these subjects. During war, the authorities made these families immobile and hostage, in view of providing protection for Portuguese *soldados*.

Phillipus Baldaeus (1958) provides a description of how Lup de Britto made use of this arrangement to neutralize a group of *lascarins* who opposed him during the 1656 Portuguese–Dutch–Kandyan war. De Britto led 150 Portuguese soldiers who occupied a "suburb" of Colombo. He ordered that the Sinhalese women and children be tied to doorposts as bait for the Sinhalese soldiers. He then set fire to the roofs of all houses near the Portuguese defense, diverting the Sinhalese and gaining enough time to close the gates of the fort.

Later, the Dutch were attracted to the former Portuguese policy of "body-appropriation," or using the reproductive capabilities of Ceylonese women and Company men (Arasaratnam 1988). Despite their low numbers, men of mixed Portuguese and Sinhalese descent who fought alongside the Portuguese were seen as largely responsible for the stiff and prolonged resistance. Dutch Governor Johan Maetsuyker found that "free-burghers" could not compete on even remotely equal terms with local "Muslims." The children of mixed marriages, he averred, were better acclimatized than those of pure European parentage (Boxer 1990). In this, women and men were seen as sets of discrete functioning mechanisms, bodies that could be controlled, exploited, and coerced to produce a new race.

Dutch authorities desired the production of bodies that looked Dutch but were as strong as the Sinhalese. They believed that, after the second or third generation, the offspring differed little, if at all, from the complexion of pure Netherlanders (ibid.). Although the Dutch were specific about the bodies and wombs they wanted to employ, they encountered some resistance. Allegedly, Muslim women deliberately aborted the babies of Christian men (ibid.).

The Dutch "body appropriation" and the policy of miscegenation produced a reasonable *mestizo* (mixed race) community, but it failed to produce the anticipated results. The Dutch were not successful in attracting their preferred bodies, that of high-class, high-caste Christian or proselytizable women. "Although it was a patriarchal society," argues Jean Grossholtz (1984: 3), "elements of a matriarchal past, Buddhism, and the idea of land-use rights ... gave [Lankan] women ... [a] more flexible position."

Within this broadly sketched position, the specifics are quite striking. The choices available within Lankan gender relationships were broad. The loss of virginity in women was less of a taboo than today and a loose form of trial marriage was common (Knox 1981; Davy 1821). Women had substantial freedom and made most decisions regarding marriages and domestic organization. The Sinhala-Buddhist precepts which incorporate diverse moral codes were more guidelines than commandments, and monogamy, polygamy, and polyandry were customary in various segments of the society (Grossholtz 1984; Jayawardena 1992; Tennent 1999; Tambiah 2011). One option was to enter into a virilocal *diga* marriage in which the bride was given a dowry and had no further claims to inheritance. The alternative was the uxorilocal *binna* in which the woman was entitled to an equal share of the inheritance when her father died, her husband was subject to expulsion at will, and the marriage contract could be dissolved by mutual consent (Jayawardena 1992).

A determining factor of this system was that marriage was not a mode of transferring cultivation rights to a family living outside of the village, irrespective of the gender of the person who relocated (Grossholtz 1984). Unlike the situations of the orphans of the king or of women in many parts of South Asia, dowry was not a way of "bribing" a man to marry a woman, but a way of substituting immovable rights to land for movable property in a society in which land was not commodified.

Dutch colonialism transformed these relationships, displacing the older system with the patriarchal Roman-Dutch legal system and enforcing new marriage and inheritance laws (Jayawardena 1992). Patriarchal inheritance, for example, a more individualistic orientation to material gain, was rooted in the European Enlightenment and required a nuclear family structure. Given indigenous practices, women of upper-caste, upper-class families did not have much of an incentive to liaise with Portuguese or Dutch men.

Those who were attracted by the prospect of living with a White man in the fort were largely from lower castes, presumably meaning non-*Goyigama* caste womenfolk (Roberts *et al.* 1989). For Dutch authorities, the final outcome was the most undesirable: Dutch children born in the Indies were derogatorily called "liplaps" (Stavorinus 1798). Moreover, the children of mixed marriages drew the contempt of the European-born and the Ceylonese, viewed to inherit the vices of both races and the virtues of neither, and their defects were ascribed more to their Eurasian blood than to their upbringing (Boxer 1990).

A Women's Third Space

Despite the rhetoric of male superiority, European women were better adapted to climatic and cultural conditions in Ceylon. The perceived mysteriousness of Portuguese women was integral to the discourse that represented them as inferior to the *conquistadors*. Paradoxically, men died in large numbers in the tropics whereas the women adapted and indigenized faster. Moreover, the willingness to mingle with Ceylonese and slave women helped colonial women create a third space for themselves, instigating the subversion of colonial gender control and maps of spatial subjectivity.

The prevailing rhetoric projected Portuguese women, and their adaptations, as deranged and inferior. In Pieris' (1983: 116) words:

> When at home these women wore a *Baju* of fine muslin ... varying in quality with the wealth of the wearer, wound round their waists, and loose sandals or slippers on their feet. All their spare time ... was devoted to chewing of betel leaf; their food was chiefly rice and curry with some pickled mango ... they invariably ate with their fingers ... drank water in the Oriental fashion from gorglets, which were never applied to the lips. They were very cleanly in their persons, having learnt the Oriental custom of frequent baths ... and were fond of scents, using sandal wood and similar articles on the body like Indian women.

Socially conditioned to think that they were superior, the men did not give much credit to the versatility and adaptability of their women. Instead, they perceived Portuguese women as physically inferior, not tough enough to acclimatize to the tropics. Queiroz wrote in 1687 about the women's frailty: "Even nowadays the pregnancies of Portuguese women almost invariably terminate fatally for both mother and child" (in Boxer 1969b: 129). Whether supported by political or medical knowledge of the time or not, this dominant notion must have justified the thinking of Portuguese women as physiologically, mentally, and morally inferior beings.

Women spoke in a language not fully comprehensible to men and conducted themselves by rituals that defied male reasoning (see Guha 2000). In large part, men's inability to recognize and/or control the processes of transformation experienced by women seem to have contributed to the perception of the women who wore *baju*, hung sandalwood articles on their bodies, and drank from gorgets as some sort of strange beings. Within hegemonic structures of masculinist privilege, unrecognizable transformations can only become so much of a potential threat before the order in the gendered landscape of power is reasserted by redirecting or stopping such change. Projecting the male "lack" onto women to reproduce male superiority, men absorbed the difference that this uneven gendered indigenization produced into a dichotomous system defined by superior–inferior and good–bad.

Like the Portuguese, the Dutch authorities also projected male shortcomings onto women. The lack of strong family and communal life was aggravated by the alcoholism that plagued Dutchmen in Colombo, which was also a problem in the metropole. Cape Town had acquired the reputation as the "Tavern of Two Seas." The authorities blamed women and imposed restrictions on Dutch (colonial) marriages with the intent of ensuring the desirability of women; the usual test applied was the regularity of attendance at church and the women's knowledge of the Christian religion (Arasaratnam 1988).

The Dutch community was hardly stable. At the beginning of Dutch rule, owing to the relative absence of Dutch women on the island, the colonists married Portuguese widows, *mestizo* girls, or Christian Ceylonese, all belonging to very different cultures. The intermarriages created a global village whose inhabitants had very little in common. According to Sinnapah Arasaratnam (1988), once uprooted from their own society, the Sinhalese women who converted to Christianity and married Dutchmen tended to fall into what he calls the corrupt life of that place. It must have been rather difficult for any Ceylonese woman to relocate herself within the Dutch colonial community that was also searching for its own identity, form, and culture.

Within this instability, slaves, mostly of south Indian but also of African origin, became the progenitors of a women's third culture. Language, a prime component of any culture, was molded by the slaves who played a crucial role in reproducing Portuguese within the colonial community in an "Indianized" form. In the early nineteenth century, Robert Percival (1990), a Briton, was surprised that the Dutch ladies in Colombo hardly spoke Dutch, a fact he ascribed to their frequent interaction with slaves, all of whom used "Indianized Portuguese." Each of the 409 households within Colombo in 1694 held an average of 4.31 slaves; in 1761, slaves were 53.5 percent of the city population (Knapp 1981).

The significant role of female slaves in bringing up children was central to the establishment of the third culture. According to Percival (1990), who is unimpressed, the children imbibed manners, habits, and superstitious notions of the slave population. Instead of occupying the slot assigned to them by the colonial authorities and assimilating into the colonial system, the slaves incorporated Dutch women into their culture, including their language.

A major condition that helped the development of the third culture was the dissonance between men and women. Women had spent their entire lives apart from males. Ladies and gentlemen led separate lives not just at home but in the public realm as well. Percival stresses (1990, 137–8):

> The conversation of women ... forms very little of a Ceylonese-Dutchman's entertainment. Although ladies make part of the company, yet they experience

none of that attention and politeness to which fair sex are accustomed to in Europe. After the first salutations … the men seem to forget that the ladies are at all present.

This disjuncture represents a considerable displacement of colonial social and spatial order, developing a competing public sphere for women in the colonial community. This third culture originated within residential space and the female community, but it made its way to the public activities. Manifestations, such as women wearing *bajus*, smelling like oil, speaking in Indo-Portuguese, and socializing together, became naturalized and violated both the hierarchical separation of public–private and public–domestic spaces. This transgression disabled the ability of the male-dominated public sphere to subsume the domestic sphere associated with women.

The new roles and spaces were further strengthened and expanded by Dutch intermarriage practices. Despite the desire of Dutch authorities for apartheid, within a few months after the takeover of Colombo, about 200 Dutchmen married Indo-Portuguese women (Goonewardena 1959). During subsequent decades, Dutch soldiers and officials lived in boarding houses run by *Tupass*, a Dutch term used to identify the darker people of mixed Portuguese and Sinhalese descent, those born out of wedlock, and Asian converts to Christianity. This often resulted in intermarriages (Roberts *et al.* 1989).

Ceylonese women crossing the divide to join the colonial community bolstered this process, and they constructed their own segment of the third space, aided ironically by European women. The women who braved the disdain of their own community and contracted unions with Dutchmen or other Europeans did not simply transform themselves into passive subjects in the new society. While the possession of slaves was especially pleasing for them, these women tended to put on "airs," become "ladies," and wish to be waited on (Roberts *et al.* 1989).

Mixed marriages were instrumental in the development of a remarkable Indo-Portuguese culture within the Dutch colony, of which the *lingua franca* was an Indianized-Portuguese—for Europeans, the Kandyan court, *Mesticos*, *Tupass*, Ceylonese headmen, and other local people. After the British takeover in the late eighteenth century, the Dutch language waned quickly, but use of the Portuguese Creole continued. Even as late as the 1860s, this language was not restricted to the Burghers and *Tupass*, but extended to the urban notables from Bharatha, Colombo Chetty, and other Asian communities (Roberts *et al.* 1989). It is this language that seeped into the women's sphere of the colonial community through the slaves, unifying the women's third spaces with the quotidian culture and the non-formal public sphere within Colombo. While this language is still spoken by a few communities, many of the words used during this time were also absorbed into Sinhala, including "*Thuppahi*," a derogatory term developed out of *Tupass*.

The British Reproduction of Gender Subjectivity

British Colombo was radically different from that of the Portuguese and the Dutch. The British held firmly to apartheid; spatial segregation and control were highly organized. There were more English women living in Colombo than Dutch or Portuguese women during their rule, but the proportion of British women in the city was still small. According to James Cordiner (1807), the British circle in Colombo initially numbered nearly 100 gentlemen and 20 ladies. In the 1840s, Colombo's White population of 2,100 consisted of only 400 females (Roberts *et al.* 1989). These figures include the Dutch and other Europeans who lived in Pettah, the European/Eurasian residential zone. In regard to both number and power, therefore, the gender imbalance in Colombo continued, and the fort continued to be a male domain of the colonial community.

The British colonial society, marked by the principle of exclusiveness, did not recognize miscegenation. Percival, for example, showed extreme prejudice against the Creole population; he was appalled by the lack of "polite" or cultured conversation among Dutch ladies, their "superstitious notions," their use of "barbarous" and "vulgar" Portuguese language, their habits of betel chewing and applying coconut oil to their hair, the odors of which "quite overpower the senses of a European, and render the approach to these women disgusting" (Percival 1990, 139–41; Roberts *et al.* 1989). The British continued the same discourse of the "indigenized-witch," but directed toward other European and Eurasian women, not to their own kind.

The gendered spaces were thus more clearly demarcated at the everyday level. King (1990) demonstrates how the relative absence of women in colonial Delhi led to specific colonial institutions such as the bachelor chummery and the club, and to the allocation of disproportionate space for recreational activities for young male officers, including race courses and riding tracks, which were separated from the local bazaar, which was used by both men and women. Colonial Colombo was no different. In the world outside work, the Ceylonese were kept at a distance and were not admitted into home, club, or social setting. Clubs were principally for men of the colonial community, and ladies were also excluded from meetings.

Entertainments involving women were occasionally provided by both main clubs, but they took place in the country and in the fort, not on club premises; when women were present, there was dancing (Cordiner 1807). The further separation of sociality for men and women would, thus, exacerbate the temporalization of spatial control and the subordination of women.

The officials who made the mistake of marrying Ceylonese women, rather than keeping them as concubines, ruined their careers; the so-called European "ne'er-do-wells" were quickly deported (Roberts *et al.* 1989). The Colonial Office further tightened controls by sending out a circular in 1909 prohibiting civil servants from liaising with local women (Strobel 1991; Jayawardena 1995). Complementary to the intense stratification was the unwritten rule of colonialism that there should be no breach in the ranks.

Englishwomen bore the burden not only of maintaining this social integrity, but also of being considered the guardians of the purity of the race. White women who had local friends were, therefore, accused of "going jungle," and their socializing with local men was seen as racial betrayal (Jayawardena 1995). Confining them to the particular allocated spaces, the British ostracized those English women who had stooped to marry Ceylonese, disparagingly referring to them as "landladies' daughters" (Roberts et al. 1989).

Despite the hardening of British exclusiveness over the years, these apartheid policies never fully materialized. Upper-crust British tended to marry into Burgher elite families with greater frequency in the early part of British rule (Roberts et al., 1989). The loosening of the seemingly tighter British control was quickened by the movement of lower class British across the lines of segregation into associations with the Ceylonese; some even lived with Ceylonese women. Although its characteristics may have transformed, women's third spaces were further reinforced.

From Third Space to Public Space

During British rule, there was a marked increase in the number of European women who disrupted the colonial system of gender control in Colombo. They became increasingly involved in the social, cultural, and political activities of the island. The wide range of out-of-the-ordinary European women—from a colonial perspective—included holy rollers, spinsters, busybodies, eccentrics, divine mothers, fanatics, and prostitutes who disrupted the gendered maps of control to those who more overtly exported the idea of social change to Ceylon, such as agitators, anarchists, and communists (Jayawardena 1995). More prominent in the early years were those who brought Christianity, Western education, social reform, women's rights, and other modernizing processes to Asia within the framework of British colonialism. Toward the latter part of British rule, Ceylon saw the emigration of women who were rejecting Christianity, negating Western values, and rediscovering indigenous religions and cultures in a context of self-rule, nationalism, and socialism. These women were inspired by social beliefs that motivated many of them to abandon their home countries to live and die in South Asia (Jayawardena 1995).

Missionary women were the first to explicitly subvert the colonial structure of gendered space. Their mission required contact with the indigenes, so these women boldly crossed the colonial divide. As those who carried out the broader colonial objective of Westernizing the Ceylonese, missionary women were entitled to occupy the public sphere. Through occupying these new spaces, and crossing the colonial divide, missionary women not only subverted the colonial map of gender control, but also achieved what was denied to them at home. Through their presence and activities, they expanded women's third space into the formal public arena and, physically, to ecclesiastical spaces in the middle of the city, such as churches, convents, missionary schools, and plazas.

In the early phase of British rule, missionary schools for Ceylonese women undertook the narrow objective of producing good Christian wives for male converts. Higher education, almost equal to that for boys, granted Ceylonese women access to professions and employment in the formal economy. Women medical practitioners among the missionaries drove this social transformation even further.

Dr. Mary Rutnam (née Irwin, 1873–1962), who had earlier been involved in charity and religion, not only worked in the field of gynecology but also campaigned in Ceylon for maternal healthcare, hospital facilities for women, childcare, and temperance, half a century before independence. Rutnam, who Kumari Jayawardena (2009: 33) claims is "the forerunner of women's struggles in Sri Lanka … and the inspirer," began her practice in 1906, drawing women who preferred to be treated by a woman doctor. As women's health was linked to birth control, she pioneered sex education and opened a family planning clinic in Maradana in 1937 (ibid.). She also believed in extending the male suffrage to women and in women having a say in framing the laws of the country. Moreover, she pioneered women's groups such as the Ceylon Women's Union (1904), the Tamil Women's Union (1909), the Women's Franchise Union (1927), and the Lankan Mahila Samitiya (1931) (Jayawardena 1995). Despite being a "foreigner," she was elected to the Colombo Municipal Council from Bambalapitiya ward in 1937 (Jayawardena 2009).

Toward the end of colonial rule, educated European women indigenized much faster and crossed deeper into the Ceylonese side of the colonial divide. In so doing, they accelerated the Westernization of Ceylonese women and their movement from an indigenous domestic sphere to the colonial public sphere.

Another group, consisting of theosophists, Orientalists, and holy mothers who rejected the "noble savage" hypothesis, wanted to "civilize" the colonized. For them, Asia had

> achieved a degree of wisdom and spirituality far superior to the materialist development of the West … they were particularly attracted by the concepts of woman's power (*shakti*) in Hinduism, by androgynous deities, female goddesses such as Kali, and by the claims of high status of women in ancient Hindu and Buddhist societies. These perceptions placed them in a position of direct antagonism to colonialism, which they saw as a destructive force.
>
> (*Jayawardena 1995: 4–5*)

The Russian Helena Blavatsky and the American Mary Foster were key figures in the revival of Buddhism in the late nineteenth century.

As they were going against the grain of the colonial system, women who took part in these movements did not perceive their role as exporting Western ideas. Moreover, both men and women of this category did not directly occupy the colonial public sphere, but bifurcated it, developing room in it for the Ceylonese. This public space was built around the new Buddhist institutions in Colombo, particularly the Mahabodhi Society, *vihares* (temples) at Kotte and Kelaniya, *piriven* (Buddhist universities) at Vidyodaya and Vidyalankara, printing presses, publishing houses, and Buddhist schools in Colombo (Chapter 1).

In the early twentieth century, some European women directly took part in the struggle for independence and socialism in Ceylon. These socialists rejected Kali and local gurus and wanted the Ceylonese to free themselves, politically from foreign rule and, with regard to women, from socially oppressive structures and traditional religious and cultural practices. In 1942, Hedi Keuneman (née Stadlen)—who married a leader of the Communist Party—was elected as president of the Rendapola Co-operative Society (Perera and Gunasekera 2009).

The British rulers were clearly rattled by the boldness of these Western women who were undermining White supremacy by consorting with the colonized. They were considered far more dangerous than the "indigenized witches" of the early colonial era. If missionary women developed a niche in the public space for them, socialist women directly contested the validity of the colonial public space and threatened to replace it with an alternative. Bringing the involvement of Western women to a peak, Doreen Wickramasinghe (née Young), who married the leader of Ceylon's Communist Party, defeated her own Sinhalese in-law who represented the ruling party, to become the first foreign-born woman to enter the Parliament in 1952.

Lankan Women Join the Process

For almost the entire colonial period, upper-class, upper-caste Lankan women were not central to feminizing the city. As discussed above, there was not much for them to gain by liaising with the foreigners; they did not even live in Colombo during the early colonial period. Their move to Colombo was largely as family members of the political and economic elite who emulated colonial roles and residential preferences in Muttuwal, Kollupitiya, and Cinnamon Gardens, successively. It was Western women who helped their Ceylonese sisters enter the Modern (colonial) society, largely through education. Eventually these women, too, crossed the colonial divide to create their own third space, a Modernized and Westernized version of the Ceylonese world.

When compared to other countries in Asia, Ceylonese women had a head start in education. Yet the literacy rate of women in 1881 was a mere 3 percent, and among Buddhist women only a few had a "systematic" education. Modernized Buddhist men were reluctant to marry uneducated women, preferring the products of Christian convents. In Buddhist culture, where the woman is considered the agent of cultural continuity, Buddhist men marrying Christian women, some non-Sinhalese, was viewed by some as a threat to the Sinhala-Buddhist identity.

Buddhist women's schools were established in the late 1880s. Henry Olcott, a leader of Buddhist revival in Ceylon, was interested in providing opportunities for women based on the idea that the "mother is the first teacher." Responding to the inaction of the Buddhist Theosophical Society, a group of women organized the Women's Educational Society and began four major schools. Sangamitta School at Maradana (Colombo) was in English medium (Tampoe 2013). Following Olcott's ideals, at its entrance was the motto "From daughter to wife, from wife to mother."

Learning English was considered an important part of upward social mobility. Yet it was hard to maintain Sangamitta School. Among other Westerners, German Marie Musaeus Higgins was invited by the theosophical women to become the principal. Later in 1894 she began Musaeus College (ibid.).

The first English-medium high school, Buddhist Girls' College was established in 1917 (and renamed Visaka Vidyalaya in 1927) (ibid.). All the principals and most teachers of the school were women of European origin, and some were Burghers. The first Sinhalese-woman principal of Visaka Vidyalaya was appointed in 1967, 19 years after independence. The number of girls enrolled in schools rose from 50,000 in 1901 to 396,000 in 1946. Their proportion rose from 27 percent to 42 percent, and the literacy rate for women from 3 percent to 83 percent during this period (Jayawardena 1993).

Education opened up a broad avenue for Buddhist women to enter the public sphere. Most crucially, it enabled Buddhist girls to gain status-enhancing value without totally relinquishing their Sinhala-Buddhist identity (Tampoe 2013). Values like respect for elders and Buddhist respectability did not allow ballroom dancing. Although Sangamitta tried sari, the Buddhist Girls' College did not, nor was Buddhism in the curriculum. All religious activities were conducted outside of the main syllabus. However, the students observed eight precepts on full-moon days which were school holidays. The Buddhist middle class thus had a school which provided English-based modern education and social accomplishments associated with élite status.

These were not the lower-caste, lower-class women who helped European women indigenize and develop a third space; rather, the upper and upper-middle classes and castes were the helpers. They were helped by educated, middle-class European women who were creating a space for themselves in their own Western world. Selestina Rodrigo, the activist who established Buddhist Girls College, was a successful business woman, respectful benefactress, and a pioneer of women's rights. She was honored with Member of British Empire status in 1929. Yet she was not interested in moving to Colombo, but lived in Panadura.

Few educated Ceylonese women such as Selena Perera (née Pieris) and Vivian Goonewardena directly challenged—with their male compatriots—the colonial rule. They were original members of the socialist (*Sama Samaja*) party formed in 1935.

The major group of actors who brought about the feminization of Colombo's core was the women of the "Black City," the unsung heroines. These mostly lower-class women lived in the indigenous part of Colombo during the entire colonial period. When Percival (1990) claimed in the early nineteenth century that, for its size, Colombo was one of the most populated places in "India," and the meeting place of a large number of races and ethnic groups, he referred to this part of the city. This was also the most women-friendly area in Colombo, where women defied most official restrictions imposed upon them and engaged in public activities, particularly vending. Although some of them might have fallen prey to miscegenation, police brutalities, and other discriminatory policies of colonial regimes, it was these poorer women, with their men, who continued to contest the European and male claims to Colombo throughout the colonial period. These women and their families built and maintained their city adjacent to the colonial city and, along with the new migrants, eventually transformed the White male city into a more women-friendly city.

Feminizing the City

European imperial powers strategically used social space, especially the separation between the colonial community and the colonized as well as the domestic and public spaces, to make cultural and ideological impositions on the bodies and the minds of the colonized. As illustrated, Portuguese, Dutch, and British colonial maps of gender control were not as efficient, efficacious, or complete as their discursive representations suggest. Neither the Portuguese nor the Dutch authorities were able to induce a significant number of "respectable" women to emigrate to the colonies, nor were the Portuguese males able to engage in miscegenation to a degree that it would become a crucial instrument in the colonization of Ceylon.

Simultaneously, subordinate groups redefined the maps of gender, race, class, and ethnic control through their everyday practices. If separation was a key strategy of control, women on both sides of the colonial divide made use of their mobility to subvert the socio-spatial map of colonial control, enhancing the number and prominence of women in Colombo. While slave and indigenous women helped their European counterparts to both indigenize and carve out a women's third space, European women facilitated the entry of upper- and middle-class Ceylonese women to modern society. Later, missionary women of European origin expanded the third space into the public arena and the socialist women helped Ceylonese women, and men, to occupy the public sphere. Complementing the long-term residents of the "Black City" who never relented, the Ceylonese socialist women joined their male compatriots and the immigrant women who were in the process of creating an alternative public sphere and space; some like Gunawardena and Perera ascended to the leadership. Although these small transformations neither solved the larger gender discriminations nor addressed all issues of social justice and equity, the above actors emerged out of the colonial assignment of space and asserted themselves.

In the long run, women's third space progressed from a "semi-private" sphere to a public sphere. First nestled within the domestic arena, the third space was developed, during Dutch rule, into an alternative space within the colonial public sphere, and a representation of women's resistance to colonial control. The progress in regard to feminizing the city was not linear: The authorities periodically reproduced the order within the gendered spaces of power by obstructing the movements of subversives at the boundaries of masculinist privilege; for example, the Dutch authorities stopped the "adventurous women" from traveling to colonies. At every stage, however, the women developed everyday practices that would resist and undermine that order. What we see are successive cycles of reestablishment and subversion of the gendered landscape of power in colonial Colombo within which women were able to gradually progress their standing.

Notes

1 For earlier versions of this study in different contexts, see Perera (2002, 2009).
2 According to Abeyasinghe (1966), many of the *soldados* who came to the East were men pressed for service from the Lisbon jail, the *Limoeiro*, and the worst of the Portuguese in the East tended to be posted for service in Ceylon.

References

Abeyasinghe, T. (1966) *Portuguese Rule in Ceylon 1594–1612*, Colombo: Lake House.

Arasaratnam, S. (1988 [1958]) *Dutch Power in Ceylon 1658–1687*, New Delhi: Navarang.

Baldaeus, P. (1958) "A True and Exact Description of the Great Island of Ceylon" trans. P. Brohier in *The Ceylon Historical Journal*, vol. VII (July 1958–April 1959), Maharagama, Colombo: Saman Press.

Blunt, A. and Rose, G. (1994) *Writing Women and Space: Colonial and postcolonial geographies*, New York and London: Guilford Press.

Boxer, C.R. (1969a) *The Portuguese Seaborne Empire 1415–1825*, New York: Alfred A. Knopf.

Boxer, C.R. (1969b) "Portuguese and Spanish Projects for the Conquest of Southeast Asia, 1580–1600," *Journal of Asian History* 3: 118–136.

Boxer, C.R. (1975) *Women in Iberian Expansion Overseas 1415–1815: Some facts, fancies and personalities*, New York: Oxford University Press.

Boxer, C.R. (1990 [1965]) *The Dutch Seaborne Empire 1600–1800*, London: Penguin Books.

Brohier, R.L. (2000 [1984]) *Changing Face of Colombo (1501–1972): Covering the Portuguese, Dutch and British periods*, Colombo: Lake House.

Cordiner, J. (1807) *A Description of Ceylon Containing an Account of the Country, Inhabitants and Natural Productions; With narratives of a tour round the island in 1801, the campaign in Candy in 1803, and a journey to Ramisseram in 1804*, 2 vols, London: Longman.

Davy, J. (1821) *An Account of the Interior of Ceylon and Its Inhabitants, with Travels in the Island*, London: Longman, Hurst, Rees, Orme and Brown.

de Silva, C.R. (1972) *The Portuguese in Ceylon 1617–1638*, Colombo: H.W. Cave.

Garber, J.A. and Turner, R.S. (1995) "Introduction" in Judith A. Garber and Robyne S. Turner (eds.) *Gender in Urban Research*, Thousand Oaks, CA: Sage, x–xxvi.

Goonewardena, K.W. (1959) "A 'New Netherlands' in Ceylon: Dutch attempts to found a colony during the first quarter century of their power in Ceylon," *Ceylon Journal of History and the Social Sciences* 2: 203–43.

Grossholtz, J. (1984) *Forging Capitalist Patriarchy: The economics and social transformation of feudal Sri Lanka and its impact on women*, Durham, NC: Duke University Press.

Guha, R. (2000) "Chandra's Death" in R. Guha (ed.) *Subaltern Studies Reader 1986–1995*, New Delhi: Oxford University Press, 34–62.

Jayawardena, K. (1992) *Feminism and Nationalism in the Third World*, London: Zed Books.

Jayawardena, K. (1993) "Sudu Gahanu, Arrakku Salli ha Balika Adyapanaya" [White Women, Arrack Money, and Girls' Education] (in Sinhala) *Pravada* 5 (October–November): 13–22.

Jayawardena, K. (1995) *The White Woman's Other Burden: Western women and South Asia during British colonial rule*, New York and London: Routledge.

Jayawardena, K. (2009) *Dr. Mary Rutnam: A Canadian pioneer for women's rights in Sri Lanka*, Colombo: Social Scientists Association.

King, A.D. (1990) *Urbanism, Colonialism and the World-Economy: Cultural and spatial foundations of the world urban system*, London and New York: Routledge.

Knapp, G. (1981) "Europeans, Mestizos and Slaves: The population of Colombo at the end of the seventeenth century," *Itinerario* 5: 84–101.

Knox, R. (1981) *An Historical Relation of Ceylon Together with Somewhat Concerning Severall Remarkeable Passages of my Life that hath Happned Since my Deliverance out of My Captivity*, Colombo: Gunasena.

Nandy, A. (1994 [1983]) *The Intimate Enemy: Loss and recovery of self under colonialism* (8th edn.), New Delhi: Oxford University Press.

Percival, R. (1990 [1803]) *An Account of the Island of Ceylon Containing its History, Geography, Natural History, with the Manners and Customs of its Various Inhabitants to which is Added the Journal of an Embassy to the Court of Candy*, New Delhi: Asian Education Service.

Perera, N. (2002) "Feminizing the City: Gender and space in colonial Colombo" in S. Sarker and E. De (eds.) *Trans-Status Subjects: Genders in the globalization of South and Southeast Asia*, Durham, NC: Duke University Press, 67–87.

Perera, N. (2009) "People's Spaces: Familiarization, subject formation, and emergent spaces in Colombo," *Planning Theory* 8, 3, 50–74.

Perera, M. and Gunasekera, R. (eds.) (2009) *Colombo: Excluding women – The struggle for women's political participation in Sri Lanka*, Colombo: Social Scientists Association.

Pieris, P.E. (1983 [1914]) *Ceylon: The Portuguese Era*, 2 vols, Dehiwala: Tissa Prakasakayo.

Roberts, M. (1984) "Colombo in the Round: Outlines of its growth in modern times," Paper presented at the *Second International Conference on Indian Ocean Studies* held at Perth, Western Australia, December, 5–12.

Roberts, M., Rahim, I., and Colin-Thome, P. (1989) *People in Between: The Burghers and the middle class in the transition within Sri Lanka 1790s–1960s*, vol. 1, Colombo: Sarvodaya.

Rosaldo, M.Z. (1974) "Women, Culture and Society: A theoretical overview" in M.Z. Rosaldo and L. Lamphere (eds.) *Women, Culture and Society*, Stanford, CA: Stanford University Press.

Russell-Wood, A.J.R. (1998 [1992]) *The Portuguese Empire, 1415–1808: A world on the move*, Baltimore, MD: Johns Hopkins University Press.

Sarker, S. and De, E. (2002) *Trans-status Subjects: Gender in the globalization of South and Southeast Asia*, Durham, NC: Duke University Press.

Spain, D. (1992) *Gendered Spaces*, Chapel Hill, NC: University of North Carolina Press.

Stansell, C. (1987) *City of Women: Sex and class in New York 1789–1860*, Urbana, IL: University of Illinois Press.

Stavorinus, J.S. (1798) *Voyages to the East-Indies*, London: G.C. and J. Robinson.

Strobel, M. (1991) *European Women and the Second British Empire*, Bloomington, IN: Indiana University Press.

Tambiah, S.J. (2011) *Polyandry in Ceylon with Special Reference to the Laggala Region*, Colombo: Social Scientists Association.

Tampoe, M. (2013) *The Story of Selestina Rodrigo (Mrs Jeremias Dias): Pioneer in Buddhist girls education*, Colombo: Social Scientists Association.

Tennent, J.E. (1999 [1859]) *Ceylon: An account of the island*, New Delhi: Asian Educational Services.

3

SPACES OF SURVIVAL

People's Adaptation of a War Zone in Sri Lanka

War is physically more brutal than colonialism. The way the Sri Lankan separatist war (1983–2009) was perceived, conceived, and executed by politicians and journalists constructed a totalizing view of Sri Lanka defined by two opposing ethnic groups and an "ethnic conflict" between them. The descriptions and analyses of the war as represented in political statements, newspaper reports, and scholarly work were built around Tamil–Sinhala, the Liberation Tigers of Tamil Eelam (LTTE)–government forces, and Colombo–Jaffna binary oppositions. This is partly due to the lack of cognitive tools that help pinpoint the actors or actor-groups and partly deliberate politics. Nonetheless, this discourse privileged the war and the warring parties as the agents capable of making peace.

This chapter focuses on (third) spaces between and outside these dualities. It attempts to bring to light how ordinary people, subjects of the war-zone, lived and constructed their own spaces. The chapter contextualizes what it perceives as a separatist–sovereignist war within postcolonial state-making. It is one among many processes through which the postcolonial nation-state, particularly the positions of ethnic groups within it, is socially and spatially restructured. Sri Lanka has radically transformed since the 1970s from a state largely defined by its colonial past to a nation-state of its "own" creation, but influenced by colonial and "traditional" pasts and global and regional processes.

The trope of the "ethnic conflict" reifies the nation with regard to ethnicity, making the ethnicity-based classification of people common sense. This leads to the "unmixing" of mixed and hybrid populations into Sinhalese and Tamil (see Rajasingham-Senanayake 2002). This classification also marginalizes other people, groups and politics, including income, ethnic, religion, gender, and class-based politics that the signs of "ethnic" and Sinhala–Tamil fail to register. This chapter draws attention to other narratives and their corresponding spaces that lie beyond and within the interstices of this hegemonic ethnic duality.

Space was central to the separatist struggle: It was about territory. Both the state and the LTTE presumed a direct link between a homogeneous Tamil group and a particular territory to which it naturally belongs. This highlights a geographical determinism. The LTTE claimed what it called Tamil Eelam for Tamils. The sovereignists believed in the inviolability of the sovereign territory of Sri Lanka that geographically cognates with the whole island. They feared the breakup of this "natural" national territory. Yet social space is neither natural, nor authentic or static. It is socially produced through messy and complex historical processes of contestation, collaboration, accommodation, and negotiation.

With regard to scholarly work on violence in Sri Lanka, Rogers *et al.* (1998) highlight three principal strands of thought: historical-revisionist, crowd-centered, and victim-centered. This study focuses on the survivors and their spaces. Despite the richness, the literature lacks well-developed engagements with the role of space in the conflict. The narratives tend to treat space as a given or as a container of social action, fixing and depoliticizing it. Some geographers such as C.M.M. Bandara and G.H. Peiris attempt to apply their ecological frameworks to explain and even solve the conflict, but they neither question the politics of these maps nor their politics; they do not examine the conflict from the standpoint of social space. Moreover, as Homi Bhabha (1994: 2) emphasizes, "In-between" spaces provide the terrain for elaborating strategies of selfhood—singular or communal—that initiate new signs of identity and innovative sites of collaboration and contestation, all the while attempting to define the idea of society itself.

The spaces of those who lived through the separatist war were not determined by it, but were built through various responses to the context largely defined by the war. The responses arise not at the national or regional scale but at tangible scales as part of trying to live through the war as meaningfully as possible. The people both adapted themselves to the brutal social and spatial contexts and also transformed space to suit their own needs and practices to the degree possible.

Cathrine Brun (2001) argues that re-territorialization may be understood as the way internally displaced people establish new or expanded networks and cultural practices and define everyday spaces in the process. She builds on bell hooks' (1990) idea of "home-places," conceived as "safe" places that act as positions from which to negotiate worlds. Similarly, this chapter investigates how spaces are adopted, adapted, and transformed by examining the geographies of war as instigated by the LTTE and the government, and how people on the ground acted upon these geographies.

As I examine the spaces in a war zone, it is clear that I have not been able to map a "complete" geography produced by the LTTE or the people. This is not my intention. My objective is to map the basic contours of select spaces and spatial structures produced outside and in the cracks of Sri Lanka's hegemonic binary imaginations. I shall first map the new spatial duality constructed by the LTTE, both following its separatist agenda and displacing a postcolonial Colombo–Jaffna binary. I will then highlight some significant spaces and the spatial structure of the northern region that people developed.[1]

Postcolonial Geographies

The postcolonial ethnic binary is spatially represented as the Colombo–Jaffna opposition. In this chapter, I use Jaffna for the city; the Jaffna region and the peninsula will be so mentioned. Ironically, the separatist war has displaced the (post) colonial geographical imagination of a Tamil homeland, particularly the primacy of Jaffna city and peninsula, the Colombo–Jaffna binary, the hierarchy, and directionality. The government held Jaffna, what used to be the capital of "Tamil territory," since 1995. Yet it had to fight for another 14 years to bring the north under its control. In the meantime, the LTTE negotiated a territory in Vanni and created its own spatial structure, contesting the Colombo–Jaffna duality; the final battle too took place in eastern Vanni (Figure 3.1).

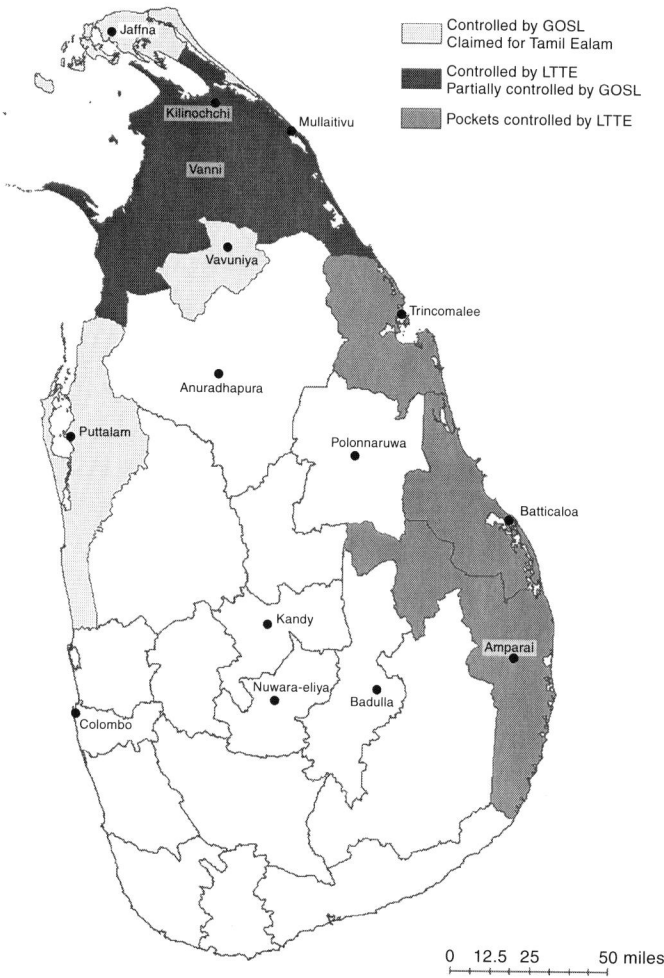

FIGURE 3.1 Areas Controlled and Claimed by the LTTE (2002) (credit: Kaushalya Herath; source: Wikipedia).

The hegemonic Sinhala–Tamil binary is largely an elite construction of the 1920s and 1930s. Yet its spatiality is vague. The Tamil homelands conceived by leaders such as Ponnambalam Arunachalam and S.J.V. Chelvanayakam were largely social and lacked spatial definition. Tamil ethno-politics focused more on the rights of the Tamils. The homeland idea was always present in the discourse, but the focus was on the electorate from which to draw political support and on an area that needed protection from Sinhalese encroachments. As the discourses suggest, the cognitive maps of the Tamil leadership loosely envisaged Tamil space as Jaffna-centric.

Yet, the Tamils did not represent a single community. The Ceylon Tamil League founded in 1922 was largely limited to the Jaffna peninsula; Jeyaratnam Wilson (1994) stresses that even the enormous reputation of Arunachalam was not sufficient to bring the Tamil population from Northern and Eastern Provinces under one banner. The Tamil United Liberation Front not only assumed leadership but also brought the idea of an independent state to the center of its campaign in 1976. The physical delineation of this social imagination continued to be vague.

The response of the "leaders" to the vague physicality of the Tamil homeland was to ethnicize colonial maps. The hegemony achieved by colonial maps in Sri Lanka is evident in the postcolonial adoption of colonially inscribed provinces, districts, and their capitals as culturally and politically neutral objective facts (Perera 1998). Rather than mapping ethnic territories, the Tamil leaders attempted to make colonial provinces represent ethnic groups. As the Tamil political parties relied on rural voters for power, their imaginations were centered upon the electorate. Post-colonial governments have modified and redrawn the electoral map, but within colonial territorial imaginations. Despite the seeming homogeneity of the electorates, the electoral power was uneven. The de facto Tamil territory consisted of a core and a periphery with the political power concentrated in the Jaffna peninsula, reducing as it moved outwards, but with spotty concentrations of power in select electorates. Hence, the homeland was defined by a frontier, very different to homogeneous states demarcated by boundaries.

The LTTE paid more attention to the territory and produced maps of Eelam. They, too, relied on colonial divisions: The LTTE created its Eelam primarily out of Northern and Eastern Provinces and Puttalam District in the Northwestern Province (Figure 3.1). This can be contrasted with how, in 1990, LTTE leader Kittu (Sathasivam Krishnakumar) defined the desired territory: "Take a map of the island. Take a paint brush and paint all the areas where Sri Lanka [the government] has bombed and launched artillery attacks during these past several years.... The painted area that you see ... is Tamil Eelam" (in Satyendra 1993). Kittu's imagination is based on ground conditions, but it does not correspond with administrative divisions of Sri Lanka drawn for other purposes. Neither he nor the LTTE has drawn a map that corresponds with ground conditions either.

Most crucially, the area lacks the ethnic exclusivity that the ethnic state demands. Ethnic diversity exists in particular areas, especially in the border region (Rajasingham-Senanayake 2002; Thangarajah 1995). Second, the area is also concentric in the sense that the intensity of Tamil-ness is almost total in the peninsula and either non-existent or very thin at the periphery.

Instead of reconsidering the map, the LTTE opted to change the ground realities. A notorious LTTE strategy was to expel non-Tamils from the region. In addition to sporadic attacks on non-Tamil villages in the claimed area, in October 1990, after the Indian Peace Keeping Force (IPKF) left in March, the LTTE issued an eviction notice to all Muslims living in the northern districts of Mannar, Mullativu, Kilinochchi, and Jaffna: Leave or be killed (UTHR 1991).

Both the extant geographies and other social agencies (especially the government) caused the LTTE to negotiate both the map and the larger imagination. What the LTTE held in the last decade was the Vanni area, the mainland area of the Northern Province of Sri Lanka, which includes Mannar, Mullaitivu, and Vavuniya districts, and most of Kilinochchi District (Wikipedia 2007). The LTTE-held territory began just south of the peninsula with the southern border stretching from Mannar on the west coast, to north of Vavuniya at the center, and Kokkuthuduwai on the eastern seaboard (see Tamilnation 2007).

Vanni is a large area of about 7,500 km² (2,950 square miles), but much smaller than the projected Eelam.

Vanni is a unique area made up of forest tracts and a distinct social life. It is home to historic settlements with Buddhist, Hindu, and other archaeological remains. In the post-Raja Rata period (which some historians call the "medieval" period), this area was ruled by Vanniar chiefs who are believed to be Tamil in ethnicity. A Survey Department map of 1852 describes Vanni and the North Central Province as "unknown country" (Brohier and Paulusz 1951).

Vanni was further isolated during the war. The Colombo–Jaffna (A9) road and the northern railway line which link Jaffna and Colombo go through Vanni. Both the LTTE and the government viewed these thoroughfares as one-way connections that facilitated Colombo's authority over the north; the government also used these to move its military. The LTTE laid landmines along both the road and the railway. Later, the militarily instantiated isolation of Vanni was complemented by the restrictions of movement imposed on ordinary people by both the LTTE and the military.

The "isolated economy," especially between 1990 and 2002, continued until 2009. Turning the isolation into a separation, the LTTE introduced different taxes, laws, and a justice system, highlighted by the adoption of a border tax and a different no-building zone in tsunami-affected areas (200 m as opposed to the national norm of 100 m). The tax system was formalized and justified by the LTTE's engagement in public works projects, such as road construction, more vigorously during the truce between 2002 and 2006. These structures and activities gave substance to the de facto geo-body. The maintenance of the old timezone, when the rest of the country changed its clocks back to Greenwich +5:30, made the separation tangible.

The resultant geo-body is neither congruent with LTTE maps, nor the combined Northern and Eastern Provinces offered as a package to devolve political power. It resulted from the military power of the warring parties.

Along with carving out a territory on the ground and negotiating who would inhabit it, the LTTE also transformed the regional structure. As part of its fight against the military's dominance over the city, it deliberately sought to undermine Jaffna's power in the region. In effect, the LTTE displaced the centrality of both Jaffna and the peninsula with regard to the imaginations of the Tamil homeland.

Jaffna is a European colonial product and home to Westernized, middle-class Tamils and Tamil parliamentarians. Its coloniality is marked by the continued importance of its location near the sea as an external entry point to the peninsula and its grid-like urban layout. Most institutional buildings in the city, such as schools and administrative buildings, are largely from the British colonial period, built in neoclassical and gothic architectural styles. In positioning Jaffna as a regional center, colonial authorities also shaped its hinterlands and the spatial structure of the region. This is particularly evident in its radial road connections to all corners of the northern shore of the peninsula, with a fort at the center to defend the city (Figure 3.2).

Jaffna was the center of the postcolonial Tamil leadership. The most significant monument to this leadership, the Chelvanayakam Column, was built in the city (Figure 3.3). It was also the city Sinhala communalists attacked and the government desired to hold. After the government recapture in 1995, the LTTE effectively displaced its centrality.

Even earlier, the LTTE did not ascribe much strategic value to Jaffna but favored Nallur and the outlying areas. Since the mid-fourteenth century, the northern

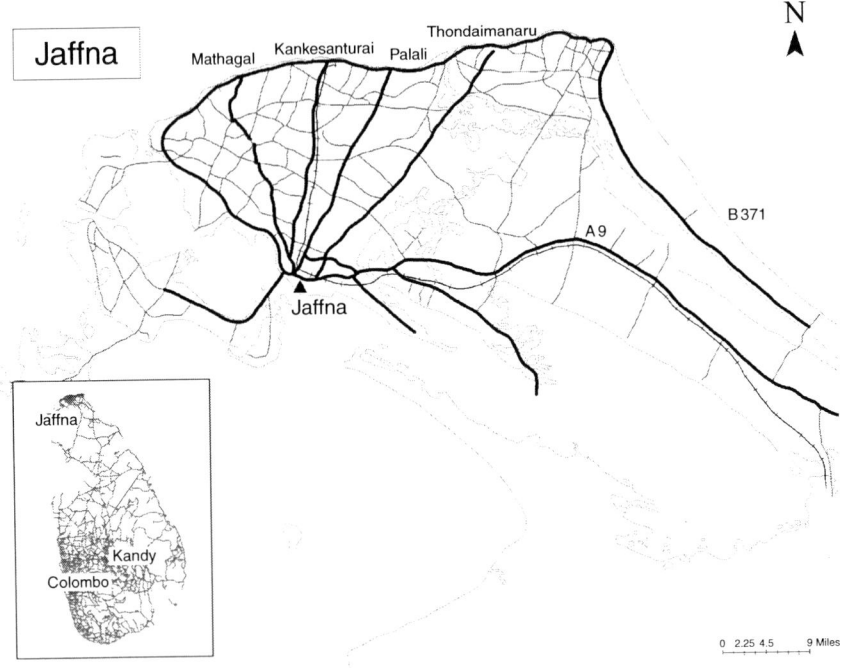

FIGURE 3.2 The Centrality of Colonial Jaffna (credit: Kaushalya Herath).

FIGURE 3.3 Formal (Colonial) Landscapes (credit: Nihal Perera).

territories had achieved independent political power, except for a short period in the sixteenth century when subjugated by the Kotte Kingdom. Located about 4 km to the northeast of Jaffna, Nallur was the capital of Nallur Rajadhani, the last (Tamil) kingdom. It still holds functional and symbolical significance among the Hindus, not least because of the sacred Kandaswamy temple.

In contrast to the rebuilding of Chelvanayakam Column by the authorities, the LTTE paid attention to Nallur and other parts of the peninsula such as Valvet-tithurai and Chavakacheri (Figure 3.4). During the truce, the LTTE managed to steer to Tellipalai the major cancer hospital that the government wanted to build in Jaffna.[2] The memorials of the martyr Lt. Col. Thileepan who died after a 12-day hunger strike protesting the occupation of the IPKF and Kittu were also placed in Chavakacheri. This way the LTTE built its own symbolic landscapes outside of Jaffna city.

Regionally, the LTTE developed its own urban structure with its dual centre— Kilinochchi and Mullaitivu—in Vanni. Killinochchi became the unofficial capital of the "Tiger Territory" in 2000, after its capture along with a large area occupied by the Sri Lankan military (Dissanayaka 2004). Unlike Jaffna, which was externally

FIGURE 3.4 The Sea Connection: Velvatithurai and Prabhakaran's House (credit: Nihal Perera).

produced through colonial encounter, Kilinochchi's significance grew from within the region as a result of separatist resistance. Further establishing its position, the LTTE used the cessation of hostilities (2002–2006) to develop the town and the Vanni region around it (see Bulathasinghala 2005). Yet the military and political command center in Mullaitivu was largely a hideout. It represented the LTTE's status as a rebel group and not a government.

Unlike national capitals that impress their subjects, these were command centers from which the LTTE's authority was exercised and expanded through cadres operating in a clandestine landscape. Thus, the LTTE effectively displaced both the centrality of Jaffna city and the significance of the Jaffna peninsula by making Kilinochchi and Mullaitivu its capitals and Vanni the heartland of its struggle.

Moreover, the LTTE also produced new social practices. An exemplary spatialization of such practices is the grand Mahavira cemetery in Kopay, where fallen fighters were buried (Figure 3.5). It had a high profile and was maintained to a high standard. The cemetery was a means of awarding the fallen their "proper" place, a military rank, and a physical memorial. Hence, the cemetery played a highly significant organizing and morale-lifting role for the cadres. Hindus principally cremate the dead, but the LTTEs attributed special value to the corpses of fallen cadres, even awarding positions and titles to deceased fighters. When the government forces entered Jaffna, the LTTE cadres took away and buried the corpse of Thileepan, so it would not fall into enemy hands. As one of the most significant symbolic elements in the Tiger landscape, the cemetery was destroyed by government forces in 1995 and quickly rebuilt by the LTTE. It was again destroyed at the end of the war in 2009.

In myriad ways, the LTTE was building its own space and writing its own story in the landscape. Other monuments include those to commemorate watershed events and heroes. These spatial transformations displaced the Colombo–Jaffna duality and former notions of the Tamil homeland. The LTTE reshaped an equally insidious spatialized ethnic polarity in its place wherein Kilinochchi and Mullaitivu displaced Jaffna as the center of the Tamil territory, and Vanni replaced the Jaffna peninsula as the heartland of Tamil Eelam.

The new landscape that consists of places to perform ordinary functions, towns, command centers; specific elements as checkpoints and monuments, and elements that represent new traditions such as cemeteries unsettled and contested the landscape of postcolonial Tamil parliamentarians. With the military attacks on Kilinochchi and Mullaitivu at the end of the war, the government, too, engaged LTTE's new spatial structure. Although the war is over, and the material traces of conflicts have been erased by the government, these spatial structures and practices will have a long-lasting impact, particularly with the memory and desires influencing the meaning of the landscape.

Everyday Practices and Emergent Geographies

As the government and the LTTE battled for power and remapped the region, people in the war zone also continued to reproduce their lives. As they adapted

FIGURE 3.5 Tiger Landscapes (credit: Nihal Perera).

their social practices to the context of war, people created new practices to fulfill their needs and achieve their desires, developing another layer of social space. Everyday space-making materialized on a dwelling scale and shaped both urban and regional geographies. At times, these people's spaces reinforced, and other times they contested and/or displaced, the government and/or LTTE spatial structures. This section examines these ordinary spaces developed in the north during the war, at dwelling, urban, and regional scales, thus teasing out a "people's geography."

At the immediate level, the conflict made the areas where the Tamils lived, particularly the north, east, and Colombo, materially and perceptually unsafe and unstable for average people. After a brief period of relative stability under the LTTE, the IPKF–LTTE war (1987–1990) destroyed the region's civilian life and space (Swamy 1994). The instability continued for more than ten years, until the ceasefire of 2002, with two brief respites in 1990 and 1995 (Rogers *et al.* 1998). The last battle (2006–2009) totally transformed the power and spatial structures in the region; I focus on people's production of space within the structure of conflict prior to this battle.

The immediate reaction of a large proportion of people who could afford to do so was to escape the conflict. By 1992, about 300,000 Tamils had sought asylum in the West, and 200,000 in India (UTHR 1993). Once the strong memories of the 1983 riots subsided, many Tamils also migrated to the Colombo area, first to the older Tamil area of Wellawatta and later to new areas such as Ja-ela and Mabole, north of Colombo. In 2001, more than 6,500 Sri Lankan Tamils lived in the Wattala-Mabole Urban Council area compared to 15,300 Sinhalese.

As a result of out-migration, the population of the northeast dropped by almost half within five years: from 1.7 million in 1987 to 900,000 in 1992. The population of the Jaffna peninsula dropped by one-fifth, from 743,000 in 1981 to an estimated 589,000 in 2004 (Department of Census and Statistics, Sri Lanka 1982; District Secretariat 2005a, 2005b, in Satyendra 1993).

The remaining population was largely displaced, and their livelihoods were highly disrupted. By July 1990, there were 880,000 people displaced in more than 600 camps; Jaffna became a temporary home to 355,000 people in 352 camps (US Committee for Refugees 1991). The war also displaced people of other ethnicities, particularly Sinhalese and Muslims, many of whom were forcibly removed. By 1992, Jaffna district lost well over 100,000 jobs (UTHR 1993). In addition to the reduced buying power of the people, the government imposed embargoes, and the LTTE taxation limited the goods entering the region, further increasing the prices. The taxation was reinforced during the ceasefire.

The majority of the people had moved in and out of their homes, hometowns, and refugee camps at various points in the war, finding safe places and better living conditions. Saving their own lives and building livelihoods were activities far more central to these moves than taking a side in the war. One of the biggest movements in the region was the exodus from Jaffna before the government forces entered in 1995.

The LTTE instigated a panic, encouraging many people to move out with them to Vanni. In his annual November speech, LTTE leader Velupillai Prabhakaran said: "We are relieved that our people have safely escaped from the military siege and the political trap behind it" (in Swamy 2006: 256). Questioning the absorption of the people's reaction within the separatist discourse, most people eventually returned home. The exodus had more to do with people's concern for their own safety, security, and basic needs than supporting the LTTE. Similarly, people returning to Jaffna had little to do with any endorsement for government control or sovereignty.

Building Homes

"Returning home" is a common desire of those involuntarily displaced. Anna Lena Lösnäs (2005) found that Muslims in the village in Vanni where she conducted her research did not trust the LTTE. Still, they chose to return to the LTTE-controlled area because they wanted to return "home." The "displaced" Tamils, too, wished to return home, even if their houses were close to military camps. About half the population of Alaveddy, adjacent to a military camp, also moved back.[3]

This does not mean that everyone wanted to return home. Unfortunately, most displaced people did not have the luxury of returning home as their original homes were not safe. The government/military map had clearly demarcated security zones of about 3,000 hectares that were emptied of people (District Secretariat 2005a). While the coastal belt across Palali, Kankesanthurai, and Karainagar, and some thoroughfares, belonged to the highest level, villages like Alaveddy and Maviddapuram belonged to the next level largely because of nearby military camps. People also had their own maps: the rumors about landmines and other war-related "knowledge" discouraged people from moving back to many areas. Hence, home was more nostalgia than reality for most.

The majority of the internally displaced people were first confined to refugee camps. The camps were shelters of the most basic and temporary nature; they lacked water and sanitary facilities. Many families lived in temporary shelters for more than a generation. A major location of displaced people was around the Jaffna railway station: The station allegedly contained landmines, but people lived in the vicinity in self-built housing. Most of them attempted to improve their dwellings, and they sometimes built smaller individual shelters of their own. By developing particular social interactions that intersected at their present location, they transformed the new (and old) locations into their own places (see Brun 2001). As they familiarized these unfamiliar locations, they also developed their identities in relation to them.

As the region was redefined by the war, even "homes" were displaced, and places were defamiliarized for many. Sina Nona of a displaced Tamil family at Vinayagapuram was happy her family lived close to schools, healthcare, and similar facilities during wartime. However, the members of her family were only allowed to travel with special passes and were frequently harassed by the military as suspected terrorists (Refugees International 2001). The displaced, whether at "home" or away, worked hard to develop a livelihood, identity, and place within new contexts. The taking up of new opportunities had radically changed the subjects and their spaces.

Brun (2005) well illustrates how the loss of familiar livelihood due to displacement encouraged Tamil and Muslim women to look for new opportunities. A major consequence was the change in patterns of gender control. Many young Tamil women who did not have sufficient social capital to escape violence by marrying within the global diaspora viewed joining the LTTE as the better local alternative. They increasingly got involved in military activities.

Many Muslim women, who were not otherwise "qualified" to apply for political asylum abroad, opted to work abroad. Those who were able to pay employment agencies preferred to go abroad in order to restore assets and rebuild lives rather than work locally as agricultural labor. Transforming extant gender roles, many Muslim women played greater roles in income-generating activities, largely abroad. In this, the northern women radically transformed their identities, gender relationships, and spaces.

At the level of the built environment and shelter, a large number of families lived in spaces they saw as "usable," behind the ruined structures as well as quickly built minimalist shelters. People's agency in creating social space was evident in how they adapted to the ruined environment and reused the remaining environment to their highly reduced needs simultaneously (Figure 3.6).

The desire to go beyond the minimum shelter provision and regularize life at a domestic scale is evident in the repaired and reconstructed buildings. The neatly piled stacks of salvaged material, especially bricks, from destroyed houses represented hopefulness and testified to the ongoing rebuilding processes. In a situation where the government (national or rebel) paid very little attention to the needs of the people and where NGOs were unable to help much, people created their own shelters and more basic spaces by improvising in their (and others') ruined houses, moving into relatives' houses, personalizing refugee dwellings, and building temporary shelters.

Rebuilding Community, Transforming Cities

In addition to rebuilding and maintaining lives, conducting social and economic activities such as buying and selling helped (re)produce neighborhoods and cities. All towns and small urban centers where people live maintained places of commerce, at least a set of boutiques and *santhi* (see chapter 10), along with the social relations they represent. The cities and neighborhoods so reproduced were similar to what they used to be, but not the same.

With a population of 135,000 in 1995, Jaffna was still a second-tier city in Sri Lanka behind Colombo (City Population 2006).[4] As the city most affected by the war, Jaffna saw many of its most educated, economically better-off, and Westernized people flee the conflict. These expats moved overseas or sometimes to Colombo, leaving behind those who evinced weaker support of the formal society and economy.

Many Chavakachcheri businessmen who had a substantial presence in Jaffna moved their capital back to their hometown, about 20 km east of Jaffna. The

FIGURE 3.6 Ruined Environments: Living and Reconstructing (credit: Nihal Perera).

reduction in the original population was matched by the migrants who moved into the city in search of a better place, leaving Jaffna with the same number of inhabitants but a vastly different composition. Most notably, the business-oriented *tivu* people (the islanders) from the surrounding islands where the economy was badly affected by war moved in to fill part of the investors' gap. Making use of the relative stability during the 2002–2006 truce and the opening of roads, the city regained a strong population and economic base.

Demographically and economically, Jaffna continues to be the primary city in the peninsula and the north. Because Jaffna was of strategic significance to the government, resources were provided to maintain infrastructure (and abstract space) necessary to keep the city and government-controlled areas safe and functioning, both to protect the city from the enemies and to win the support of the subjects. Public amenities included the city administration, schools, university, library, and market. The remaining local leaders, the business community, and upper classes with stakes attempted to enhance the resources by leveraging various sources, including NGOs and their own investments.

The government kept reproducing the connections with Colombo, particularly in regard to government functions. It maintained public transportation between Colombo and Jaffna; it used the air force base in Palali as the airport for civilian flight services by Lionair and Serendib Express. As the government center in the region, Jaffna also attracted international missions and NGOs.[5]

The intervention of institutions, organizations, and people is key to the reconstruction of everyday life. Small improvements in services substantially upgraded the quality of life in Jaffna. The city thus maintained a large public sphere and public space. Despite the damaged buildings and environments in surrounding areas, not much destruction was apparent in the city center. Most buildings were reasonably well maintained.

The (old and new) entrepreneurs also strove to reproduce and maintain the economy and society. They attempted to serve the region during a long period of isolation. As the war and the embargo isolated the north, its investors attempted to produce basic provisions such as soap and aerated water within the region. While most of these factories were ruined, some continued to operate during the ceasefire.

The ceasefire increased the number of visitors to Jaffna city and the peninsula, and investors were quick to identify new opportunities. As foreigners, members of the diaspora, and other Sri Lankans began to visit during the truce, a tourist industry emerged. Although few in number, guest houses sprang up and are largely located in the area of foreign missions. Old cars—particularly Austins—that represented Jaffna's isolation became fashionable. Along with the landscape of disaster in which they were driven, these old cars existed for the consumption of tourists. The landscape of war and the images of economic stagnation were thus commodified.

As new buildings were a rarity, Jaffna continued to be defined by the architecture of its colonial past. Main institutional buildings, including City Hall and the university, were built during the colonial period. Outside the city center, the conflict has also preserved "traditional" buildings with courtyards, entrance structures, and *thinnais* (verandahs). With regard to dwellings, Mayooranathan (2002) confirms that "traditional" courtyard houses with entryways and Dutch-influenced houses with open verandahs are still in use. The stagnant economy has done much to conserve these climatically suitable and culturally identifiable built forms. These aspects make Jaffna a unique city in Sri Lanka with regard to its built environment and space.

At a more personal level, the display of wealth in the landscape is not conspicuous. Except for a few large houses built during the colonial period, almost none of the others visually stand out. The houses are functional places to "live in," and Jaffna citizens have not "modernized" these as in Colombo, nor have they added embellishments (see Arasaratnam 1994). Thus the landscape was conservative and was less of an indicator of unevenly distributed wealth.

According to Jaffna resident and architect Shanthini Balasubramanium,[6] the lack of modernization is not a direct effect of the war; rather, it reflects the inhabitants' notions of modernity. Even before the war, the people of Jaffna did not invest much money in building grand houses. Savings usually took the form of land, a simple house to live in, houses for their children, and gold. The war made security an extra concern: Many people feared that a display of wealth might attract the undue attention of LTTE and/or government forces.

Yet Jaffna was dynamic, and the modernization of its spaces continued slowly and incrementally throughout the war. In addition to rebuilding, to a very limited degree, new construction and the renovation of public buildings also took place. The movement of goods, people, and ideas during the truce began to transform the city. The most visible new buildings were outside of Jaffna; the market complex and private commercial buildings, particularly the Millennium Restaurant in Chavakachcheri, stood out in the peninsula (Figure 3.7). With blue glass curtain walls, this restaurant did not demonstrate much conservativeness. Two main restaurants in Kilinochchi also demonstrate the use of imported materials and building styles from Colombo.

These "modern" buildings, when taken in isolation, looked very much like those in Colombo or similar cities around the world and performed similar economic roles. Hence, the "people's struggle," as read from the business landscape, did not reject Colombo; instead, it involved a competition with Colombo and other "large" cities in the region.

Nonetheless, transcultural ideas were apparent in the investments made by the diasporic community in the Tamil neighborhoods of Colombo: a trend began to build luxury condominiums targeting Tamil customers. These also bear names like Sellamaal Court, making them Modern and Tamil simultaneously. However, the flow of ideas into the north struggled against the censorship and constraints of war.

Today, the overall landscape is made up of components that represent destruction, reproduction, and growth. The largely destroyed environment is mixed with buildings that continue to be maintained and is punctuated with temporary housing and more-permanent modern buildings that imply possible future trends.

FIGURE 3.7 Emerging Environments (credit: Nihal Perera).

Shaping the Region

In negotiating their livelihoods, inhabitants in the north have also restructured urban centers and generated a regional structure in the cracks and the margins of the spatial structures created by the government and the LTTE, but building on their infrastructures. While Jaffna and Kilinochchi became significant nodes in the system, a series of towns such as Chavakachcheri, Mullaitivu, Puthukkudiyirippu, and Point Pedro developed the second tier of the settlement structure of the north.

Chavakachcheri produced entrepreneurs who had invested in Jaffna. Many entrepreneurs who did not emigrate moved their capital back to Chavakachcheri and also made new investments in it. It was heavily damaged by the war; for example, its hospital was totally destroyed. Yet, with the investment of more capital, it became the other significant town in the peninsula. It thus replaced other secondary towns such as Kankesanturai. Unlike in the more subdued Jaffna, as discussed above, the new investments in Chavakachcheri caused the "modernizing" of its built environment.

Some of the towns that did not face large-scale destruction to their infrastructure also belong to this tier. On the mainland, before the final battle, Puthukkudi-yirippu, about 20 km from Mullaitivu, was left with its historic landscape and hospital intact. It was more vibrant than Mullaitivu and benefited from the instability surrounding Mullaitivu. Less damage to infrastructure made it a desirable place for people who strove to reconstruct their lives and livelihoods. The population increases in towns such as Valvettithurai and Mullaitivu highlight that they were perceived as safe and more desirable.

As people moved in and out of various places for safety and survival, Kilinochchi grew into the center of Vanni. Before the war, Kilinochchi was not a big town, and, by the truce of 2002, most of the 65,000 people in the area were displaced. According to Kilinochchi Government Agent R. Rasanayagam (in *Daily News* 2003), more than 90 percent of the town's population had fled to the jungles at one time or another. The location of a few major LTTE institutions provided some stability, and the rebel center grew into LTTE's political and administrative locus. With the location of new organizations such as the Peace Secretariat, the government provision of funds for factories during the truce, and more NGOs moving in, Kilinochchi became an established town. Kilinochchi thus developed into a commercial hub and an active town on the Colombo–Jaffna road. The air-conditioned restaurants with tinted glass walls stood as testimony to its modernity. The settling of ordinary people and the building activity of citizens made it a town.

The changes were hardly one-sided. The town lost its former function as the regional vegetable collection center to cities such as Vavuniya and Dambulla. It had electricity during the day, but most people lived in the dark by night. However, the efforts of the civil society, on top of those of the LTTE, turned it into an inhabited town with life. Shops and restaurants lined the main road, offering various food items brought from outside the region.

In this, people and institutions adjusted to the conditions of the town and adapted its environment for daily practices. The Kilinochchi Central College building was bombed into a shell with no walls, windows, or doors. According to Principal Veerakarthy Rajakulasingham, about 1,500 landmines were found on its playground. Under his leadership, the school was turned into a place where 1,500 students learned math and languages (in *Daily News* 2003). The opening of the Colombo–Jaffna road, the reduction of restrictions to the movement of people, and the greater access to goods all worked in Kilinochchi's favor during this period. Its population rose to 149,000, more than doubling its pre-war numbers, and matching Jaffna.

The biggest town that people created, with almost no help from the government or the LTTE, was Vavuniya. Vavuniya and Mullaitivu had the highest annual growth rate of 2.2 percent per annum between 1981 and 2001 (Department of

Census and Statistics, Sri Lanka 2001). Vavuniya's population grew from 18,500 in 1981 to 53,000 in 2001, and the population of Vavuniya District almost doubled from 95,500 to 164,000 during the same period (City Population 2006).

Most crucially, it was the Tamil population that increased dramatically. During its 1996 offensive in Vanni, the LTTE asked people to leave the town. However, the population swelled due to the migration. Vavuniya was thus the town of choice for most people who remained in the northeastern region. It is a place with a substantial social and physical infrastructure that can support the rebuilding of lives; it is also the furthest town from the war that is not "inside" Sinhalese territory. It is perhaps the safest for Tamils, but it is the furthest from the core LTTE area. It is government-controlled, but not fully. It is a people's creation.

What people created in Vavuniya is an ethnically mixed town. Tamils here were joined by Sinhalese and Muslims who wanted to do business in this expanding gateway town. Even before the war, the town had a pattern of coexistence. It was a place where ethnic and caste-based spatial segregation was counterbalanced and interpolated by social mingling and linguistic hybridity (Rajasingham-Senanayake 2002).

Vavuniya is a nexus between the north and the south. The level of disruption was very low for a town in the war-zone. Except for a few interruptions, bus services from the south operated throughout the conflict period linking the north and the south. Vavuniya is not in the center of any ethnic territory, but rather it is both a liminal space in between the north and the south and a hybrid place where the Tamil and Sinhalese lands overlap. It questions the validity of an absolute and ethnicized Sinhala–Tamil duality.

During the strife, the ethnically mixed Vavuniya developed into a gateway and frontier town between the north and south. As it is on the main Colombo–Jaffna highway, and because it might have been the least "dangerous" of the towns discussed above, the opening of the highway turned the city into a pivotal connection between the north and south, and a highly desirable place for business. The government also provided basic infrastructure facilities such as roads, wells, and electricity. Demonstrating its competitiveness, Vavuniya took over some of the collection and distribution of goods from Kilinochchi.

The high number of internally displaced persons and the ongoing pass system Vavuniya had for movement between government- and LTTE-controlled areas continued to cause hardships for local people. Although less affected by the war compared to northern towns, the constant patrols of army vehicles and heavy security were stark reminders of its location on the frontlines of the war. According to Vavuniya District Secretary K. Ganesh, the people began to feel there was free movement between government- and LTTE-controlled areas during the truce (in Herath 2002). In response to the war, people reinforced and redefined the city's hybridity, ambivalence, and its liminality into a nexus between the north and south.

In short, responding to the conditions imposed by the conflict and their own needs, people struggled to maintain and rebuild their lives throughout. In so doing, they created a series of new social spaces, spatial structures, and a new geography in which some cities prospered and others withered for a time. Along with creating living spaces, they restructured the urban system along the A9 road. Its principal nodes are Jaffna, Kilinochchi, and Vavuniya, and the second-tier cities include Chavakachcheri, Valvettithurai, Point Pedro, Puthukkudiyirippu, and Mullaitivu. Vavuniya, located at the most ambiguous location and intersection of Tamil- and Sinhalese-dominated areas, is the defining articulation of people's agency and their intervention into the larger spatial organization: It defies the notion of "ethnic conflict" based on absolute and essential Sinhala–Tamil opposition.

Spaces of Survival

The stories and spaces of war and peace are multilayered, multifaceted, interwoven, and changing. There is not even one Tamil–Sinhala duality: The parliament-based postcolonial opposition and the government–LTTE war produced and represented different social and special realities through this conflict. It is impossible to understand these within simple binary oppositions that created polemical, binarized, and ethnicized understandings that efface the activities of the majority of social actors in the region: the ordinary people. The spaces they produced are messy, contested, complex, and ultimately hybrid and intertwined.

The separatist–sovereignist struggle itself inverted many postcolonial spatial discourses. Jaffna had been under control of government forces for over a decade, but it took over a decade for the government to bring the north under its control; Jaffna did not prove as strategically powerful as the conventional Colombo–Jaffna duality suggests. The LTTE had subverted it. While the Tamils have particular attachments to Jaffna, the city is no longer the undisputed center of the north or of the Tamil people. The LTTE fought to accomplish its objectives, but the territory it controlled in Vanni was a small segment of its map of Eelam.

Despite clear spatial perceptions, maps, and formal articulations of both the government and the LTTE, the messy spaces of the conflict were defined by non-contiguous territories held by the government and the LTTE and the contested spaces within and without these landscapes that were lived, performed, and (re)produced by ordinary people. In accommodating, adapting to, and building within and upon the context, ordinary people and small institutions created new spatial and temporal structures within, in the cracks, beyond, and besides those of the separatist–sovereignist duality. At one level, they adopted, reinforced, and expanded the spatialities created by the warring parties, for example, in Jaffna, Kilinochchi, Mullaitivu, and Mannar. At the same time, the spaces of the warring parties were undermined, redefined, and adapted by people to serve their everyday needs.

In effect, Jaffna city and the peninsula underwent demographic change, and Chavakachcheri developed into an enterprising and modernized town. The people also moved into and developed small towns such as Point Pedro.

Most significant is the people's choice to move away from the war zones to Vavuniya, the southernmost town in the north, a liminal space between the north and the south. With Vavuniya becoming a major town in Sri Lanka, a new structure of cities has emerged, made up of Jaffna, Killinochchi, Vavuniya, and the second-tier towns such as Chavakacheri, Puthukkudiyirippu, and Point Pedro.

The spatial organization of the north is, therefore, different than what the well-organized hegemonic discourses suggest; it is a palimpsest of spaces negotiated by the government, the Tamil parliamentarians, the LTTE, and, most importantly, by the people, through war, based on everyday social and cultural needs and practices. These spaces cannot easily be captured within mappings that fix and reify a system of (post)colonial provinces and districts, because these are parts of multiple identities and narratives. These new spatialities, especially the people's geography, present new political constraints and possibilities beyond the war.

Notes

1 For earlier versions of this study in different contexts, see Perera (1997; 2009).
2 The Central Engineering Consultancy Bureau led a number of construction projects in the northeast. I draw on personal communications with its Director of Architecture, Praneeth Amaratunga, December 2007.
3 Personal communications with Gopalakrishnan Kalaeswaran, January 2006.
4 Before the war, Jaffna's population was 118,000, and the peninsula had about 750,000 (City Population 2006).
5 Toward the end of the war, the government expelled many NGOs.
6 Personal communication with Shanthini Balasubramanium, February 2005.

References

Arasaratnam, S. (1994) "Lanka's Tamils: Under Colonial Rule" in M. Chelvadurai and B. Pfaffenberger (eds.), *The Sri Lankan Tamils: Ethnicity and identity*, Boulder, CO: Westview Press, 28–53.

Bhabha, H.K. (1994) *The Location of Culture*, London and New York: Routledge.

Brohier, R.L. and Paulusz, H.O. (1951) *Lands, Maps and Surveys: Descriptive catalogue of historical maps in surveyor general's office*, vol. II, Colombo: Ceylon Survey Department.

Brun, C. (2001) "Reterritorializing the Relationship between People and Place in Refugee Studies," *Geografiska Annaler* 83: 15–25.

Brun, C. (2005) "Women in the Local/Global Fields of War and Displacement in Sri Lanka," *Gender, Technology and Development* 9, 1: 57–80.

Bulathasinghala, F. (2005) "Report: Dateline Jaffna," *Himal: South Asian*. Online. Available: www.himalmag.com/2003/february/report_1.htm (accessed 10 December 2005).

City Population (2006) Online. Available: www.citypopulation.de/SriLanka.html (accessed February 2, 2006).

Daily News (2003) "Kilinochchi Residents Yearn for Peace," *Daily News*, November 15. Online. Available: www.dailynews.lk/2003/11/15/sec03.html (accessed February 5, 2006).

Department of Census and Statistics, Sri Lanka (1982) *Census of Population and Housing: 1981*, Colombo: Government Press.

Department of Census and Statistics, Sri Lanka (2001) *Census of Population and Housing: 2001*. Online. Available: www.statistics.gov.lk/census2001/index.html (accessed August 3, 2006).

Dissanayaka, T.D.S.A. (2004) *War or Peace in Sri Lanka*, Mumbai: Popular Prakashan.

District Secretariat (2005a) *Statistical Information: Jaffna district*, Jaffna: District Secretariat.

District Secretariat (2005b) *Statistical Information: Kilinochchi district*, Kilinochchi: District Secretariat.

Herath, A. (2002) "Vavuniya." Online. Available: www.priu.gov.lk/Vavuniya/Home.htm (accessed August 3, 2006).

hooks, b. (1990) *Yearning Race, Gender, and Cultural Politics*, Boston, MA: South End Press.

Lösnäs, A.L. (2005) "Resettlement and Rehabilitation of IDPs in Post-conflict Sri Lanka: A case study of a village in Vanni," unpublished Master's thesis, Lund University, Sweden.

Mayoornathan, R. (2002) "Understanding the Architectural Traditions of Jaffna," *Sri Lanka Architect* 104, 1: 21–28.

Perera, N. (1997) "Territorial Spaces and National Identities: Representations of Sri Lanka," *South Asia*, 20: 23–50.

Perera, N. (1998) *Society and Space: Colonialism, nationalism, and postcolonial identity in Sri Lanka*, Boulder, CO: Westview Press.

Perera, N. (2009) "Rebuilding Lives, Undermining Oppositions: Spaces of war and peace in Sri Lanka" in Cathrine Brun and Tariq Jazeel (eds.) *Spatializing Politics: Culture and geography in postcolonial Sri Lanka*, New Deli: Sage, 168–93.

Rajasingham-Senanayake, D. (2002). "Identity on the Borderline: Modernity, new ethnicities, and the unmaking of multiculturalism in Sri Lanka" in N. de Silva (ed.) *The Hybrid Island: Culture crossings and the invention of identity in Sri Lanka*, Colombo: Social Scientists' Association, 41–70.

Refugees International (2001) "IDPs in Sri Lanka: Visual mission March 2001," *Refugees International*. Online. Available: www.refintl.org/files/1900 (accessed July 10, 2007).

Rogers, J.D., Spencer, J. and Uyangoda, J. (1998) "Sri Lanka: Political Violence and Ethnic Conflict," *American Psychologist* 53, 7: 771–77.

Satyendra, N. (1993) *Tamil Eelam Struggle for Freedom: Boundaries of Tamil Eelam*. Online. Available: www.tamilnation.org/tamileelam/boundaries/index.htm (accessed December 15, 2007).

Swamy, M.R.N. (1994) *Tigers of Lanka: From boys to guerillas*, Delhi: Konark.

Swamy, M.R.N. (2006) *Inside an Elusive Mind: Prabhakaran*, Colombo: Vijitha Yapa.

Tamilnation (2007) Online. Available: www.tamilnation.org/tamileelam/defacto/index.htm (accessed January 21, 2007).

Thangarajah, Y. (1995) "Narratives of Victimhood as Ethnic Identity among the Veddas of the East Coast" in P. Jeganathan and Q. Ismail (eds.) *Unmaking the Nation: The politics of identity and history in modern Sri Lanka*. Colombo: Social Science Association, 191–218.

US Committee for Refugees (1991) "Sri Lanka: Island of refugees," Issue Paper, US Committee for Refugees.

UTHR (University Teachers for Human Rights) (1991) "The Politics of Destruction & the Human Tragedy." Online. Available: www.uthr.org/Reports/Report6/Report6.htm (accessed August 3, 2006).

UTHR (University Teachers for Human Rights) (1993) "Rays of Hope Amidst Deepening Gloom." Online. Available: www.uthr.org/Reports/Report10/Report10.htm (accessed January 15, 2006).

Wikipedia (2007) *Tamil_Eelam*. Online. Available: http://en.wikipedia.org/wiki/Tamil_Eelam (accessed April 23, 2015).

Wilson, A.J. (1994) "The Colombo Man, the Jaffna Man, and the Batticaloa Man: Regional identities and the rise of the federal party" in C. Manograran and B. Pfaffenberger (eds.) *The Sri Lankan Tamils: Ethnicity and identity*, Colombo: Social Science Association, 126–42.

4

FROM RESISTING TO FAMILIARIZING IMPOSITIONS

Living in the World Heritage Site at Galle Fort, Sri Lanka

With Sanjeewani Habarakada

> On Peddler Street, opposite Peddler's Inn, there is a house without a roof. [The occupants] were repairing the fallen roof, but the Department of Archeology stopped that. They have an approved plan, but the Department wants to take them to courts. Yet [the Department] does not take any speedy action [allow construction or sue]. I believe that it is because the officials want a bribe.
>
> *(Hussain, personal communication, 2011)*

In 1988, UNESCO declared Galle Fort in southern Sri Lanka a World Heritage site (Figure 4.1). The fort then had 449 buildings and 2,128 inhabitants (Department of Census and Statistics, Sri Lanka 2001).[1] Liyana_Arachchi (2009) of the Galle Heritage Foundation (GHF) claims this is the largest preserved historic, walled, living settlement in Southeast Asia. World Heritage, in this sense, is a physicality that represents universal (abstract) human history, not belonging to any time or place. During fieldwork, the built environment was made up of some houses with European-looking verandahs and columns and others without roofs (Figures 4.2, 4.4, 4.5). This chapter focuses on the people who live in this monument, particularly their predicaments and responses to the same and the environment.

Galle Fort has been integral to Sanjeewani Habarakada's life and identity: She not only attended 13 years of school in it, but she also studied the fort for her undergraduate capstone project. During the early years, the fort was an everyday space where she attended school, hung out, and played with friends and family. She never felt the aura of a World Heritage site. Undergraduate research exposed Habarakada to the outside-in viewpoint of the World Heritage committee and to the local operations of this abstract reality. She observed how the Planning Committee of the Foundation made decisions and implemented them. However, the meeting she attended confused her: She was unable to fathom the connections

FIGURE 4.1 Street Layout of Galle Fort (credit: Sanjeewani Habarakada).

between committee decisions and the idea of World Heritage designation. She also sensed a gap between heritage conservation efforts and the aspirations of the inhabitants for their neighborhood.

As the objective of this study is to learn about people's spaces, an exhaustive discussion of the fort, the World Heritage designation, and all gaps in the World Heritage project would be superfluous. Yet it is important to note that the idea of the World Heritage site, particularly whose idea, for whom, and the significance of the designation are hardly questioned by practitioners or scholars. The phrase "living

FIGURE 4.2 Landscape of the World Heritage (credit: Nihal Perera).

settlement" is mentioned in the GHF (1994) documents, but the focus of preservation regulations and project implementation is on the physical environment, especially the outward appearance and form of the houses rather than the life in Galle Fort. It became a struggle for the inhabitants to conduct their daily activities and socio-cultural practices within the constraints imposed by the World Heritage designation.

This chapter focuses on people's struggle to survive and familiarize the strange environment of the World Heritage designation and the spaces produced in the process. It will first map out the abstract space of the Galle Fort World Heritage site and then examine the inhabitants' spatial practices in relation to it. The study focuses on what the fort used to be, how the inhabitants contest the space of the World Heritage site, and how they are re-familiarizing the neighborhood.

Physical Environment and Outsider Claims

UNESCO first established the World Heritage List in 1972 to acknowledge places with universal/global significance. As the nation-states also lobby for nomination, the listing is a highly political process. The World Heritage project in Galle is based on a particular understanding of the fort and its history. Criteria number four under which UNESCO (1972) declared that Galle Fort is a World Heritage site considers the fort "an outstanding example of a type of building, architectural or technological ensemble or landscape which illustrates a significant stage in human history." The declaration refers to the universal significance of town planning, architecture, civil engineering, and hydrology of the Dutch colonial era (ibid.). UNESCO's (1988) justification highlights the ramparts, the street grid, the streetscapes, courtyard architecture of the houses, verandahs with columns, and the underground storm-water drainage system. Despite the reference to universal history, the World Heritage site designation focuses on the designed physical environment created by the Dutch colonials (1640–1796).

Galle Fort is a diverse living settlement shaped by multiple colonial powers and indigenous groups, including Muslims, Sinhalese, and Burghers. Branding the fort Dutch colonial marginalizes all other actors. Yet it is a colonial product. Expelling the Muslim traders who had developed a port city (Ruberu 2003), the Portuguese established a fort on the current site and further developed it, in 1595, into the more solid *Forta Leza* (Black Fort). What the Dutch conquered in 1640 was a well-developed fort with buildings and roads, a small component of which still remains. The Dutch established an administrative center with a grid layout of streets, a familiar form in the Netherlands. It was symmetrically organized around King's Street (the British renamed it Queen's Street), which provided access to the fort and connected significant buildings and structures (Figure 4.1). It connected a cluster of massive warehouses on the western edge with a group of public buildings on the eastern end. The most important buildings, such as the Captain's House, the flagstaff, the courthouse, and the city assistant's office, were located on this main street.

The British—who took over Ceylon in 1796 and ruled the entire island from 1815 until 1948—adopted Galle Fort as their administrative center for the south. They did not make any substantive physical changes to it, but transformed its meaning and landscape by introducing British spaces, building elements, and new technology. Unlike the Portuguese and the Dutch, who expelled the Muslims from the city, the British pushed all other Europeans out of the fort.

The British reorganized the fort into three zones: administrative, residential, and institutional, which had their own plats. Instead of erasing the environment built by the Dutch, the British superimposed their own spaces. The creation of a new entrance decentered the original entrance and King's Street. Newly designed buildings and formal urban spaces were then added, displaying military strength and civil grandeur. In the new structure, institutional functions were at the entrance court, the administrative functions along King's Street, and residential buildings on the south. This way, the British transformed both the spatial organization of the fort and the meaning of its components.

The fort is thus a hybrid, composed of Portuguese, Dutch, British, and Sri Lankan structures and built elements. While the first rampart on the landside originated during the Portuguese time, the protection on the seaside, the street grid, streetscapes, courtyard architecture of the houses, verandahs with columns, and the underground storm-water drainage system were built by the Dutch. All of these were transformed and/or redefined by the British. It is this eclectic fort that UNESCO redefined as Dutch and ICOMOS (International Council for Monuments and Sites) consultants and the Heritage Foundation opted to represent largely through columns, verandahs, and courtyards to the detriment of other elements. Even if select environments and/or elements were produced by the Dutch colonials, they belong to the colonial third culture, the Dutch culture in Galle which is influenced by the locals. In short, they are not totally Dutch.

The World Heritage project's interjection of Dutch history into the fort (Kuruppu 1992) both familiarized and historicized it within a Dutch history while defamiliarizing and dehistoricizing it for the inhabitants and Ceylonese. Questioning the politics of historic preservation in the USA, Gail Dubrow (2003) argues that places chosen for preservation, like heritage sites, landmarks, and historic monuments, reflect the distorted and incomplete history of the elite and the powerful found in mainstream narratives. Furthermore, she (ibid.) argues that because women and minorities had little power throughout American history, the selection of "beautiful" buildings from the past for preservation inadvertently constructs and reinforces a white male history. The hegemonic preservation narrative in the USA has erased the historical experiences and contributions of locals and, more importantly, the existence of people belonging to other ethnic and religious groups and women. In Galle, ironically, it is a piece of colonial history that has become a World Heritage site.

After the British left in 1948, the fort was reclaimed by Burghers—mainly people with Dutch ancestry but also others of European descent—and the local Muslim, Tamil, and Sinhala people. Together they developed it into their neighborhood. The diverse physical environment consisted of houses, schools, hospitals, churches, a mosque, a Buddhist temple, offices, and commercial buildings. Most Burghers felt unable to live in Sri Lanka, especially with the rise of Sinhala nationalism, and a large proportion emigrated to Australia. As a result, the Muslims became the majority in the fort. Since the World Heritage designation was conferred, they, too, have been leaving in large numbers.

The Grand Discourse

The idea of conserving the fort is a British colonial idea. The first significant attempt to conserve the fort was made in 1940 with the adoption of a private members bill to transfer the protection of Galle Fort to the Department of Archaeology of Sri Lanka. After three decades of relative inaction, damage caused during the 1971 insurgency prompted the department to declare the fort a protected monument under the *Antiquities Ordinance No. 9 of 1940*, incorporating all structures within 400 yards of it (Silva 1998).

The new regulatory framework that followed the declaration comprised the *Galle Heritage Foundation Act No. 7 of 1994* (GHF 1994) and special regulations of the Urban Development Authority (UDA 2009). This connected preservation with planning and wedded the future with the past. While making the GHF responsible for its protection, the act spells out the government's plan for the fort: i.e., to "make the World Heritage Living City of Galle Fort a cultural tourist center of excellence" (GHF 1994: 3). The regulations that followed focus on preserving the Dutch–British hybrid architectural character but with more bias toward a Dutch colonial architecture that the authorities and consultants defined in terms of verandahs and columns.

The Galle Fort "project" was not one, but many. Those with the power to define had their own projects: For UNESCO, it was protecting a part of "universal" history. The state of the Netherlands incorporated Galle Fort into Dutch history. The Sri Lankan government initiated a tourist project. The project officers interpreted regulations and acted in a "practical" sense.

On the ground, the *Galle Heritage Foundation Act* created a complex administration to take care of the physical form of Galle Fort and any changes to it. The administrative organization is made up of the Department of Archaeology, the Urban Development Authority, and the Galle Municipal Council. In addition, the local court is used for litigation and the police department for law enforcement. Authorities and professionals who carry out the regulations and the officers who enforce these make up the crucial interface between the anonymous World Heritage project and fort residents. These changes made the fort an alien place for its inhabitants.

People's Heritage

Prior to World Heritage site designation, the inhabitants of the fort were ordinary citizens who maintained a high sense of community. The inhabitants knew each other well, and the community had a unique lifestyle supported by the specific environment of the fort. For residents, Galle Fort was a place with clean air, safe roads, and loyal, respectable people. Families lived there for generations, adapting to the place and transforming the environment to support their lifestyles. They had a strong sense of belonging: They were people of the fort. Women had their own space. Most women spent the daytime at home but coordinated their daily routines with others. They came out of the houses in the morning, greeted neighbors, and continued the dialog throughout the day. Unlike in most other areas of Galle town, in the fort, street vendors with vegetable carts came right to the doors of the homes, stretching commercial functions up to the domestic space. Women bought fruits, vegetables, and fish together in small groups. These activities allowed them to enjoy each other's company; they commented on prices, compared the quality, and discussed what each of them wanted to buy, cook, and eat, along with other matters of significance. This was the women's public sphere (see Chapter 2). As the public sphere penetrated the private, for women the road was an extension of their comfort zone, which began from homes and extended into the city and beyond. Women also banded together to visit the town and planned their days together. These interactions developed a strong sense of place and community.

Such a sense of belonging was not limited to women. It was a diverse neighborhood where Muslims, Sinhalese, Burghers, and Tamils lived together, sharing and celebrating their cultures, festivals, and food. This inclusiveness was evident in the physical environment: A Buddhist temple, a mosque, and two churches exist inside the fort where people watched, shared, participated, and enjoyed cultural practices of other religious groups. Vesak of the Buddhists and Ramadan of the Muslims were the most popular festivals. During Vesak, most government and private institutions used to decorate their buildings and roads with lanterns and flags. The Buddhists erected *dansal*, where donated food and refreshments were served free of charge to passers-by; many Muslims and those from other cultures voluntarily supported these activities. During Ramadan, Muslims shared food with others. More

FIGURE 4.3 The Rampart (credit: Nihal Perera).

than the communities outside of the fort, the fort residents celebrated cultural events together. The diversity was not simply accommodated, but celebrated in the fort.

The rampart was their main public place (Figure 4.3). In the evenings, women went to the rampart in small groups with their children. While the children played, mothers chatted and shared news. Women had up-to-date knowledge about the neighborhood in areas of their interest. Children grew up relating to the rampart; they belonged to that space.

Cultural differences were built into domestic spaces. The inhabitants organized their houses based on their own understandings of the fort and their own needs. Most Muslim households were concerned about privacy and the lack of front verandahs is largely attributed to this; most families covered the front verandah. Some residents also constructed new buildings, the architecture of which is clearly not colonial. Many newer houses consist of a front garden and a parapet wall at the road. The fort holds a diverse population and mixed physicality.

Defamiliarizing the Neighborhood

In a context characterized by a sense of belonging and ownership, the residents view the World Heritage project as an intrusion, but they are not strong enough to stop it. The inhabitants' responses range from organized protests to individual actions, from protesting against officials to collusion, and from open to hidden space-making processes. These reactions both accommodate and resist the imposition.

At first, the inhabitants protested against the World Heritage proposal in 1987. After the designation, they formed the Galle Fort Old-House-Owners Association (locally known as Isuru Welfare Association) to fight for their rights. The government did not relent, the organizations weakened, and many residents left the fort. The fort also became more attractive to investors. In this context, a trend emerged among Muslim inhabitants to sell their property, especially to foreigners who paid higher prices, and use the proceeds to buy one or two houses in Colombo. According to interviewees, the most desired husband-candidates for their daughters work in Colombo. Hence many residents prefer to have a house in Colombo.

The people who fought were not ignorant. Nazar Hussain is a successful businessman and statesman who cares for his community and represents it. He is weary of losing his neighborhood, the sense of place, and the sense of security. He helped advocacy groups and made many representations himself. He still advertises the fort, its sense of place, and community to potential property buyers; he prefers to sell property to those who embrace the fort's values.

The prohibition of new construction and then restoring incompatible physical structures into "Dutch" styles affected the people who lived in that environment. As interviews indicate, for the officers and consultants, the World Heritage site is a frozen space, an architectural image stuck in colonial buildings with verandahs and columns (Figure 4.4). According to Gunathilaka Perera:

> [The GHF] chose my house for the 60-Houses project. The project team decided everything. They did not ask anything from me. In my house, as long as I remembered [for about 50 years] the front façade was a closed one. But the project [officials] constructed Dutch type pillars. Now my own façade is unfamiliar to me. Also I lost a part of my house [that used to be

FIGURE 4.4 Perera's House Façade after 60-Houses Renovation Project (credit: Sanjewani Habarakada).

interior space]. Now we cannot use that space for our family purpose because it is an open verandah.

For generations, families have lived in the same house. When a Muslim girl marries, she receives a house from the family as her dowry. Families with one house subdivided it among the girls; some subdivided the land. The new couple turned the dowry into an apartment, but many extended families shared one kitchen. The World Heritage project prohibited such physical changes and, thereby, these cultural practices. Replacing those moving out were foreigners and Sri Lankan upper classes, both of whom saw a secure and valuable neighborhood in the fort. According to residents, there was only one European resident in the early 1990s, and he was married to a local woman. Since then, many Europeans bought land—as well as in many other parts of Sri Lanka—until the government began charging a 100 percent tax on foreign ownership. In 1998, immediately after lifting the tax, households owned by foreigners rose to over 5 percent, up to 105 houses (Liyana_Arachchi 2009).

The moving in of "outsiders" further weakened the community and its struggle. The newcomers were mostly well-to-do people, including the famous cricketer Kumar Sangakkara. According to Hussain, the newcomers could be individualistic and may even be absentee landlords. This could transform the vibrant neighborhood into a dull gated-community, turning the extant inhabitants into workers of the rich newcomers.

Tourism further eroded the inhabitants' sense of place. Tourism superimposed cultural practices of different scales and forms, relating their public/semi-public spaces such as streets and the rampart more to tourism. The neighborhood became a strange place with verandahs used for restaurants and some living areas used as tourist shops. It has become increasingly harder for women to recreate in the rampart, gossip on verandahs, and casually buy vegetables on the street.

Inhabitants' Responses

The inhabitants were never passive recipients of the imposed identity and space of the World Heritage site. For inhabitants, submitting to the rigid rules of World Heritage status meant the loss of identity. As the oppositional struggles yielded few results, they resorted to more imaginative and creative ways of negotiating the onslaught of the project. They transformed spaces to meet their own needs, and thus reproduced their place, but within particular limits imposed by the project. Early efforts to restore their activities and spaces were evident behind private houses, particularly from the alleyways and, later, behind the façades and at night.

All inhabitants negotiate their own (hybrid) living environments. Although no one has fully failed or succeeded, people's responses can be organized into three broad categories: The most conservative group chose to go with the flow of the project, transforming themselves into subjects. Some inhabitants opted to not accept the project as having any major impact on their lives; they continue to create the (lived) spaces they need, desire, and/or aspire. The majority is in between; they also opted to create their own spaces, but sometimes avoiding surveillance and other times directly negotiating with the authorities.

The Heritage of Disaster

As part of the World Heritage project, the GHF restored 60 private houses. The project was supported by a seven million rupees (USD 55,000) Cultural Grant from the government of the Netherlands and directed by the Centre for Heritage and Cultural Studies of the University of Moratuwa (Manawadu 2011). The project incorporated the 60 most conserved houses. Although the owners were not allowed to change the houses, the GHF began using them to erase the twentieth-century look in the fort and "restore" the environment to a Dutch colonial style. While some owners volunteered their houses for the project, almost everyone kept complaining about the pathetic living conditions in those dwellings, and more active owners looked for ways to benefit from the project.

When the majority of residents resisted the GHF's meddling with their properties, Fatin Farred, 48, became the first to volunteer her house on Middle Street. As project officials came with university professors and archaeologists, she expected genuine work from them. For them, Farred's house was unique.

The finding of emblems increased the value of the house. The first symbol indicated that the structure was the Galle Night Club, and the project officer who found it decided to exhibit it on her front wall. However, there is no indication where the night club was and/or what it was like. Similarly, a professor of architecture found the Dutch East India Company logo on the front door. There is no indication of what this vague representation meant, but the owner is bound to protect the old logo.

"Thickening the plot," the officers identified the structure as the Dutch governor's house. Yet while one of its pillars was in Dutch style, the other followed British architecture (Figure 4.5). Erasing this conflict, the house was situated within a "Dutch" colonial history. The consultants and officers are highly attached to this narrative, not least because their own identity depends on this history. They are bound to protect it, but the onus is on the owner. Farred also had her own expectations, especially to get her house repaired. All but two walls are of Dutch origin. These thick walls built in limestone are difficult to maintain, especially after centuries. The roof was leaking but, due to the size, she could not afford repairs.

Farred's was the first house to be renovated, presumably as a showpiece of the project. She believes that her house got the best building materials, workmanship, and supervision. In the process, she developed a close relationship with project representatives like Tharanga Liyana_Arachchi, project planning officer of GHF, and ICOMOS experts like Samitha Manawadu. These relationships enabled her sons to learn the historical value of the house of which she is proud.

The same structure deprives her of her dreams. Despite Farred's desire, it is a challenge to keep a historic house neat and clean, especially as she hardly owns this

FIGURE 4.5 Farred's House: Limestone Wall with Dutch- and British-type Columns (credit: Sanjeewani Habarakada).

World Heritage site and is not allowed to make any changes to the structure. The house is big, but it has only three rooms. She desires to convert the (unused) stable and storage area into a room for tourists and paint the ceiling, but the regulations do not allow these changes. When she made a request, the GHF highlighted the historic value of her house and advised her to maintain the old look.

Nonetheless, the officials used her house for their purposes. It has been a model house for television dramas. For this, project representatives asked her to paint the walls with *samara*, a natural ochre pigment commonly used in Sri Lanka. As she had used rubber paint on her walls for the ease of maintenance, she refused. As this demonstrates, each party opted to push the boundary between them, trying to gain more from the other.

Farred is reluctant to make changes due to the fear of breaching regulations and, more importantly, the relationship with project representatives. Hence, she maintains a World Heritage property, suppressing her desires to create the house she wants. It includes a "Dutch period" stable with no use for it.

Gunathilaka Perera, 48, never volunteered, but his house and small shop on Sudharnalaya Street was chosen by the GHF for the 60-Houses project. The project team and consultants decided to restore the house to a "Dutch" character and changed its front, which was over 50 years old, possibly from the British period. Perera had no problem with the façade. What he needed was more rooms for his children and to make the house more comfortable. Perera was not allowed to make any decision about the renovations to his own house. Ignoring his aspirations, the project officer decided to create history out of this house. He was displaced in his own home.

Asoka Weerasinghe, 62, a retired police officer, follows preservation regulations. His two-storied house on Hospital Street is believed to be the first guest house in the fort. The roof is in very bad condition; it leaks during the slightest rain, and the wooden floor at the second level is too unstable to use. The family has lived in it for three generations, over 50 years, but Weerasinghe does not legally own the property. As property values in the fort are increasing, Weerasinghe's ownership has been questioned in court.

Despite the low use value of the house, the officers are attracted to its exchange value. The house not only has a significant written history, but is also considered to have unchanged character and popular historic narratives around it. Many films, television dramas, and documentaries are filmed at this venue. Architecture and archaeology students also learn about the house. The project officers treat this house as common property and lend it for a fee to documentary and film-makers who need a colonial-era setting. The officers require Weerasinghe to welcome any visitor at any time and let the students and film-makers film, photograph, draw, and document the house.

This deprives him and his family of domestic life, space, and privacy. He is uncomfortable with the publicity. With two young daughters, he and his wife are very uncomfortable when strangers enter the house unannounced, especially the male project officer. Habarakada had direct experience of the project officer walking into Weerasinghe's house without prior notification to show her an old Dutch house. Weerasinghe's daughter was very uncomfortable. For the young girl, this is her home, but for the project officer this is a monument and a part of a World Heritage site. Weerasinghe is tired of living in a showpiece.

In the eyes of project officials, the 60 houses are minimally changed, have unique historic stories relating to the Dutch period, and have maintained an authentic character. They are linchpins of the larger space of the World Heritage site. The project officers tend to exercise tight control at the expense of inhabitants.

Yet these ideals and spaces are contested, and the meanings of the houses, the project, and benefits are negotiated from both sides. The project incorporates the houses through little gifts to home-owners, like including them in the 60-Houses project and by letting artists represent them. The owners, too, gain by being participants of the project; they may be granted roof repairs and permitted to stay in their homes.

The project has disempowered the residents. The Perera house represents an extreme in which the owner was not allowed any rights. After the 60-Houses project repaired Farred's roof, it is still leaking. She justifies the project by saying that "even the king's palace is leaking. It is okay for my roof to leak a little." Although Farred and Weerasinghe are not satisfied with the ways the project has affected their lives and properties, they do not seem free to express their feelings.

Although their houses are claimed to have the authentic Dutch look, Farred and Weerasinghe have not been able to benefit from tourism.

Most disgusting for people, especially the families with girls, is the officers' disregard for their privacy. One explanation is that project officers conduct side business by leasing time to television and cinema. Second is the attitude, a superiority developed through pseudo-Western science, gender relations, and sheer ignorance. The officer believes that his notion of Galle Fort is scientific, derived from global knowledge, and uncontested. Hence, there is no need to worry about people's privacy or a girl's protection. Third is sexism; treating girls and women as inferior. Fourth, the lack of culture in a person is called *nehedichchakama* in Sinhala. This may be a personal attribute, but it affects the supposed cultural project and its management.

Corruption is also a major topic of discussion in the fort. Some project officers and consultants have improved their own livelihoods. The officers who worked on this project for a decade have built their own power within the project and the fort and have produced their own projects within their desires, interests, and needs. According to people, project officers have possessions that cannot be afforded by their salaries.

Despite its weight, Farred and Weerasinghe still find ways to work with the World Heritage project and try to accommodate their daily practices and fulfill their aspirations. Farred maintains a good relationship with the officials related to this project; she does this with the belief that in the future she might get other help with home repairs if they are needed. As evident in refusing to paint with *samara*, she has found room for negotiation. In this, these people also try to construct a history that can enable the fulfilling of their own goals as well.

Intercepted Life Journeys

Most fort residents have partially achieved their dream dwellings and are working to improve their livelihoods. They had begun their journeys to fulfill their aspirations by overcoming the regulations and authority imposed upon them. For many, their surreptitious processes were intercepted by the project staff before completion. These interceptions have produced a landscape of disaster with unfinished houses and failing roofs (Figure 4.6). People do not see these "stalemates" as end results, but as temporary suspensions that need to be overcome. They are optimistic and believe in change.

In order to begin her married life, Suha Farid, 40, converted her dowry teashop on Light House Street into a house. After becoming a mother, she dreamed of providing individual rooms for her sons and an outdoor space to dry clothes. In 1998, she added a floor to the house without touching its outer appearance. The Department of Archaeology sued her, and the court stopped construction. Since 1998, she has lived in the unfinished house. The pressure of living in it led her to build her dream house outside the fort.

Farid is both in and out of the fort, but she does not want to move out. She was born and grew up in the fort; that is where she belongs. Farid is contemplating

FIGURE 4.6 Shoba Fashion House during and after the Court Case (credit: Sanjeewani Habarakada).

potential opportunities generated by tourism. She uses the front area of her house as a shop to sell small tourist items such as chains, handicrafts, and greeting cards.

Nimal Jayawardhana, 70, is a retired government officer who bought his house on Church Street in 1980. The house was a boarding place used by Tamil people in the 1970s. In 1998, when the authority was the Department of Archaeology, Jayawardhana began repairing the bedroom and replaced a couple of windows and walls. Using the police, the new authority, UDA stopped Jayawardhana's repair work in 2001. He submitted a plan of the intended changes for approval, but the UDA found the house to be taller than 30 ft., the legal height limit.

For 11 long years the house remained in a state of disrepair. Furthermore, a UDA representative asked Jayawardhana to demolish the "illegal" part of the house, which is confusing to him. According to him, he has not added to its original height of 32 ft. As much of the house is now unusable, the family lives in only the front area. Jayawardhana, too, anticipates change.

Harsha Sooriyaarachchi, 35, lives outside the fort but bought his business premise on Peddler Street from a fort inhabitant in 2011. He transformed the salon and rental house into a jewelry and antique showroom. As he is getting into the tourism business, he wanted to provide a new look to the building while maintaining the old character. He installed a new front door and converted the interior into a showroom. When he attempted to replace the wooden trellis of the second-level balcony, GHF stopped the work. He will not be allowed to change the balcony, but he is happy that he renovated the first floor before the authorities intervened.

As these stories indicate, the resultant spaces of this group are half finished, destroyed, and/or deteriorating. Each person initiated her/his own process to achieve the desired space. The residents believe the "system in the fort" is highly corrupt and say it is difficult to get permission for the changes they want. Contextualizing within their own perception of the World Heritage structure, they try out compromises without breaching aspects such as the façade, which they believe is the most important for project officers. They simply go ahead with their plans behind those façades.

Within the strange environment created by the World Heritage, the way the authorities intercepted and responded to what they saw as unauthorized construction has made their own dwellings strange. They live in unfinished buildings. They have lost their sense of ownership and place, have become strangers in their own homes, and live in a landscape of disaster.

Adding another dimension to this story, most locals believe the officials discriminate against locals. They are puzzled by how foreigners begin construction immediately. According to "normal procedure," it takes nearly six months for a local to get such approval.

In their view, but in our words, the officers have established a highly corrupt and uncontrolled bureaucratic system. Some officials have built a monopolistic personality toward local people: Those who are not willing to listen and with no close relationship with them face a lot of difficulties when they need services.

Also, most of the top officials are political appointees, and those with aristocratic family backgrounds do not like to consult the general public. Assuming privilege, they maintain distance with local people. This attitude of the higher-ranking feudal-like officers enables officers with low qualifications to obtain more power, making the "system" unfair.

In addition to placing ordinary people at a disadvantage, this structure provides fertile ground for corruption and bribery. According to community leaders, some officials use the resources of Galle Fort for their personal needs and to make money, but they do not do much good for the majority of ordinary people. As a result, many residents live in deteriorating buildings and half-built houses with no roofs. Yet they are hopeful and work for change.

Ideal Lived Spaces

The above narratives make it seem that the World Heritage designation creates a prison or a disaster. Yet people have subverted the dominance of this script. They see and interpret the project in different ways, depending on their personal capacities, economic backgrounds, political and personal views, and immediate constraints. Within this perceived space, and beyond the boundaries of the heritage project, people conceive aspirations and strategies to achieve them. Yet everyone is not able to achieve their goals smoothly; at times they are compelled to accommodate demands, negotiate external forces, and/or compromise the project.

Thirty years ago, Somasiri Gamage, now 70, bought a dilapidated house on Leyn Baan Street. Although there were small bushes inside and a large tree on the front wall, for the newly married clerk it was affordable and he was willing to overlook a few minor issues. The house got inundated every time it rained due to its very tall, arched front door. Beginning with fixing a shorter door, he repaired the whole house. Thinking of the future of his two sons, but before the fort became a

World Heritage site, he subdivided the house into three units. He chose to live in the middle unit. Today, both sons rent their apartments as offices and live outside the fort.

The 2004 tsunami flooded Gamage's house up to 6 ft., and he wrote to the president of Sri Lanka asking for funds to repair the house. The president (or his office) granted an undisclosed sum of money and advised, in the same letter, to add an upper floor to be safe from future tsunamis. In 2006, Gamage decided to build a separate dwelling unit in the backyard with the intention of establishing a tourist restaurant. Following UDA regulations, he got a chartered architect to make the design, which cost him Rs. 75,000 (USD 570), but the planning committee rejected the plan. He simply began construction. The Department of Archaeology, with the help of GHF, sued him, and officials constantly asked him to stop construction, but Gamage completed construction before the court ended the hearing. Whenever an official visited his house, he told them he had permission from the president to build an upper floor as a safety measure from future tsunamis. When the court ordered him to stop construction, he used the same letter.

By using the president's letter as a "weapon of the weak," Gamage repaired his house and constructed a restaurant. He believes that the Galle Fort Planning Committee rejected his plan with the intention of getting a bribe. After spending money on the architect's plan, he was not willing to spend more money to get the approval. He is happy with his decisions, and he has his dream property.

The owners of Shoba Fashions, Mala and Sachini Gunasekara, are locally famous as "the Shoba sisters." As they began to repair the unstable roof of their Peddler Street business, the Department of Archaeology and the GHF ordered them to stop; for nine months they lived in a house without a roof (Figure 4.6). This stopped their business and disrupted their lives. The sisters submitted a petition to the government stating that their human rights were violated on a daily basis by the government organizations involved in the project. The authorities also sued, but the courts fined them Rs. 50,000 for destroying a historic monument and permitted the sisters to construct a new building designed by a chartered architect.

Businessman Sisil Liyanapathirana, now 66, moved to the fort with his parents in the 1940s, when he was six years old. He bought his current house on Peddler Street in 1980 for his two sons, his wife, and himself. The house was in poor condition, and he requested permission to make repairs. There was no response from the Department for eight years. Due to the dilapidated condition of the house, Liyanapathirana went ahead with the repairs. He added a new front door, two windows, and a front wall; this changed the façade. The UDA, which became the authority for planning and construction, sued Liyanapathirana. After three years of debating, he obtained the court's approval for the changes he made.

Later he gifted two perches (160th of an acre) of his six-perch lot to his elder son; he now has four perches of land. Seeing the potential of tourism, Liyanapathirana reconstructed his house. This time he hired an architect who works for the Department of Archaeology and got approval for a two-storied house, but with "Dutch" pillars in front. Liyanapathirana himself changed his house twice, and the present house is a totally new structure. His early experience made him more careful with construction, and he found ways to get plans approved before construction the second time around.

Firyal Majid, 26, and her son live at her husband's house with his parents on Peddler Street. Not satisfied with her husband's income, the couple opted to tap into the tourist market. Peddler Street is a crossroad used by tourists. Since her husband is a good cook, the couple converted part of their house into a restaurant. They changed the façade by replacing the front door and two windows by a band of trellis work. By moving the wall about five meters back, they created a restaurant on the verandah. Separating the restaurant from the house, they added a wall. Even during the off-season, they earn enough to cover the renovation expenses, she said.

Majid did not have any problems with the conversion; in her own words, she and her husband followed the "normal way" of doing construction. They changed the façade but maintained the old look by adding a "Dutch-type" trellis. She also completed the changes within two days. It is possible that they constructed at night. Majid is aware of the problems that other people have faced when making home improvements. She believes the authorities interfere only when someone complains about construction and that her project did not garner any complaints.

Lalani, 29, moved to the fort after her marriage to Vimal Jayasekara, a native of the fort. The couple then converted the house they received from Vimal's parents into a hotel and restaurant and settled in it. They kept the façade with Dutch pillars and a wall with Dutch-type trellis, but added two more floors. They totally refurbished the house and gave it a new look. Now it is a four-storied house with five rooms, each with an attached bathroom. The first floor has a verandah, a living room, which is also the welcome area for guests, and a kitchen. There are two air-conditioned rooms with attached bathrooms on each of the second and thirds floors; these floors are finished with ceramic tiles. The fourth floor has just one room with a bathroom and an open verandah. The family uses this floor as their living quarters, but during the tourist season they rent out this room, too, temporarily moving out of the fort.

According to Jayasekara, the family did not face any problems during construction. Like Majid, Jayasekara also believes that nobody complained about their construction. They did not change the façade, so nobody knew they were adding new floors. The location of the house makes it difficult for anyone to see its four floors from outside.

Engaging in a totally different activity, Wasantha Rathnayake, a 45-year-old fisherman, cultivated a six-perch lot of land between the rampart and sea by Hospital Street. He received this land from his father, Jinadasa, who also lives on Hospital Street. Responding to a food shortage in 1970–1971, the government engaged in a *wagasangramaya* (war of cultivation). The government appealed to the people to grow food on uncultivated land and authorized the use of uncultivated land through gazette notification (using executive powers). People across the nation began to grow food crops on uncultivated land. In Galle Fort, according to Jinadasa, some people even cultivated the land in front of the entrance to the fort. Later, the father handed the land over to Rathnayake.

At present, the land contains a lot of trees, including coconut, fruits, and vegetables. There is a wooden fence around the vegetated area. Currently, this is the only cultivated land of this size within the Galle Heritage Project area.

According to Rathnayake, tourists began to visit the fort in the early 1980s, when he was a full-time fisherman. He built a cabana close to his father's cultivated lot and served the tourists. In 1995, the Coastal Conservation Department sued him for illegal construction. They also demanded the restoration of the cultivated land back to the beach. The court ordered him to remove the cabana but allowed him the right to cultivate the land, although they would not give him ownership rights.

There are many people who have successfully achieved the houses and land uses to which they aspired. They include Majid, Jayasekara, Liyanapathirana, Rathnayake, Gamage, and the Shobas. They have used different tactics to achieve their dreams. The most successful ones have evaded the project's impositions but benefit from tourism, an outcome of the same World Heritage project.

Majid's family, which faced financial difficulties, observed the changes in Peddler Street. They changed their house by adding some "Dutch" architectural features and opened a restaurant for foreigners. Jayasekara's family invested their savings in the growing tourist industry by adding two new floors to the house, converting it into a guesthouse for foreigners.

These people found creative ways to overcome the impediments imposed by the institutional structure of the World Heritage designation and the officers who maintained the restrictions. When Liyanapathirana began to repair his decrepit house, his project was blocked by the Department of Archaeology and the UDA. Through his own forms of negotiation, he managed to construct a new house with three additional rooms for tourists. Majid and Jayasekara were well aware of the issues they could face with the Department and GHF, especially if they were caught while making changes to existing structures. Those who were stopped by the GHF took different paths. The Shoba sisters went to court and completed the construction by paying a penalty. These inhabitants are creating their own version of the World Heritage, a version that acknowledges their presence.

World Heritages

In summary, the "World Heritage Project" is not one, but many. UNESCO's project is about humanity as defined within Western humanism. It dominates the larger discourse, but it hardly touches the ground. The project was brought to Sri Lanka by the national government, which wanted to create a tourist economy. If successful, the fort will depend on foreign tourists with a greater spending power. It was brought to Galle by ICOMOS consultants and state organizations such as the Department of Archaeology, which redefined it in design and legal terms. GHF, UDA, courts, and the police developed their own mechanisms to support and implement aspects of the project. There are substantive gaps between these projects and the Galle Forts they imagine. The gaps were shaped by negotiations between the various creators and implementers of the project. At the operational level, it is the project officers who fill the gaps. They make use of the gaps between projects and the ambiguity such gaps produce to develop and empower their own definitions, both tightening the project and constructing power and privilege for themselves.

The declaration aptly refers to the involvement of people in shaping the fort's built environment. The UNESCO idea itself is ignorant and/or contradictory: It is impossible to transform the fort into a Dutch environment and also let the place continue to function in the people's own ways; the consultants and the implementers hardly attempted to accommodate people. The Sinhalese and Muslims form the largest groups in the fort, and there is no way to get them to adopt Dutch practices, or to remove them. Turning the fort into a place in a particular history is impossible. The ICOMOS consultants, the people know, are interested in private projects to earn money and the (GHF) project officers take a lot of favors. It is therefore impossible to make the World Heritage project a total success.

People also use these gaps and cracks in the project—or between projects of different power-actors—to assert their needs and desires. Foreign populations, basically of European origin, made the best use of their "white-skin privilege" to buy property despite the prohibition, to get projects approved much faster than locals could, to include built elements they want such as swimming pools, and to prevent others from encroaching onto their space, even visually, by not allowing windows on buildings that face their properties. They create a strong private space. The (local) upper-middle classes who bought property follow this model.

The conflict between the imposed World Heritage project, particularly its local version created by ICOMOS consultants and GHF project officers, and the spatial needs and aspirations of the residents are reconciled through negotiations. While the GHF officials use power, the people use weapons of the weak. Many people do not know the law; many are also ignorant of the regulations imposed by the World Heritage project. While being ignorant and practicing apathy have enabled some to fulfill dreams, others fall into trouble with the officers. Like Farid, most of them learned about the rules when construction was intercepted by the project officers.

Responses to regulations/regulators can be broadly categorized into three types: The first group accepted the imposed subjectivity/predicament. While some opted to sell the property and move out, others attempted to follow the imposed regulations. Many offered their houses for the 60-Houses project. Despite their hopes, this option hardly yielded any benefits for them. The residents largely live in monuments over which they have little control and which are frequented by GHF officials without any notice or respect for privacy.

Those who belong to the second category began to adapt to the project, but of their own definition. However, the government intercepted their construction work. Many of these houses are incomplete and many have insufficient roofs, but the inhabitants are hopeful for change.

A surprisingly large proportion of people have substantially achieved their goals. They have not been too intimidated by the project and have benefited from the introduction of tourism. These fort residents have bypassed regulations and followed what they call the "process" which includes using personal contacts, evading, bribing, and/or simply ignoring the regulations. Popular ways of getting the work done include building at night, not being conspicuous, and bribing officials. The inhabitants have thus created a heritage site of their own conception: It is largely a tourist site in which they have business and other opportunities, but also one that better accommodates their daily activities and cultural practices.

Note

1 The buildings consisted of 285 residential units, 62 private institutions, 56 commercial units, 49 government institutions, and 11 religious buildings.

References

Department of Census and Statistics, Sri Lanka (2001) *Population by Ethnicity According to D.S. Division and Sector: Galle District (Provisional)*, Colombo: Department of Census and Statistics.

Dubrow, G.L. (2003) *Restoring Women's History Through Historic Preservation*, Baltimore, MD: Johns Hopkins University Press.

GHF (1994) *Galle Heritage Foundation Act of 1994*, Colombo: Ministry of Cultural Affairs and National Heritage.

Kuruppu, I. (1992) "The Conservation of the Galle Fort and Its Environs," Director-General of Archaeology, Department of Archaeology.

Liyana_Arachchi, T. (2009) *Socio-Economic and Cultural Survey of the World Heritage Site of Galle Fort 2009*, Galle: Galle Heritage Foundation.

Manawadu, S. (2011) "Preservation of Historic Cityscape in Fort of Galle, Sri Lanka by Restoration of Private Houses Through Public–Private Initiative: Proceedings of the 17th ICOMOS General Assembly and Scientific Symposium of Heritage," *Driver of Development*; November 27 to December 2, 2011, Paris, France, pp. 1158–62.

Ruberu, T.K. (2003) *Pratikal Jatika Ribeirogei Lanka Itihasaya*, Colombo: Godage Publishers (in Sinhala).

Silva, R. (1998) *Preservation Efforts of Recent Years at the World Heritage City of Galle*, Colombo: Department of Archaeology.

UDA (2009) *Special Regulation (Planning and Building) of "Galle Fort" World Heritage City*, Colombo: Urban Development Authority.

UNESCO (1972) "Convention Concerning the Protection of the World Cultural and Natural Heritage," United Nations Educational, Scientific and Cultural Organisation.

UNESCO (1988) "Advisory Body Evaluation: Old town of Galle and its fortifications." Online. Available: http://whc.unesco.org/archive/advisory_body_evaluation/451.pdf (accessed December 11, 2011).

5

BEGINNING SPACES

Young People's Struggles for Dwellings in Tashkent, Uzbekistan

With Hikoyat Salimova

It is normal for young people to leave their original "nests" in search of their own lives as singles, part of families, or otherwise. Building a new life requires each of them to create, acquire, or rent a dwelling. Yet the socio-economic conditions in Uzbekistan, which became independent in 1991, do not help young people in Tashkent fulfill this dream on their own. Newly wed Kseniya is clear about the conflict between her aspirations and the choices available to her:

> but, Hikoyat, we don't want just any apartment! The ones that we have seen are either in not good districts, too far from the center [of the city], or in very bad shape. We cannot afford a good apartment right now.
>
> *(Kseniya, in private conversation, 2005)*

The key questions are: How do young people begin their own lives in Tashkent? Where do they live? What kind of spaces do they produce in the process? This chapter is an exposition into young people's searches for dwellings as they seek to establish new households in the almost impossible housing environment of Tashkent, a situation which is only beginning to ease two decades after independence.

Housing for all citizens was a main goal of the former Soviet Union. The leading mechanism was for the state to provide housing for its employees as part of remuneration. Responding to the shortcomings, under the direction of Nikita Khrushchev, the first secretary of the Central Committee of the Communist Party of the Soviet Union (1953–1964), the state embarked on a program to provide a dwelling of minimum standards to every family in the country (Chernik 1957). In Tashkent, modern high-rise apartments were built after the 1966 earthquake. As these interventions did little to alleviate the housing deficit, the state allowed individual housing construction in the 1980s (Stronski 2003; Tokhtakhodjaeva 2007).

Independence brought the Soviet system of production and distribution of housing in Uzbekistan to a halt. Most state enterprises in trade and service sectors were privatized in the 1990s, and between 1998 and 2005, about 80 percent of state enterprises in other economic sectors were transformed into share-holding companies, with the state holding 25–50 percent. Goskomimuschestvo, the state committee for the management of state property, also allowed foreign investors to hold the rest of the shares (Embassy of Uzbekistan in Austria 2005).

The newly independent state—burdened with many other issues—did not consider housing a priority. It neither had the capacity nor the will to provide housing for citizens. The state began privatizing the housing stock in 1992, with the state agency, Housing and Communal Services (*Uzkommunalhizmat*), continuing the responsibility for utilities. Every household that lived in an apartment had the opportunity to own it.

The state continued to provide free housing for the military and employees of select ministries, but other enterprises were financially incapable of constructing housing for their employees in the necessary quantities. The emerging private sector firms have not shown an interest in providing housing for their employees either. There is hardly a private building industry to fill this gap. Houses are supplied to the market by "Gabus" and UzJSB (Uzbekistan Housing Construction Bank) in limited quantities and are very expensive. It has been almost impossible for ordinary families to find housing in Tashkent unless they already have a dwelling. This chapter concentrates on those who became of age to establish new households after the country gained independence.

The stagnant housing supply was complemented by a huge increase in housing prices and rents in Tashkent from 2005 to 2008 due to a rapid increase in the national GDP.[1] House prices grew steadily between 2000 and 2004, from 50 to 200 percent per annum (Ansher Capital Research Report 2004). Then they drastically increased by 250 percent in the first half of 2006 (Kudryashov 2006). According to real estate expert Murad Abduhakimov, this inflation in housing prices was triggered by foreign investments and remittances from overseas workers (Ansher Capital Research Report 2004). To seize the profit-making opportunity, wealthy Russian and Kazakh entrepreneurs made significant investments. The housing prices doubled every quarter from 2005 to 2007 (Figure 5.1).

These increases made housing in Tashkent unaffordable for a large majority, especially the young. While well-off Tashkent residents, and regional and foreign investors, seized the opportunity to make quick profits, ordinary citizens became more insecure, doubting whether they could ever save enough money to buy even a small dwelling, or repay debts if they could borrow. The 2009 global economic crisis somewhat stabilized the housing market; the price of apartments dropped twice, although not to pre-2005 levels.

The housing market in Tashkent is also affected by the demand caused by migrants, called *oblastnie* (provincials). In addition to being the political, economic, and cultural center of the republic, the national capital is also where most of the best universities are located. In addition to main state institutions, Tashkent is also the

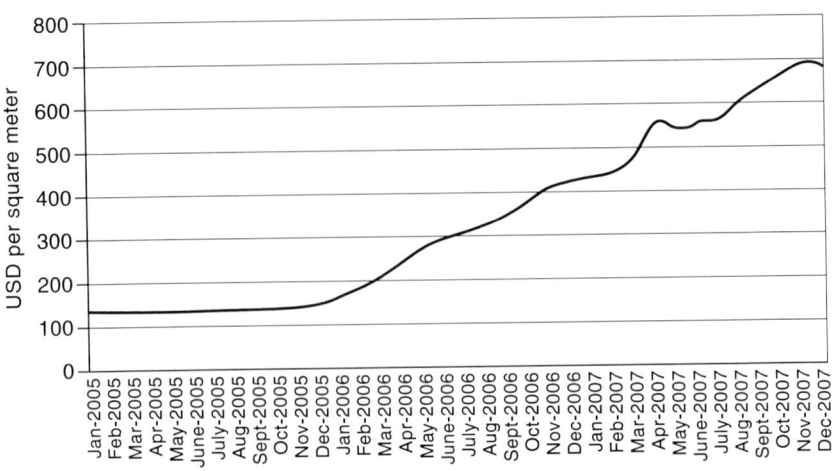

FIGURE 5.1 Average Prices of Apartments in Tashkent, 2005–2007, in USD Per Square Meter (credit: Hikoyat Salimova) (source: Sion Real Estate Agency 2011).

location of choice for foreign companies and international organizations that offer higher salaries. For these reasons, Tashkent is attractive to young people across the country.

To control migration, local governments continue old Soviet methods such as passport control and resident registration. The *hokimiyat* (the municipality) of Tashkent imposed severe restrictions on the registration of new residents after the bombings of 1999. Yet these measures could not completely stop in-migration. According to official estimates (which may not include a large number of unregistered migrants), Tashkent's population in 2009 was 2.2 million (State Statistics Committee of the Republic of Uzbekistan 2010).

Our investigation began with a broad survey of Tashkent residents, followed up by detailed interviews with 21 young people, aged 21–34, who lived in the capital for at least four years. To draw on Arjun Appadurai (1996: 3) from a different context, these young people "struggle to extend their chances of survival, to improve their horizons of possibility and to enhance their wealth and security." The stories of the young people reveal how they struggle to improve their livelihoods, particularly, to enhance their income and security, by deploying their social networks, social capital, imaginations, and creativity. They found means in their surroundings, both physical and social, family and friends, and their hometown connections.

From Coping to Negotiation

The young Uzbeks we spoke to did not back out of discussing the difficult housing situation. Their responses were wide-ranging. Significant outcomes include: home building, fringe property market, and the revival of traditional practices.

Despite the constraints, a small minority managed to build new houses. Coming out of a system of state-provided housing, in Uzbekistan capital and goods did not flow as in a market economy. A major strategy was to resort to traditional and/or customary institutions and practices that were also "modified" in the process. Some young people receive a great deal of support, from not only their close family and their extended family but also from friends and neighbors. In regard to building, they employ *hashar*, i.e., collective community volunteer work, for construction, renovation, and improvement of living environments, or they substitute labor for money.

At the same time, the Kvartirniy Bazaar (Russian for "apartment market") emerged as an institution through the matching of buyers and sellers of housing property. Although the housing stock was stagnant, some apartments fell vacant due to the emigration of Russian-speaking people following independence. Under the Soviet Union, people of different ethnicities lived in Tashkent for various purposes. The prospect of Uzbekistan separating from the USSR caused much anxiety for those who were not Uzbeks. Some began to emigrate before independence; however, the rate intensified from 1991 to 1994, and slightly dropped by 2010 (Radnitz 2006; State Statistics Committee of the Republic of Uzbekistan 2010). Although the city's population increased from 20.5 million to 27.8 million from 1990 to 2010, the "European" population—mainly Russian—dropped from 1.6 million to 1.2 million, halving the percentage, from 8.1 to 4.2 (United Nations 2009; State Statistics Committee of the Republic of Uzbekistan 2010). The dwellings that were vacated became known as the *vtorichka*, "secondary housing market."

With privatization, by 2002, 98.2 percent of the housing stock, including single-family houses and apartments, was in private hands (USAID 2002). Privatization, along with in- and out-migration, precipitated the need for a housing market.

At the end of the 1990s, people who wished to sell, buy, and rent dwellings gathered next to Hotel Uzbekistan, near Amir Temur Park. When this emergent institution, colloquially called Kvartirniy Bazaar, became noticeable in 2002, the city authorities assigned the participants a place behind the nearby main bus stop. The bazaar enabled the growth of self-declared renters, realtors, and agents. Within a few years, this market was absorbed into the city administration and moved to Chilanzar District.

Kvartirniy Bazaar is a "modern" institution. It is always busy, but it is yet to win people's trust. Most house-hunters, like Akmal, first asked friends, acquaintances, *babushka*s, *domkom*s, and "other gossip-tellers" in the target district. They want to avoid hassling with real-estate agents, extra fees for their services, and fraud. However, Kvartirniy Bazaar is an asset for rural and provincial residents who move to Tashkent, especially if they lack connections or social capital in the city. These newcomers can easily fall prey to fraud, and many migrants have lost their life savings to "black" real-estate agents. Hence, the would-be renters have to trust their intuitions and try to get a good deal. Fraud and rapid price increases led to stricter regulations and the enactment of real-estate laws. In 2008, Kvartirniy Bazaar was subject to the supervision of Goskomimuschestvo (Embassy of Uzbekistan in Austria 2005).

If Kvartirniy Bazaar is a building block of the burgeoning market economy, the modernized *mahallas* represent Uzbeks' traditional resource. *Mahalla* is a well-bonded, stable urban village physically represented in groupings of *hovlis*, "traditional" court-yard houses that share common open spaces. It is hard for outsiders to enter *mahallas*. New buyers of *hovlis* are recommended to get the permission and/or blessing from the *oksakol*, its elderly person, and the head, the *rais*. In Jane Jacobs' (1972) terms, *mahallas* make up a vital part of a city's organism and provide uniqueness to it.

Yet, Uzbek planners and city officials view future Tashkent as a modern city following Western environments. With the increase in land prices, especially in the city center, the old residential neighborhoods became the target of redevelopment. Previously, under the Soviet Union, traditional *mahalla* lost its status, but was not abolished. In 1993, the government of Uzbekistan established the Mahalla Foundation with the aim of reviving *mahallas* as community unifiers and supporters.

As the state was unable to provide sufficient social support for low-income families due to budget shortages, *mahallas* assumed this responsibility. These residential associations organized self-help (*gap, hashar*) mechanisms, recreating mutual bonds within communities. The adoption of the *Law on Community Self-Government* of 1999 increased the role of *mahallas* in citizens' lives, but absorbed the independent self-supportive community-organizations into the administrative system. Unlike *oksakol*, who is chosen by *mahalla* members, *rais* is now appointed by the state. *Mahalla* is still considered a prime community resource by a significant proportion of residents. People use it as a source of social capital and a tool to negotiate with the state.

Physically, some *hovlis* have been subject to *Evroremont*, meaning luxury repair with the best possible upgrades. The "modernizing" of traditional *hovlis* has resulted in hybrid houses that incorporate many features of Western houses, yet maintain the spirit of local ones (Figure 5.2). Similar to the example of *havelis* in New Delhi

FIGURE 5.2 *Hovli*: Existing and Modified Courtyards (credit: Hikoyat Salimova).

(Hosagrahar 2005), and the houses in Daanchi (Chapter 8), Uzbek *hovli*s equipped with Western amenities create an architecture of "indigenous modernity." Although these houses are not Western houses, the term "Euro-style" indicates the use of high-quality imported materials and furnishing in construction and decoration. Along with Kvartirniy Bazaar and (limited) new house construction, the revival of *mahalla*s indicates the people's ways of fulfilling their housing requirements and wants in a harsh housing environment.

Living Independently

The young are not passive. The lack of housing first paralyzed them, forcing them to continue to live with their parents for longer periods, even after marriage. Born and raised in Tashkent, Alexander and Kseniya, both 28, tried to live on their own; their stories reveal the difficulty of the market. Yet living with family, as Albina, also 28, highlights, is not always a problem.

Kseniya got married at 24. She and her husband worked for foreign companies and earned higher-than-average salaries for several years, but they could not afford an apartment at an appropriate location. After marriage, they rented an apartment from a friend who left for Russia, but the owner unexpectedly returned in a year. After changing a few apartments, and having a child, they returned to the home of Kseniya's parents-in-law.

For years Kseniya dreamed of a separate dwelling for her family where she hosts, lives by her rules, and has desired privacy. They are not qualified for the state mortgage program for young married couples because her husband is over 30. They think of emigrating, but only if both of them can find jobs that match their education and experience. As with many Russians, their primary choice is Russia, but they fear that it could become "nowhere." They value what they have in Tashkent.

After eight years of marriage and moving to five rental apartments, Kseniya and her husband bought an apartment. It is in the same building as her mother's, only a few floors above. While wanting to live separately, most young people prefer to live close to their parents. In addition to maintaining close family relations, the proximity allows the grandparents to provide childcare. Sobir's story (below) resonates with this.

The apartment became affordable because Kseniya bought it from a childhood friend who emigrated to Russia. She allowed Kseniya to pay in installments over a year. The apartment needs major repairs, but these can be accomplished slowly, as the couple abandoned plans for emigration.

Although not married yet, *Alexander* tried to live "independently," in his words. He could not afford the rent for long, and in a year he returned to his mother's one-room apartment. Rooms refer to "dwelling rooms" such as living, dining, and bedrooms. "Auxiliary rooms" include the kitchen, loggias, and toilets (Figure 5.3).

To create another dwelling room, they transformed the kitchen into a bedroom and moved the kitchen to the loggia (Figure 5.3). Adding a room is common when

FIGURE 5.3 Modified Loggias (Balconies) (credit: Hikoyat Salimova).

a family needs extra space for grown children. The law allows changes within apartments if the changes do not disrupt the structure of the building. A common strategy is to transform auxiliary rooms into dwelling rooms (Figure 5.3). Another strategy is to use a particular space for multiple purposes. The kitchen usually serves dining functions.

In contrast, Tashkent native *Albina* lives happily with her family. She never looked for housing. She has her own room and enjoys a comfortable life at her grandmother's apartment. She has a good job with a foreign company, and her family and friends live in Tashkent. The grandmother subjected the apartment to *Evroremont*, which is highly valued among the local population and drives up the price of the apartment. With such a settled life, Albina does not want to think too far into the future. Her housing needs have always been met by her family.

The "traditionalists" believe that it is good for young Uzbek families to live with their parents and that extended families help revive and maintain cultural values. Today, these extended families live in smaller apartments designed for nuclear families. While this practice provides social energy to respond to market failures, this traditionalist view also camouflages issues such as lack of privacy and freedom for young people like Pavel, below.

The Dreamers

Most young people are between their original homes and their own homes. Although living with parents, Tashkent native *Aliyar* dreams big about his own house. He shows confidence in achieving it. He is the only interviewee who described his dream house in detail. He identified his family as Europeanized, implying that his future nuclear family will live in a separate residence. According to Uzbek customs, as the oldest son Aliyar is likely to leave his parents' home to establish his own family.

At the time of the interview he lived with his mother and younger brother in a three-room apartment. It was originally a two-room apartment that his father received from his job. When the boys were growing up, the parents transformed the kitchen into a bedroom and moved the kitchen functions, which include dining, into the spacious loggia.

Having experienced life in Europe, Aliyar wishes to have a European-like house in Tashkent. He wants a large estate with a lake, lawn, garden, driveway, and other features of a European country house, but he prefers the center of Tashkent. Aliyar understands the conflict between these ideas and the market, but he has seen a few houses in the city that would satisfy some of his desires. Although acquiring his dream house may take many years after marriage, Aliyar purchased large apartment in the city center for which he used a loan from Ipoteka Bank.

Sobir, 22, and Nadejda, 24 (not discussed), are also dreamers who came from Bukhara and Fergana, respectively, as adults to study and work. Born in the Namangan Province, Shakhzod, 26, migrated to Tashkent as a child, with his parents. Yet to have their own families, the three live with their parents, but reveal the journeys of migrants and their dreams of getting their "own" dwellings.

Sobir arrived from Bukhara to study and work. He had some family members in Tashkent who gave him accommodation. He is still unable to move out. He came to Tashkent immediately after high school and majored in finance and auditing, a popular trend due to expected higher salaries. After four months of looking for an appropriate job, Sobir went to Moscow. Within a month, he was employed as an accountant's assistant in an international company.

Although Sobir's salary was four times as high in Moscow as in Tashkent, it was still inadequate for living; he spent 40 percent of it on housing. Moreover, the Moscow environment was hostile for Central Asians. Sobir was subjected to constant discrimination: His employer paid him a significantly lower salary and the Russian *militsia* (police) demanded monthly bribes, despite him having a work permit. He returned to Tashkent after eight months and the rest of his family also moved to Tashkent.

After some struggle, Sobir was hired as a financial analyst in a Turkish company. Although the position was flattering for a young man, the salary was one-third of what he had received in Moscow. As he is in a familiar environment and close to his parents and friends, this job feels more satisfying for him.

Sobir resides with his mother and sister in a smaller-than-average, $45\,m^2$, two-room apartment. He transformed the original bedroom into a study-bedroom for himself. His mother sleeps in the living room and removes her bedding during daytime, converting the space into a family room. The family also changed the two small loggias into rooms, one of which is for his sister. Sobir's family repaired the apartment by themselves. They insulated the loggias, replaced old wallpaper with plaster, and painted the walls in different pale colors, providing a Europeanized Uzbek style. Many locals who want *Evroremont*, but cannot afford it, create their own imitations.

As the only son, Sobir is expected to live with his parents after marriage. However, he does not want to be bound by this Uzbek custom. He wants to live close to, but separate from, his parents.

As for *Shakhzod*, his father migrated to Tashkent for better employment. Although the demand for his artwork was not as high as expected, his father earned enough to support his family of four. In 1990, he bought a spacious four-room apartment in Akmal-Ikrom District; the apartment was cheaper because it is far from the center of town.

As Muslim families provide separate rooms for boys and girls, Shakhzod's younger sister needed another room. For dining, they transformed the loggia into a traditional-style living room with *topchon* (large traditional platform), *homtakhta* (low table), *dasturhon* (table cloth laid on the floor, if no table), *kurpacha(s)* (long and narrow traditional padded quilts), and *yostik(s)* (long and rounded traditional pillows) (Figure 5.3). It is common among Uzbek families living in apartments to have at least one traditional-style room, incorporating familiar comforts to apartment living (see Chapter 8). This room is where the family spends time together, especially during morning and evening meals and tea conversations.

In 2001, the family decided to subject the apartment to *Evroremont*, especially to install new wallpaper and paint the walls. The renovation turned out to be expensive; they could afford new furniture for all rooms but the living room. That room was furnished by Shakhzod's young bride.

According to Tashkent customs, the groom's family provides a living space for the couple—a house, an apartment, or a separate room. The bride's family provides interior furnishing, sometimes filling an empty apartment or certain rooms. The main item is a *stenka*, wall-sized furniture in the living room that could hold a variety of items including television, books, dishes, and an alcohol bar. If the bride's family is unable to afford so much, they provide bedroom furniture—a bed and wardrobe. The dowry is negotiated between the families before the wedding.

As the only son in his family, Shakhzod did not leave his parents after the marriage. His wife and children live at his parent's apartment, which he will eventually inherit. The family will give his sister her share of the money or another form of inheritance.

As a devout Muslim, Shakhzod dreams of buying a *hovli* in a *mahalla* where the community strongly adheres to the Islamic faith. "I want to be closer to land [not on an upper floor]; I want to pray on the ground," he said. *Hovlis* are relatively expensive as they are located in the city center.

Shakhzod also shared his plan: He expects to save a substantial amount of money in the next five years and raise the rest by selling his parents' apartment. If his current salary doubles, he expects to buy the house sooner. Then both his family (after marriage) and his parents will live as one family, respecting Uzbek traditions, in his dream house in a *mahalla*. Recently, Shakhzod returned from Sweden where he obtained his master's degree; the expense drained much of his savings.

The young people who shared the stories above do not simply cope with bad housing. Rather, they have dreams and are hopeful of achieving them. While Aliyar works toward a suburban-style European house, Shakhzod hopes to live in a traditional *mahalla*; Sobir expects help from his family to buy his own apartment. The stories highlight how young people make use of "modern" and "traditional" resources and thinking and the ways they try to achieve their dreams through small amendments to their lives and the spaces they build.

Moving Abroad

Bekzod, 22, and Pavel, 28, represent a group of young people who have sought a better future abroad. Bekzod, who has worked for several years in Moscow, is planning to buy an apartment there. Pavel choose to migrate to the neighboring Kazakhstan, where his parents moved several years earlier.

Zarafshan-native *Bekzod* came to Tashkent in 2004 on a scholarship from a foreign joint-venture located in his hometown to study at the International Business School, Kelajak Ilmi. All five students who received the prestigious scholarship were contracted to work for the company-sponsor after graduation. However, in 2006, the foreign company sold its shares to another company, nullifying previous contracts including scholarships and potential jobs.

His housing journey began at a classmate's apartment. Although his stipend was equivalent to the average monthly salary in Tashkent, Bekzod lived with a friend from his hometown. The friend arrived earlier and had rented an apartment from an acquaintance. The one-room apartment was minimally furnished with beds, a wardrobe, table with chairs, and a refrigerator. There was no television, but the friend allowed Bekzod to use his computer. The two also had a slow dial-up internet connection and a telephone. The apartment was warm in the winter and "bearable" in the summer. His share of the rent, 15,000 soums, was less than one-third of his monthly income.[2] The stipend allowed Bekzod not to worry about his living expenses, and he became one of the best students in school.

For Bekzod, the apartment in the Chilanzar District was a bit far from school; it involved a 30-minute commute. The size of the dwelling was a greater concern: The only room ($3.5 \times 5 \text{m}$) was used as both living room and bedroom; the kitchen was about $2 \times 2.5 \text{m}$, and the loggia ($1 \times 1.5 \text{m}$) was not usable during cold months.

In his second year of studies, he moved to a separate dwelling. An acquaintance from Zarafshan found a lady who wanted to rent a spare apartment in Yunusabad District. He was fond of the one room apartment, especially its location and conditions. It was renovated and had one big living room and modest-size loggia remodeled into a well-insulated bedroom with windows. The living room had a standard set of Soviet furniture—a *stenka*, two armchairs, a couch, a small coffee table (*zhurnal'niy stolik*), a small night-table, and an ironing board, which was a bit unusual as people usually use a table for ironing. In the kitchen there was a dining table, a couple of chairs, and parts of a kitchen furniture set.[3] In the hall there was another standard Soviet piece of furniture: a *prihojaya* (antechamber). The apartment was more comfortable, but the rent was also 50 percent higher than the previous apartment. His generous stipend enabled Bekzod to afford it.

The situation suddenly changed. In the fall of 2006, the company's new management decided to stop financing Zarafshan students. The family pooled resources up to 40 percent of Bekzod's tuition; the school covered the rest from a Eurasia Foundation contribution. His parents partially funded his living expenses. He still had to significantly reduce his expenses, so he moved back to his classmate's apartment. Bekzod also found part-time employment but could not sustain this as his studies were intense and he needed high grades to maintain his tuition scholarship.

After graduation in 2008, he returned to his hometown. After four months of unsuccessfully searching for employment, his former internship supervisor offered him a full-time position in Tashkent to do the same job he did during his internship. Upon his return Bekzod rented the second apartment. This time the rent had doubled because the owner had done a *kosmeticheskiy remont* (minimal, refreshing repair), changing wallpaper and repainting the apartment. Yet it was not too far from the city center and was within his budget. After two years, he moved to Moscow and hopes to buy an apartment there.

Among the *oblastnies* interviewed, *Pavel* has lived the longest in Tashkent. Originally from Nukus, when he was 14 his parents decided he would get a better education in Tashkent and sent him to his uncle's house in 1996.

His uncle has a spacious, four-room apartment of $80 \, m^2$, in Yunusabad District. In these higher-quality 77-series apartments, rooms are relatively large. According to Pavel, "you can play football [soccer] in it." The uncle remodeled the kitchen into a bedroom for Pavel, moving the kitchen and dining to the loggia, which was of the size of a medium-size bedroom ($8 \, m^2$).

Linked to the loggia, Pavel's room had little privacy. He did not like this, especially because his uncle desired to have some supervision over him.

Two years later, his family moved to Tashkent. They sold their apartment in Nukus and bought a three-room apartment near his uncle's residence. The apartment was not as good as his uncle's, but they did *kosmeticheskiy remont*. Pavel had more freedom with his parents. After two years, in 2000, the parents sold the apartment and moved to Almaty, in neighboring Kazakhstan.

With his parents' support, the second-year college student moved in with his cousin who rented a one-room apartment in Sergeli District. They shared the rent of 35,000 soums per month. The living room, loggia, and kitchen were all large in the $45 \, m^2$ spacious apartment, which had separate toilets. However, the apartment was far from the city center.

After graduating from university in 2003, Pavel got a job. He and his girlfriend rented a one-room apartment in Chilanzar District, closer to the city center and near a metro station. It was a short and tiny $20\,m^2$ apartment: "I could reach the ceiling with my stretched arm," he said. It had an average-sized living room, combined toilet and bathroom, and a kitchen just large enough for cooking. The living room also served as the bedroom. As the young couple lacked the space for entertaining guests, they spent their evenings out.

Although this apartment was close to the city center, it was in a neighborhood where a lot of drug and alcohol addicts loiter. The rent was 40 percent of Pavel's salary; they could not move to a better place as it would cost even more.

A year later, Pavel and his girlfriend got married and moved to a two-room apartment near Victory Park that belonged to Pavel's wife's relative, who did not live there. They were not charged rent, but they were expected to take care of the apartment and pay utility bills. Pavel liked the dwelling, particularly the large rooms, high ceilings, separate toilet and bathroom, good neighborhood in *mahalla*, and close proximity to a metro station. However, they decided to move closer to Pavel's parents, in Almaty, Kazakhstan, leaving Uzbekistan altogether.

Materializing Dreams

Unlike most others, Anna, 28, Hamida, 26, Farida, 30, Igor, 28, and Ravshan, 28, established their own homes in Tashkent. Anna and Hamida live with their own nuclear families, whereas Farida shares an apartment with her sister. Igor was lucky and found the perfect window of opportunity in which to buy an apartment. Ravshan's father built his own house.

The majority of young people who are able to obtain housing do so with the help of family, mainly parents, but sometimes relatives and friends. Out of 111 survey respondents, only one used the (state) mortgage program provided by Ipoteka Bank, introduced in 2006 (*Uzbekistan Today* 2007). Many, including Kseniya, claim that loans are inaccessible to the public because Ipoteka Bank expects the borrower to have a stable, above-average salary. Among interviewees only Aliyar managed to get a bank loan. Most young people do not have enough money for the required down payment, and there is no guarantee they will receive the salary on time. Studies conducted by international organizations also confirm that housing and mortgages are unaffordable for the majority of citizens (UNDP 2010; World Bank 2007).

With fewer resources and power, finding accommodation requires young people to identify smaller gaps in the system, find opportunities, be more agile, and exercise their agency vigorously, tactically, and in a timely manner. Their responses are highly varied, but due to the financial constraints, most young people resort to social capital, particularly to informal financial aid from their social networks and to traditional methods that are also modified in the process. The journey of Anna, a native of Bukhara, is long and complicated, but it provides insights into most journeys. The stories of Igor and Ravshan provide depth and diversity.

Anna migrated to the capital after her higher education. She was invited by a friend from Bukhara to share a rented apartment in Tashkent with her and three university students. The three-room apartment was conveniently located near Oybek metro station. These girls wanted to escape dormitory life. Anna was the only non-student, but even as a worker she was unable to afford a separate apartment. The apartment was unfurnished, and the girls slept on the floor on mattresses brought from their parents' homes.

Most amenities including elevators in the 16-storeyed building relied on electricity. There was at least one power outage every two months, lasting for 10–12 hours. Anna still thinks that living conditions in Tashkent are better than in Bukhara, where the water supply is limited to certain hours, and hot water is a luxury.

The girls lived in the apartment for 18 months until they all, except Anna, got married and moved out. They shared all living costs, including rent, which was 12,000–14,000 soums per girl. Once the roommates were gone, Anna could not afford the "Oybek" apartment on her salary of 50,000 soums.

She received money and provisions from home. Every month, her mother visited with groceries from Bukhara, especially meat which was five times more expensive in Tashkent. Anna spent all her savings from Bukhara in three months, just looking for employment.

She moved in with another friend from Bukhara who had a three-room rented apartment near Gorky metro station. The area is known to be Europeanized and is populated with Russian and "Russified" people. The apartment was fully furnished, with a television, telephone, internet (a rare service), and a computer that Anna could use. Although cheap (40,000 soums), she had to walk for 15 minutes to the nearest public transport system; the path was poorly lit and relatively dangerous for a young girl to walk alone, especially after dark.

Anna found another rental apartment at the Kvartirniy Bazaar and moved back to the city center, the Darkhan area, close to Hamid Olimjon metro station. The only downside to this recently renovated two-room fully furnished apartment was the rent: 110,000 soums. She invited a friend to share it. Instead of accepting, she offered to share her rental apartment near Drujba Narodov metro station, so Anna moved in with her. The roommate did not pay her rent, and Anna moved out again to an apartment she found through Kvartirniy Bazaar. Again, the surrounding area was dark.

Anna invited an acquaintance to live with her; the arrangement lasted for only two months. She met a friend who was working in Tashkent and was looking for an apartment. The friend thought of living in an apartment a classmate had rented. The classmate was male, and Anna was worried about social norms, especially the inappropriateness for non-blood-related unmarried young people of different sexes to live in the same apartment.

Anna made the difficult choice. The three-room apartment afforded each of them a room, had necessary amenities, and was in a good location in Chilanzar District, three minutes to the main road and seven minutes to the nearest metro station. The roommates were from different ethnic backgrounds: Anna, Korean;

her friend, Tatar; and her classmate, Russian. They lived for ten months with no significant problems.

Bringing this eventful journey to another turning point, in 2006 Anna's family bought an apartment for her near Gorky metro station. It was vacant for some time and was in disrepair. Her parents brought some furniture from Bukhara and made it livable. She invited a friend to join her for company (with no rent); they shared grocery and utility bills. Eventually the friend decided to move closer to her workplace. In 2008, Anna got married to a friend from Bukhara, who also came to Tashkent for better employment. Both of them had relatively high incomes, up to three times the average income in Tashkent, and enjoyed a comfortable life in their own apartment. They migrated to Canada in 2012, seeking an even better life.

Tashkent native *Igor* bought a two-room apartment; he resides with his wife and daughter in a desirable neighborhood. According to Igor, he was lucky to purchase an apartment just before the housing prices went up in late-2005. He borrowed money from his parents and friends and soon repaid the loans.

He now lives near Gorky metro station, close to the most significant places in the city, including work, school, and recreation. He can also walk to visit his parents at any time, quickly and safely. Most people in this district are Russian-speaking, Europeanized citizens, similar to Igor's family culture.

However, his roof leaks. Igor's apartment is on the top floor of the building. ZhEK (house management association) regularly collects money but does not maintain the building well. He decorated the whole apartment before moving, but the first rains of the winter ruined the rooms.

Due to potential roof leaks, top-floor apartments are not favored in Tashkent where most apartment buildings are outdated and need capital repairs. People learn about repair issues from friends and acquaintances before moving.

Igor anticipated such possibilities, but his ability to afford a property was limited. This is definitely not his dream house, but he hopes to move to a better apartment once he saves enough money. It may take decades for Igor to upgrade his current lodging.

Ravshan followed his father to Tashkent in 2003 after completing his bachelor's degree. In preparation for the arrival of his brother and mother in 2005, his father bought a detached courtyard house in a *mahalla*. The *mahalla* consists of about 200 *hovli*s, or several apartment buildings (Figure 5.2).

His father demolished the old house and built a new one in a Europeanized style. The new house has three large bedrooms of 15–20 m², a living room, an entrance hall, and a big kitchen which also serves as the dining room. Unlike traditional Uzbek houses in which the kitchen and bathroom facilities are separate from the main house, the new house incorporated all auxiliary rooms. It has a gas stove, European-style bathroom, and a separate toilet. Since he worked in a construction company, the building was completed in a mere three years.

Ravshan's family is not that traditional; he does not get involved in *mahalla* activities; only his grandmother participates. Being young and on his own, he does not think he needs *mahalla*'s support. Second, Ravshan spends most of his time at work and is usually too tired for evening social gatherings. Third, it is not customary for younger family members to make decisions at *mahalla* committees; they simply follow the decisions made by the elders. The young people are connected to culture and tradition, but also far from these. In a way they do not live in any traditional, modern, or a third culture that combines these two. The spaces of the youth are better understood on their own terms.

Race, Gender, Discrimination

The (housing) journeys of the young people we spoke to were not smooth; competition, derogatory views, and discrimination were a part of their stories. The terms they used, the situations they described, depictions of the environment in which they grew up, and the cultural peculiarities they applied to houses were revealing. Kamila, 29, directly clashed with boys at her lyceum and with the neighbors of her rental apartment. She called them "*haripi*," colloquial for "uncivilized" people. The term is commonly used by the "Europeanized" (Russified) for uneducated Uzbeks. Although Kamila is partially Uzbek, she emphasizes her Russian upbringing and refuses to associate with these Uzbeks. This conflict led to her expulsion from the dormitory.

There is a strong opposition between "Europeanized" and "traditional," and each notion implies a particular set of stereotypes. At independence, many Uzbeks shared nationalist views, and some were openly hostile toward Russian-speaking people. Now, the young people largely get their inspiration from the West. Almost all elements of young Uzbek Aliyar's ideal house are Western, yet his current life very much resembles that of the traditional Uzbek family.

Housing preferences also follow ethnicity, religion, and identity. The representations include: "I wanted to live among the Muslims [Uzbeks]" and "I chose this district because it is more Europeanized [has a large Russian-speaking population]." Uzbekistan has a multiethnic population; Tashkent is more so. While their histories intertwine, there is still clear distinction among particular ethnic groups. After the privatization of housing, people began to move closer to their relatives. This fostered ethnic enclaves. One such distinctive group is the Koreans; among all ethnic groups in Uzbekistan they are the most concentrated due to the history of their relocation to Central Asia (Yalçin 1999).

The stories also reveal aspects of gender in student dormitories, shared rental apartments, and established households. The Soviet system radically transformed the predominantly Muslim Uzbek society (Stronski 2003). It Europeanized Uzbekistan, introduced many Russian aspects to daily life, and brought gender "equality." The apartment living allowed both men and women to use the entire apartment together, displacing the traditional separation of male and female quarters. National independence enabled the Uzbek traditions to creep back into Uzbek thinking, including aspects of gender.

In lyceums and university dormitories, boys and girls had equal allocation of space on separate floors. Yet a significantly low number of girls live in these.

Especially teenage girls are not sent to live by themselves in the big city. A young girl is considered an easy target in Uzbek culture; only parents or a close older relative could provide adequate safety. According to Kamila, the ratio of girls to boys in the lyceum dormitory in 1996 was 1:32. The boys began to dictate their versions of "traditional Islamic rules." Those who questioned were expelled. Kamila, too, was expelled after only two months.

Aspects of gender and space are changing. Anna and her female friend did not feel comfortable living with their male friend. As they did not see a viable alternative, they opted to disregard this convention. The three young people got along better than some random roommates of the same gender. This lack of space and related realities has enabled young people to feminize space, although in small increments (Chapter 2).

Housing Themselves, Transforming the City

The housing stock in Tashkent is stagnant and deteriorating. Finding a new dwelling seems impossible, yet the young people have housed themselves. The journeys of the young people were arduous, but all interviewees were creative in developing alternatives to the market supply. They adapted themselves to the environment and also transformed the housing environment through small interventions. As they were marginalized by the state and the market, young people resorted to cultural resources. They increasingly relied on acquaintance, traditional institutions such as *mahalla* and *hashar*, and help from family and friends. They operated at an individual level, using modest resources, but affected the city.

Some individual responses to the housing predicament produced new institutions. Kvartirniy Bazaar was developed through small initiatives made by sellers, buyers, renters, and tenant/s in the absence of a formal housing market. The formalization of this housing market by the state somewhat distanced it from ordinary people, but remains useful for migrants like Anna.

People also resorted to their traditional methods and social resources: Akmal and Kamila first checked with friends, acquaintances, gossip-tellers, and *babushkas*. All others followed family. "Tradition" is not static; *mahallas* were adopted and transformed, even a *hovli* was totally rebuilt by Ravshan's father, thus creating their present combination of modern comforts and building methods with traditions, customs, and cultural resources.

The housing journeys of migrants and Tashkent natives are different. The natives have less cumbersome journeys as they are familiar with the city and have family support. In addition to being far from "home" and unfamiliar, migrants are also subjected to administration and other forms of discrimination. They still find temporary and permanent housing in Tashkent. As Ashcroft *et al.* (2002: 12) demonstrate, "marginality ... became an unprecedented source of creative energy."

The migrants employed familiar connections to access the unfamiliar city. Before arrival, all interviewees—except students who lived in dormitories—found family, friends, or acquaintances in Tashkent and initially stayed with them. Anna,

Anastasiya, Bekzod, and Hurshid stayed with friends or acquaintances; Farida, Hamida, Nadejda, Pavel, and Sobir shared housing with family members who lived in Tashkent.

The urge to live separately is greater among the urbanites, especially Tashkent natives. It is a norm among Europeanized residents like Kseniya and Igor. Their journeys, too, are uneven: While Igor managed to purchase an apartment just before house prices increased, Kseniya struggled for years to establish a separate dwelling.

The high price of housing affects both natives and migrants. They tolerated the "horrible" living conditions in dormitories, lived on the edge of the city, spent much time commuting, and some coped with annoying landlords/ladies and unsafe neighborhoods. They kept moving, and stability was hard to find: Anastasiya, Anna, Hurshid, and Kamila had to move several times to different districts. Some like Anna, Farida, and Hamida achieved stability, but only after years of moving; others like Akmal, Anastasiya, Kamila, Nargiza, and Pavel left the country.

All interviewees made changes to apartments and houses. The changes were largely to create more space to accommodate a new adult, their own child (Alexander), or a relative (Pavel), or to make extra money. They repaired "homes," added personal touches, and some like Ravshan totally remodeled. Space was largely created by transforming what they saw as "auxiliary" spaces such as turning loggias into dwelling rooms, carried out by enclosing and winterizing the spaces. The repairs range from substantive upgrading (*Evroremont*), providing insulation, incorporating imported materials for window frames and curtains, and Europeanizing to minimal, refreshing repair (*kosmeticheskiy remont*).

The exercising of people's agency goes beyond the above interventions that fall within the scope of the chapter. Some owners of first-floor apartments have encroached outside areas. Examples include corner apartments expanding into the yard, incorporating the latter by fencing it, building a separate entrance (a door and stairway), and private driveways (Salimova 2010). Some try to make the apartment a "*hovli*" by encroaching neighborhood spaces. Some have also transformed first-floor apartments into private clinics and stores.

All interviewees relied on their social networks more than on formal structures. They found rental rooms, apartments, and houses at a time when a formal housing market did not exist and the services of real-estate agents were not affordable. Through a colleague, Kamila's father found a *babushka* who shared her home with his two daughters. When Kamila lived at her aunt's house, she was not welcome there, but the space was affordable for her father (a schoolteacher) and safe as the lyceum and was within a 15-minute walking distance.

The unavailability of affordable housing is worsened by the lack of information. Most interviewees relied on their social networks to find housing. Some, like Anna, used the Kvartirniy Bazaar to find housing. Most people prefer to trust their social networks, using word of mouth and relying on connections with neighbors, friends, acquaintances, extended family, and relatives. They lived with relatives, even though they did not like it; lived with friends, whether they went along well or not; lived with homeowners, who rented a room to generate additional income or to have company; and/or rented an apartment beyond their capacity and got financial support from their parents.

The interviewees also benefited from the flow of "social energy" (Uphoff 1996). As a contribution to her aunt's household, Kamila brought groceries from home (Gazalkent) every week. While living with *babushka*s, the sisters provided company for the "old ladies" left behind by their grown-up children in return for inexpensive housing.

Such mutual benefits were countless and varied. Friends and relatives of Aliyar, Anastasiya, Hurshed, and Nadejda owned apartments in Tashkent. The absentee owners needed someone to take care of the property. They offered to let the young people live in the house and pay utility bills. The "house-sitters" in Tashkent are usually family members, rarely friends, and never strangers. This is a great matching of needs from both supply and demand sides, creating an informal exchange, and providing unofficial housing solutions.

In building this reality, the young people have resorted to the resources they have, regardless of whether they are modern, traditional, external, or internal. They have incorporated traditional spaces in apartments, built on traditional ideas such as *mahalla*s, Europeanized (*Evroremont*), and modernized *hovli*s, thus developing their own ways of fulfilling the housing requirement. People fully enjoy the benefits of self-help practices; they tap into this source of social energy to address their housing issues; the remnants of *hashar* are still practiced in some communities and among extended families for helping the neighbors and relatives with labor work in their home improvements. Instead of being subjects of the impossible housing environment of Tashkent, young people have exercised their agency, transforming the conditions into the raw material of their journeys.

Notes

1 The growth rate of GDP in Uzbekistan's grew from 4.2 percent in 2003 to 7.4 percent in 2004, and 7.0 percent in 2005 to 7.5 percent in 2006 (www.sion.uz/content/view/1337/103/lang,russian).
2 USD 1 = 1,000 Uzbek soums at the time of described events.
3 Usually Soviet apartments do not have installed kitchen cabinets; the occupants bring a separate kitchen set, or select components, and a refrigerator.

References

Ansher Capital Research Report (2004) "Uzbekistan: Real estate, the growth story." Online. Available: www.anshercapital.com (accessed 20 August 2009).

Appadurai, A. (1996) *Modernity at Large: Cultural dimensions of globalization*, Minneapolis, MN: University of Minnesota Press.

Ashcroft, B., Griffiths, G., and Tiffin, T. (2002 [1989]) *The Empire Writes Back: Theory and practice in post-colonial literatures*, New York: Routledge.

Chernik, S. (1957) *O Razvitii Zhilishchnogo Stroitel'stva v Uzbekistane* [The Development of Housing Construction in Uzbekistan], Tashkent: State Publishing Agency of the Uzbek S.S.R.

Embassy of Uzbekistan in Austria (2005) "Destatization and Privatization in the Republic of Uzbekistan," 27 June. Online. Available: www.usbekistan.at/publish/rus/printer_129.shtml (accessed January 15, 2015).

Hosagrahar, J. (2005) *Indigenous Modernities: Negotiating architecture and urbanism*, London: Routledge.

Jacobs, J. (1972 [1961]) *The Death and Life of Great American Cities*, 2nd edn., Harmondsworth: Penguin.

Kudryashov, A. (2006) "Real Estate Prices in Tashkent Rose 2.5 Times in Six Months," July 23. Online. Available: http://enews.ferghana.ru/article.php?id=1527 (accessed June 8, 2010).

Radnitz, S. (2006) "Weighing the Political and Economic Motivations for Migration in Post-Soviet Space: The Case of Uzbekistan," *Europe-Asia Studies* 58: 653–77.

Salimova, H.K. (2010) "Housing Options in Tashkent: Journeys of young people in establishing their households in independent Uzbekistan," unpublished Master's thesis, Ball State University, IN.

State Statistics Committee of the Republic of Uzbekistan (2010) "Demographic Data (1991–2009) in Uzbek." Online, Available: www.stat.uz/STAT/index.php?%ru%&article=131 (accessed May 8, 2010).

Stronski, P.M. (2003) "Forging a Soviet city: Tashkent 1937–1966," unpublished PhD dissertation, Stanford University, Stanford, CA.

Tokhtakhodjaeva, M. (2007) "Tashkent: three capitals, three worlds" in C. Alexander, V. Buchlli, and C. Humphrey (eds.) *Urban Life in Post-Soviet Asia*, London: USL Press.

UNDP (2010) "Addressing Urban Poverty in Uzbekistan in the Context of the Economic Crisis, Tashkent." Online. Available: http://mdgpolicynet.undg.org/ext/Policy_Brief-PSIA-Uzbekistan-eng-17.03-final_draft.pdf (accessed June 8, 2010).

United Nations, Department of Economic and Social Affairs, Population Division (2009) "Trends in International Migrant Stock: The 2008 Revision." Online. Available: www.un.org/esa/population/publications/migration/WorldMigrationReport2009.pdf (accessed June 8, 2010).

Uphoff, N. (1996) *Learning from Gal Oya: Possibilities for participatory development and post-Newtonian social science*, London: IT Publications Ltd.

USAID (2002) "Assessment of Current Legal and Operational Status of Housing Partnerships in Uzbekistan." Online. Available: http://webarchive.urban.org/Uploaded-PDF/411077_Uzbek_housing.pdf (accessed June 8, 2010).

Uzbekistan Today (2007) "New Types of Services in Tashkent Ipoteka Bank." Online. Available: http://old.ut.uz/rus/newsline/novie_vidi_uslug_tashkentskogo_ipoteka_banka.mgr (accessed January 15, 2015).

World Bank (2007) "Housing Finance Development in Uzbekistan." Online. Available: http://siteresources.worldbank.org/INTUZBEKISTAN/Resources/294087-1246601504640/Housing_Finance_Policy_Note_FINAL_eng.pdf (accessed June 8, 2010).

Yalçin, R. (1999) "Ethnic Minorities in Uzbekistan: The Case of Koreans," *International Journal of Central Asian Studies* 4. Online. Availab.le: www.iacd.or.kr/pdf/journal/04/4-04.pdf (accessed June 8, 2010)

6

SPACES OF RECOVERY

Rebuilding Lives after the Tsunami in Kalametiya

There are plenty of natural- and human-induced disasters these days. There are also plenty of organizations to respond to these; the powerful and well-funded disaster-response machine is made up of global, international, national, and local institutions and organizations. As the media develops its own stories, exaggerating and dramatizing selected views or events such as killer waves, huge piles of rubble, and/or mass graves, and reports these extensively and intensively, disasters take shape as high-profile events. The media has already made natural disasters more significant than the everyday slow violence seen in poverty, discrimination, and "development."

The discourse is so hegemonic, and the disaster response machine is so hefty, it is expensive to keep it idling (Klein 2007); disaster seems a necessity. The donor countries and agencies not only assume they have a responsibility and a right to help disaster victims, but they also expect the victims to receive their help and the governments to allow the flow of outside aid. This was highly evident when the US government threatened the government of Myanmar to forcefully deliver aid for the victims of a 2005 hurricane. Social and political power is, therefore, built into the disaster discourse, privileging some stories over others (ibid.).

The Indian Ocean tsunami of December 2004 was historically one of the most devastating disasters to strike the region, affecting many countries including Indonesia, Malaysia, Myanmar, and Thailand. Responses to the disaster were quick and profound: Many global, foreign, and national agencies swiftly came to the help of victims. The story has been told many times from the donors' and providers' vantage points: The goals and achievements of their relief, response, and recovery work have been documented by the agencies themselves. This chapter concerns the survivors' recovery process.

Along with aid, the donor agencies and service providers imported their ideas and visions; most of the time these were imposed on the victims they undertook to serve. The support agencies also connected the victims and their locales to faraway places from which the resources, personnel, and aid originated and to new global and national networks, flows, and processes, thus developing a space of disaster response. This chapter focuses on New Kalametiya, a post-tsunami settlement in Hambantota District, Sri Lanka (Figure 6.1).[1]

The response to the 2004 tsunami destruction in Hambantota District was exemplary. The NGOs delivered most of what they promised, and the government, especially the Urban Development Authority, effectively controlled and coordinated the quality and quantity of donations and environments they produced. All victims identified by the government were housed within little over a year in architect-designed houses of over 450 sq.ft., built on lots over seven perches in planned settlements, with water and electricity supply (Figure 6.1). From a middle-class standpoint, this is a dream come true.

This abstract space is not complete. Conspicuously absent from this discourse are the victims, who are largely present as anonymous stereotypical figures around which the discourse was developed. In regard to the flow of ideas and finances, these settlements were well connected to the outside world, but less so to the locality and the culture of the inhabitants. The aid transformed the affected environments into something the inhabitants have not known before, and they were expected to adapt to it. Yet there is hardly any substantive discussion on the impact of aid, the methods of provision, and/or post-occupancy evaluations.

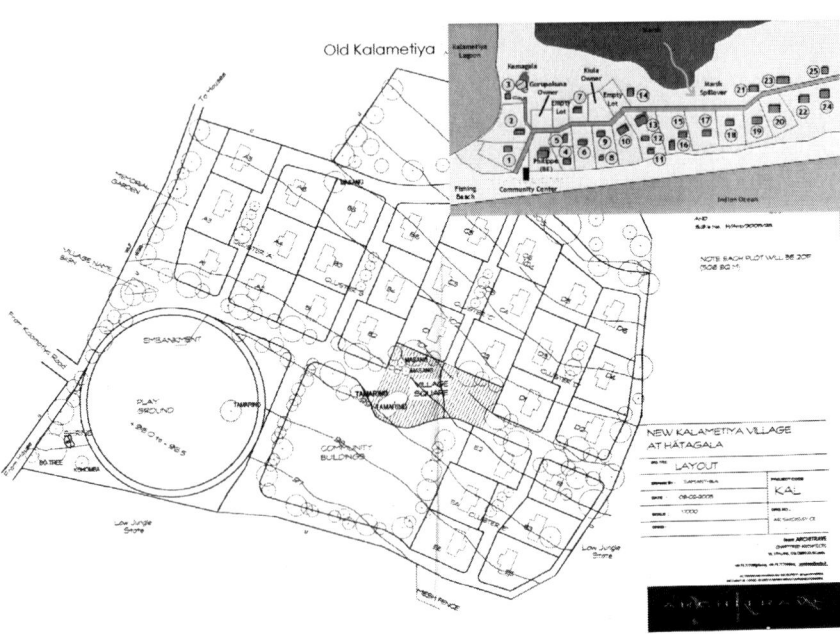

FIGURE 6.1 Old and New Kalametiyas (credit: Ashley Webb (insert); Madhura Prematilleke (plan)).

My curiosity is in the spaces and identities the survivors produce under these circumstances. What is overlooked in hegemonic narratives focused on *victims* and recovery is how the *survivors* build their post-disaster lives. How did the survivors perceive the "disaster?" How did they conceive and carry out their "normalizing" processes? What spaces do they produce for the same? Following these questions, and questioning the notion of "disaster recovery," I will investigate how survivors familiarize social and spatial environments and create their own lives, spaces, and identities.

The Destruction and New Settlements in Hambantota District

Hambantota District, which has five major post-tsunami settlements and many smaller ones (Table 6.1), is also the home of then-Prime Minister (later President) Mahinda Rajapaksa. The government and aid agencies made quick and profound responses to tsunami destruction. The government gave land, the NGOs collected money, the Urban Development Authority provided guidelines, and the people were given architect-designed houses with water and electricity in little over a year.

TABLE 6.1 NGOs Involved in Main Post-Tsunami Settlements

The Settlement	*NGOs*	*Housing Units*
Yayawatta (Tangalla)	PLAN Sri Lanka	200
	International Special Partner	90
Uhapitigoda (Amabalantota)	Theravadi Samadi Education Fund	300
	Forut Institute	101
	Bon Sri Lanka	38
Kalametiya	Sahana Project, Maine, USA	30
	Green Movement of Sri Lanka	
	Development Fund of Norway	
Hambantota	Tzu Chi Foundation, Taiwan	647
	Sabaragamuwa Provincial Council	103
	Adapty of Sri Lanka Belgium Society	35
	Omega Line	50
	Faxsa, Aflex	91
	Singapore Sinhala Association	42
	Metta Foundation	50
	Care Sri Lanka	150
Kirinda	Sithjayapura	NA
	ASPIC-GOAL	NA
	World Vision	NA
	Sonta	NA

Credit: UDA Hambantota.

As a place where such global action came together, the post-tsunami environment in Hambantota District was somewhat active and festive for the visitor. In addition to the immediate help provided by neighboring people, the agencies involved in disaster response provided the needful, particularly water, food, medicine, clothing, shelter, and media coverage. With huge banners of donor agencies and countries displayed in open air, on tents, and houses, and each project representing an NGO, the post-disaster landscapes were quite new and unfamiliar to the locals (Figure 6.2). As the disaster response coalition supplied the needful, the victims and their country became dependent on such aid.

Before the tsunami, the large majority of the families lived in fishing villages, mainly on the beach. These were not significant for outsiders except for local fish merchants, money lenders, and the like from adjacent villages and nearby urban centers. The only exception is Hambantota town, where the victims lived in a town along the shore, but, as in other villages, the main utility of the sea was fishing. In this chapter, I use Hambantota for the city; Hambantota District will be so mentioned to describe the larger area. After the tsunami, the habitats of the victims—including Hambantota—were transformed into trans-localities defined by their connections to various places across national and other boundaries. These were created by first responders, donors, helpers, volunteers, experts, sympathizers, and well-wishers, the large majority of whom—especially the ones with resources—were foreign.

Immediately after the disaster, the devastated areas became the domains of outside agencies, particularly of NGOs, with the state as the interface between them and communities. The change was much evident in Hambantota, the most populated urban center in the district where more than 10,000 people were killed by the tsunami. In a landscape of devastation, where only foundations of buildings were left and even the satellite tower had turned into a ball of metal wire (Figure 6.2), "tent cities" stood out, forming a landscape of hope. The tents were not only new, but they also bore the names and symbols of the NGOs which—perhaps inadvertently—announced and/or claimed the authorship of the new landscape—or their part of it. Moreover, especially in the downtown, the landscape was dominated by huge banners of donor agencies and countries displayed in open air and small offices that represented the NGOs (Figure 6.2).

FIGURE 6.2 Hambantota after the Tsunami (credit: Nihal Perera).

As they built temporary accommodation for victims, the NGOs became highly visible. For example, despite being a Buddhist organization, the Tzu Chi (Great Love) Foundation of Taiwan, which did a tremendous service in Hambantota, was prominent even on the property of the largest mosque in the city. The pneumatic structures they constructed for temporary living provided a spectacle (Figure 6.2). In Kalametiya, Oxfam of the UK took the lead in housing the victims (Figure 6.3). The tsunami-affected sites were a spectacle for outsiders, including researchers, donors, and middle-class tourists who visited from Colombo and other cities in Sri Lanka and abroad. For most tsunami survivors, in Hambantota and elsewhere, the aid they received was helpful and, for many, quite substantial, allowing them to get on with their lives.

At the same time, the help proved to be prescriptive and restrictive. The aid was conceived within the institutional goals and cultural frameworks of donor agencies. Along with aid, they also exported—most of the time imposed—their ideas and visions for the people they intended to serve. Such ideas included the need to serve underserved populations and support environmental sustainability. As there were no plans or information at the local government level, many donors implemented their ideas without much consideration for the local context. Architects without Borders of Oregon built a school building in Bata Atha, about 5 km from the beach that was hardly used by anyone touched by the tsunami.

In Hambantota, an NGO constructed large cisterns of about 10 m diameter and 400 mm tall for rainwater harvesting. Hambantota District lies in the driest region of Sri Lanka, but people are not used to harvesting rainwater. It has not been necessary as the district is crossed by five significant rivers, and irrigation technology has been prominent in Lanka for over 2.5 millennia. Moreover, most households have well water. The people—including myself—were confused about the purpose of these cisterns. In another place, a group from California provided solar panels for each house they built in Tangalla, abruptly introducing imported technology on disaster victims, at the exorbitant unit-cost of USD 5,000. In Kalametiya, the inhabitants received many things, including fishing boats that they could not use;

FIGURE 6.3 Temporary Housing at Kalametiya (credit: Nihal Perera).

FIGURE 6.4 Unusable Aid: Unwanted Boats and a Locked Community Center (credit: Nihal Perera).

although they are fishermen, the kind of fishing they do requires different boats (Figure 6.4).

The stereotypical "solutions" simultaneously homogenized the settlements and distinguished these from the immediate surroundings. The houses in Hambantota District—including Kalametiya—have two bedrooms, a combined sitting and dining area, front and back verandahs, a kitchen, and attached toilet. These buildings that the architects designed and NGOs provided were part of their own projects, based predominantly on ideas brought from other places. Through house designs, each settlement is stamped with the signature of the NGO and the architect involved; the designs and colors of the buildings in each settlement stand out within the extant environment.

The landscape of the region has grown, along with the society, over a long period of time, through the addition of new buildings, on new sites, replacing some of the old buildings, and infilling the extant environment. In contrast, the new settlements are uniform, mass produced, and stand out. Although "nice" from an urban middle-class taste standpoint, these are alien for the inhabitants.

This highlights a mismatch between the aid programs, as practiced, and the needs of survivors. Most crucially, the donors intervened into victims' lives and transformed them into the Other. They were subjected to medical and identity checks, counting, research, outsiders' gazes and pity, and they were required to sign many papers. This was quite new and strange for the locals whose lives were already disturbed by one disaster; they lost the sense of place and belonging and were displaced in their own habitats.

Some providers incorporated local ideas: In Yayawatta, the staff of Plan International learned that Sri Lankan culture does not promote grown-up boys and girls sleeping in the same room, unless they are married. Although this is not a strict rule the way it was understood and practiced, the NGO provided three bedrooms, but in all houses. The NGOs and designers also believe in mass production. They refer to justice and equality to all, the universal applicability of which is hard to fathom. Nonetheless, it works well for the designers and the NGOs from an economic standpoint of mass production. As Plan did not increase the house size, all rooms turned out to be smaller; couples with no children now have extra rooms, but a small bedroom for themselves. Plan also provided community gardens, heretofore unknown in Sri Lanka, but individual home-gardens, which are common in Sri Lanka, were small. As they generalized and reorganized local knowledge, the NGOs defamiliarized the environment and created new obstacles for the recipients.

From Fishing Hamlet to Global Village

The tsunami brought Kalametiya into a web of transnational and intranational flows. Before the tsunami, it was an ordinary fishing hamlet located on the beach, away from other villages. The inhabitants were self-employed in fishing or related businesses. This small community of 25 households did not have a large catch of fish, and no one paid much attention to it. Members of surrounding villages looked down upon the households. The major exception was a Belgian who maintains a seasonal home there.

The victims first took shelter in the Kiula Buddhist temple. Then, Oxfam of the UK took the lead in housing them in an L-shaped wooden row of rooms about $3 \times 3\,\text{m}$ (10 × 10 ft.). The clean-up of the tsunami-affected village was sponsored by many NGOs, including Service Civil International, and assisted by many foreign individuals. The permanent houses were funded by the Sahana Project of Maine (USA) and the Development Fund of Norway, coordinated by the Green Movement of Sri Lanka, designed by Architrave Architects of Colombo, and helped by many including the CapAsia field studies program of Ball State University, USA (iweb.capasia.bsu.edu), which the author directs. It was a large multinational project in which many NGOs participated: The Irish NGO GOAL paid the victims to clean-up the environment; others donated boats and fishing implements; and many organizations and individuals simply donated money and/or household items.

From a formal standpoint, this project was a success. Most crucially, the villagers received new houses within a year of the tragedy. Yet it was not free of mismatches: Based on its own environmentalism, the Green Movement of Sri Lanka insisted that the beneficiaries develop home-gardens, making the inhabitants feel that the NGO donated the land. Farming was unfamiliar to Kalametiyans. They are fisher folks who lived on the beach where most vegetables do not grow. Besides, they usually sit on the beach watching for fish and water currents; when the time comes, they go out to the sea. At the new location, as common in Sri Lanka, most settlers have fruit and vegetable gardens, but the NGO insisted on gardening in its way.

The way the building activity was carried out, recipients were viewed and made to feel as victims. The external interventions of providers overwhelmed the recipients with environmental changes—including new housing types—that are unfamiliar to them. Most crucially, the inhabitants do not even own their land; this displacement has been caused by government rules that do not allow them to return to their original lots. They were also not "trusted," as in any "slum upgrading" project, the project leaders fear that the inhabitants may sell their lots and do whatever they want. This may not enable the fulfillment of the project goals. In this, the inhabitants are highly subjugated to the project. The immediate impact made them passive recipients of external aid.

When the roofs leaked, people sought the help of the Green Movement workers. With surprise, the latter looked down upon the complainers; for the NGOs, the people are lazy and are asking for everything. The NGO was unable to recognize that it was its own choice to become the provider, and this choice carries particular implications and responsibilities with it. People used to build their own houses, but not these new architect-designed, contractor-built, modern-type houses. The new house was unfamiliar, and the occupants preferred or needed the help of experts to make repairs. Besides, the recipients have the right to ask for a roof that does not leak. The inhabitants were simply playing their role, an outcome the NGO was unable to recognize.

Besides, the NGO's action caused deprivations. Instead of letting the inhabitants make choices, the providers absorbed the tsunami-victims into a web of global flows. It did not question and/or reflect on its own practices. This caused a mismatch between people's needs and the provisions. The most hilarious moment that revealed this gap was when a few Kalametiyans asked for motorcycles to go to work (fishing) at the planning workshop in February 2008. Despite relocating the fishermen and their village 4km away from the sea, the aid provider did not think to supply any transportation. Hence, the people's request was reasonable, but the planners who conducted the workshop were quick to dismiss the request as ridiculous.

Just as much as the NGOs and the architects, the government also saw opportunities and incorporated the resettlement process into its plans and assumed credit. For the government, tsunami recovery was its project: It managed the funds diligently, provided the donors with norms, moved the people to safety, and set minimum standards for the provision of housing; yet it did not let the others do whatever they wanted. It also generated considerable political capital out of the enterprise.

The government's immediate response was to use a Coastal Protection Act to ban the reconstruction of destroyed buildings within 100m of the shore. Nevertheless, it donated the required land according to its own estimates, and the Urban Development Authority effectively regulated the collection and spending of donations for major settlements and maintained minimum standards for the design of houses. All the victims identified by the government were housed within a year, albeit the supply of water and electricity was erratic and inadequate.

The government, especially Prime Minister Rajapaksa, absorbed tsunami aid into its own projects. In most settlements in Hambantota District, the number of houses appears to exceed the requirement, and many families which had not been directly affected by the tsunami also live in these. In Hambantota town, the victims—and their original land from which they were removed—were absorbed into a new town that the government was building more than 3 km from the beach. The settlers include some people who were relocated due to the construction of a new harbor, road, and other projects. In effect, instead of the resettlement of the victims, the government was building new settlements which were highly unfamiliar to the inhabitants.

In Kalametiya the victims were relocated on the land-side of the bird sanctuary, 4 km away from the original village and the sea (Figure 6.1). Walking 4 km daily in this arid area is arduous. Yet having a personal vehicle is not affordable for most people. Unlike the former arrangements, the new village is to be made up of nuclear families. Hence the 25 houses in Kalametiya were replaced by 30 houses. The new settlement is organized around a single axis with a common area on one side, near the entrance.

Victimizing the Survivors

What is overlooked by the NGOs, the state, the architects, and in the mainstream literature on disaster mitigation, response, and recovery is how the survivors perceive and carry out their own "recovery" processes. Hardly anyone asked the victims—in any substantive sense—how they wished to respond to their predicament. It was simply implied that the victims lost their houses and jobs, and so providing houses and jobs equals recovery. Sometimes the victims were consulted, but largely to find ways to accommodate and/or incorporate them into the providers' processes. The gap between the providers' and recipients' perceptions was hardly bridged.

Refusing to be *victims*, the settlers began familiarizing the new environment and the new houses in which they were relocated. The *survivors* both adjusted their practices to the environment and adapted the houses and the environment for most daily activities and cultural practices, which were also transformed in the process. They made aid, other gifts, and impositions meaningful to them, i.e., their cultural practices and life journeys. In short, they transformed provided (abstract) spaces into lived spaces within their worldviews, means, and constraints, causing new cultural practices and spaces.

The Kalametiyans will never fully recover what they lost. Despite the mainstream discourse on recovery, there is hardly one on the ground. No one was trying to get back to where she or he was, whether socially or economically. The only thing they wish to recover is the land. Recovering what was lost is more an outsiders' idea; the locals have (re)begun their life journeys from where they found themselves after the tsunami.

The post-disaster journey began immediately after the tsunami in the temporary settlement. The tsunami took 11 local lives and destroyed all houses, displacing the survivors in their own land. As refugees, they first looked for food, clothing, and shelter and tried to regain part of the material life they had. When Rasika saw her children do homework on the floor in their temporary accommodation, she cried. She told me about the great house and the furniture the family had, and the high quality of life she and her husband gave to their children. While they did look to recover some of what they lost, the Kalametiyans developed and pursued their own dreams, which have been changing with the context. They are well grounded in the present.

Immediately after the tsunami, the victims were disoriented and became passive dependents. Very early on, when they were still refugees at Kiula temple, the Kalametiyans were told they were not allowed to return home. They not only became displaced, but they were also at the mercy of the authorities and other service providers. Much aid came from the outside world, especially from overseas. The processes of aid provision infused a materiality among the victims, devaluing personal agency and social capital.

For most tsunami survivors, the aid they received was helpful and satisfied some of their basic needs, but fell short of addressing their wants. The functional failure of having attached toilets and kitchens that depend on gas and/or electricity highlights the distance between the providers and survivors. Several architects, including the designer of New Kalametiya, Madhura Prematilleke, took good care to locate the toilet entrances from outside, but many inhabitants are unhappy about the toilet and the kitchen sharing a wall.

Before the tsunami, the villagers depended on each other and their own social networks. Aid made social capital worthless, making the Kalametiyans depend on external help. Initially people built very little, but had more excuses. They mostly saw what was wrong with the new location and the house they received and overexaggerated the deficiencies. Architect Hasan Fathy stressed that people have a natural urge to build. The provision of completed houses by the NGOs destroyed the people's natural urge to build[2] and socialized them into aid-dependency.

Beyond Recovery: People's Life-Journeys

The gap between the providers' and recipients' perceptions and the latter's use of agency to make use of the provisions to build their own lives is evident in their transformation of kitchens, toilets, stores, overhead water-storage tanks, and the gardens surrounding the houses. Within three years—when I did the longest substantive-stretch of fieldwork in 2008—the survivors had largely recovered from the initial shock of the tsunami and the constraints imposed by the providers, what the inhabitants call the "second tsunami." They had regained their agency and were continuing to build and shape their lives from where they were. This process is evident in changes in their livelihoods, gender relations, children's aspirations, and education.

Their post-tsunami life-journeys began with the familiarization of aid they received, including the physical environment. People thankfully accepted the land and houses they received but made substantial changes to them. This transformation was guided by both nostalgia and aspirations, as well as memory and dreams, but was firmly grounded in the present. In combining these, the inhabitants developed new cultures and spaces which can be identified as "third" or "hybrid" cultures and/or spaces at first. While the provisions by the state and the NGOs were the raw material, the immediate obstacles were the structures put in place by regulations and aid processes. People have been imaginative and creative in carrying out daily activities and cultural practices they desire, within constraints, using aid and bypassing regulations.

Sense of belonging and place is at the core of the struggle: While the old identity of Kalametiyans was in crisis, a new identity was yet to be established. Old Kalametiya was more connected to Gurupokuna, located across the lagoon. Confusingly, the latter is also called Kalametiya; although not damaged by the tsunami, some disaster aid went there, too. For Kalametiyans, Gurupokuna is the place of businessmen; they used to rent boats and fishing nets from these businessmen.

This hierarchical relationship still continues, but the Kalametiyans' standing within it has improved. They have more money and resources than before and are not as dependent as they used to be. They deposited large sums of money received as aid with Piyadasa, who lived in Gurupokuna. Piyadasa, whom the Kalametiyans called the "interest man," paid high interest on deposits.

Officially, there is no recovering of the former location. The government banned the rebuilding of damaged structures within 100 m of the sea. As repairing is allowed, most hotels and more sturdy buildings along the coasts of Sri Lanka were repaired. In Kalametiya, too, the Belgian couple repaired their house, used also as a holiday home and guesthouse. Following this lead, a few Kalametiyans are also rebuilding their houses. Hence, there is the possibility of renewed Kalametiya. However, many wish to sell their land, particularly for tourism, which may increase the price. If successful, the beach could transform into a tourist area. Although the fate of the beach is yet to be resolved, it is no longer where the Kalametiyans both live and work.

The separation of work and residence has diversified the village. The new location is adjacent to Kiula. However, Kiula residents do not consider Kalametiyans as their own. Separating themselves, Kiula people call the settlement *Tsunami Gama* (Tsunami Village). Regardless, the proximity is forging new social relationships.

Within a mere three years the village had become a new place.[3] Most parents who lost children have new babies; there were ten new babies in the first three years. New marriages have taken place, the houses are new, the organization of the village is new, and the people are transforming their physical environments. My subsequent visits confirm the continuation of this renewal process.

People are in a better financial standing than before. Many received undisclosed amounts of money and material aid. Most people seem to use these wisely. Unlike immediately after the tsunami when almost all men drank a lot of alcohol in 2008, during my recent visits, I hardly met more than a couple of people who had evidently consumed alcohol. The fishermen know their income is seasonal, and they have their own ways of managing finances; they usually buy jewelry which can be pawned if and when they need money. For people who do not have any assets that can be mortgaged, gold is the main asset.

In addition, after the tsunami, many survivors figured out how to receive the best return for their money by depositing with Piyadasa. In this, they turned around their old informal way of borrowing from individuals such as Piyadasa, at a high interest rate, into a method of savings. They have transformed the system that made them indebted into a savings mechanism, at least temporarily.

The accumulation of wealth is evident in the investments they make in new housing. At least five houses were upgraded by 2008: In three houses, the living room was expanded by annexing the rear veranda; the floor of one house was glazed; and one benefited from both of these improvements. Another owner has added an extensive three-room extension on the back; yet another has a garage in front. These processes have since accelerated.

The accumulation of wealth is uneven. Despite the provision of the same house on same-sized lots, the disparities among villagers' wealth have re-emerged. One family has a couple of vehicles and another has a three-wheeler. Through renovating houses, developing gardens, and buying vehicles, the Kalametiyans are diversifying the uniform environment created by aid-providers and regulations.

Unlike the days when it was isolated on the beach, about 6km from the Colombo–Hambantota road and beyond the bird sanctuary, New Kalametiya is well connected to the world. It is within 2km from the national road network, and three-wheel taxis are also available at short notice. These taxis link the village to places beyond walking distance, well connecting to all major places in Sri Lanka and beyond. The new location is also close to schools and other amenities. The temple, the primary school, and the Montessori are within walking distance. The Kalametiyans visit the temple and other nearby facilities more often.

The new location and its physical connections provided the context for many changes in people's lives. The new location has caused the fishermen to travel 4km to "work." Fishing has thus transformed from a vocation carried out by a community of beach dwellers to a "job" to which they have to commute. With no public transportation, and private options being expensive, most of them walk the stretch in the sun and in the dark (with no street lights).

Although most senior citizens do not fish, the displacement caused by the relocation is harsher on them. The elderly complain that it is difficult to adapt to the new environment. They even grumble about harsher climate, albeit a mere 4km away. Most Kalametiyans are not that old, and, compared to other settlements in Sri Lanka, the elders have shown greater resilience. Older men have embarked on gardening, and one has a full garden. The "short" distance between the old and new villages helps them maintain some aspects of their lifestyles and connections with old friends.

The allotment of houses for nuclear families separated generations. Yet the houses are not too far apart: Most elderly women visit their daughters' houses frequently and spend time helping them and their grandchildren. Rasika's mother, for example, helps Rasika take care of her daughter with Down's syndrome. Although the members live in several houses, the extended families are still functional due to their close proximity.

The demography of Kalametiya has changed largely due to births and marriages. All married males have brought their wives to the village, and the male population is stable. Yet women, who are key to the continuity of the village in a social and cultural sense, have left after marriage. The exceptions are the few women who are married within the village. They seem to hold a large say in the village. This became explicit at a conflict during fieldwork. While my students were a bit uneasy, these women guaranteed their safety. Also, the instability of the women population makes new women familiarize space and place quickly.

Women and children have not only led the familiarization of the new (physical) settlement, but the village is largely shaped and characterized by the way it is familiarized by women. The new gendered aspirations, roles, and spaces are quite stark. Both the beach and the village are gendered, especially during daytime. Men spend more time on the beach and keep watching currents to spot potential schools of fish. As the beach is far away now, they cannot visit home so frequently. Hence, they do not spend as much time with their families as they used to when the beach was home.

Women adapted to the new environment more easily and much faster (see Chapter 2). They have been assertive in getting their spaces organized both in temporary and new settlements. Setting up kitchens was the first building activity of the survivors, which began while they were in the temporary settlement. The temporary settlement had a communal kitchen, but no one cooked in it. Cooking is hardly a communal activity among the Sinhalese. All women who cook built fireplaces behind their individual rooms and cooked individually. This demonstrates the significance of the women's role and the kitchen.

Kitchens are also an issue in "permanent houses" (Figure 6.5). They include a small (3 × 2.5 m) attached kitchen. Kitchens in Sri Lanka are more of a socializing space, mainly for women, and are larger in size. They are usually detached, where firewood is used for cooking, especially outside of urban cores. Almost immediately after they moved in, all households in New Kalametiya—and other post-tsunami villages in Hambantota District—began building kitchens out of found material. The process became a bit easier and accelerated when Oxfam allowed the villagers how to dismantle the temporary shelter it built and take the material. Almost all separate kitchens of the permanent houses were first built out of this wood (Figure 6.5). Some built these in brick and cement mortar, making them more permanent. By 2008, all houses in Kalametiya had temporary kitchens outside the main structure; some had built attached kitchens with hearths for cooking with firewood out of more permanent material.

The house is also a center of the men's world, but in a newer sense. As in older days, the fishermen still repair and fashion new fishing nets and other implements at home. Men also make use of the locational advantage brought about by the new

FIGURE 6.6 People's Additions (credit: Nihal Perera).

settlement. In addition to fishing, several men work part-time in nearby rice fields during high seasons.

Children familiarize the environment much faster than their elders. Girls are foreseen to leave the village after marriage; hence, they do not seem to have much say in it. Boys, who are expected to stay in the village, are the main stabilizing force.

The new location added a new dimension to children's aspirations in general. The school is in the adjacent village, Kiula, and all children attend school regularly. They no longer go to the beach after school and do not get socialized into fishing and/or the life on the beach the way their elders did. The people in Kiula are not fishermen, and their children go to school with the intention of climbing the formal social ladder, becoming doctors and engineers. Going to school with Kiula children who have other plans is luring the children of Kalametiya to adopt "middle-class" values.

As the men stay at the beach for long hours, women play a central role within households and the neighborhood, establishing their place and space in a new context. The new location exposes women to the outside world, and their aspirations are taking new turns. Women have become more active: They attend meetings at schools and with public officials, representing the community.

Women have become more outgoing, perhaps because they are not tied to a routine like their male counterparts. There were two working girls in 2008: one was a bank employee and the other had completed a contract with an NGO. Those who moved to the village through marriage also continue to maintain connections with their relatives in their original villages. These connections act as channels of influence on them.

The close association with children, their main attention grabbers, also impacts women. Children have familiarized the new environment much faster. The parents, especially mothers, are vigorously pursuing new dreams for their children which lay outside of fishing. Although silent about their daughters, several mothers want their children (mainly sons) to become doctors.

The main congregation in the public area is made up of children aged 5–13. Their activities are limited to the area around the tamarind tree (Figure 6.6). When the government cleared the site for new houses in 2005, the only tree the contractor left

FIGURE 6.5 The Tamarind Tree: Before and After the Completion of Permanent Houses (credit: Wes Janz).

was the tamarind tree, somewhat in the middle of the site. The tree, used for shade during construction, continues to mark the center of the village. Currently, men converge there. When men sit near the tamarind tree, the children are pushed away and have difficulty finding an appropriate alternative. The architect has designated a playground, but it is not used by the children. As plants grow very quickly in Sri Lanka, the children are perhaps unable to maintain the playground. Mothers are, therefore, lobbying for a community center, including a meeting place and class rooms.

A community center is a contested idea in Kalametiya. There is a community center in the architects' plans, and another was built in another place on the access road to the village, but this is kept locked. Adding another dimension to this discourse, men wanted a building on the beach to store their implements and valuables. They are concerned about the safe storage of their equipment on the beach as they now live 4 km away from it. The Green Movement, which became convinced of the latter, completed the construction of a structure on the beach in May 2008. Women continue to place requests for a community center in the new village.

As this narrative represents, there are two public spaces: one on the beach and the other in the new village. The beach has largely become the exclusive domain of men who are connected to the past and continue to work with the skills they possess, modifying these to suit today's conditions. Although it is illegal to rebuild, people are possessive of their land on the beach and may use these spaces in some ways; the older generation is more connected to the beach. Women visit their former village on the beach for different reasons, but the beach is increasingly becoming less central to their lives.

Women's public space is more dispersed and runs through domestic spaces. It defies the public–private duality and calls for new conceptualizations (see Chapter 5). The houses are closer in the new village, and women visit each other more often, walking across their backyards. In addition to outdoor spaces, the public space penetrates into houses, in effect making a large area of the house a semi-public area where female friends and relatives are welcome to visit and socialize.

None of the above implies that the village is romantic; it is an ordinary village with its own issues. Yet it is a valid source for the development of knowledge. There are groupings within the village and animosities between some of them. The conflicts affect the women more as they spend most of their time in the village. This is a topic for another study.

A (Trans)Locality, Here and Now

As evident above, the survivors' needs and wants are not congruent with the imaginations of the providers of help, support, and aid. The Kalametiyans use their own imagination and creativity to conceive their life-journeys through and around aid, provisions, and the conditions that accompany these. In so doing, they figure out ways to make aid meaningful to them and to their cultural practices and life processes, and create spaces necessary for these.

New Kalametiya was first created by foreign and national actors. It was global, national, and local at the same time, created by bringing together a number of projects which are not congruent. The government, the donors, the NGOs, and the architects have their own projects in which other agents are participants. With these layers, components, and gaps, the "space" these agencies produced is incomplete. These external interventions displaced the fishermen, reduced the chances of continuing fishing as they know it, separated work and residence, and provided new kinds of houses and (abstract) environment.

The inhabitants (re)shaped and produced their New Kalametiya from within. They made use of the room and gaps between, within, and outside the above projects to reclaim their lives and fulfill their aspirations. For tsunami survivors, what they received included the necessary elements and much more, but not necessarily what they wanted. They first became subjects of abstract structures and spaces created by foreigners and the state. Over time, they familiarized the strange, transforming the abstract space into lived spaces. In this inside-out production of space, the external inputs became raw material, contexts, and constraints.

As in Daanchi, the Kalametiyans first perceived the disaster, aid, provisions, and conditions within their own frameworks. What people are constructing, as spelled out above, is beyond the imagination of outside actors who have already left the project and the community, perhaps moving on to build another one. The subjects are thus transforming their predicaments into resources, marginality into energy, and abstract space into lived spaces. They use social capital and social energy to transform the provisions into raw material for the production of their life processes and spaces. They create a locality out of the globality the outsiders created, but a translocality (see Appadurai 1996; Wind and Ferreira 2012) which is connected to and derives meaning from its connections to distant places.

Notes

1 Special thanks to CapAsia V students who helped begin building permanent houses at New Kalametiya in 2005 and the CapAsia VI team that studied its recovery process in 2008.
2 Personal communications with Vijitha Basnayaka, March 30, 2005.
3 In colloquial Sinhalese, almost all settlements outside of urban cores are called *gama*s (villages).

References

Appadurai, A. (1996) *Modernity at Large: Cultural dimensions of globalization*, Minneapolis, MN: University of Minnesota Press.

Klein, N. (2007) *The Shock Doctrine: The rise of disaster capitalism*, Canada: Knopf.

Wind, Bettina and Alexandra Ferreira (2012) *State of Translocality*. Online. Available: http://translocality.blogspot.com/2006/10/chapter-one-roots.html (accessed May 24, 2012).

7

PROTECTING THE HABITAT

Redevelopment, Illegibility, and the Strength of Dharavi

> One of Asia's most notorious slums went up for sale yesterday [30 May 2007] in a 2.3-billion-dollar project to raze thousands of ramshackle homes and create one of the world's hottest building sites.
>
> (Daily Star *2007*)

Dharavi is one of the biggest "slums" on Earth (Figures 7.1, 7.2). Four centuries ago, this location was a small fishing village, a *koliwada*, on the outskirts of Bombay (now Mumbai). Due to the city's extensive growth, Dharavi is now "centrally located," adjacent to Mumbai's new business district, Bandra Kurla. During its long existence, Dharavi has undergone many transformations, especially since the late 1940s. These changes were caused mainly by the self-building efforts of its expanding population and "slum upgrading" projects carried out by the state. No matter how "bad" the living conditions may be, the inhabitants have established a fabric of social relations critical to their livelihoods (see Simone 2010). In recent years, Dharavi has been in the news due to "Asia's largest urban renewal project," called Support Our Slums.

The term "slum" is used indiscriminately as a value-free word in India, especially among the middle class, professionals, and bureaucrats, for self-established neighborhoods of low-income people. In regard to Dharavi, this designation implies that the current "development model" is unacceptable to formal society, especially for the middle class and power-holders. The latest proposal for redevelopment was made by Mukesh Mehta, chairman of M.M. Project Consultants. The project seeks to demolish the old "slum" and replace it with residential towers, industrial parks, golf courses, a sports complex, and hotels, thus replacing the grime with glitter. The numbers reveal the project's magnitude: 600,000 people, 535 acres, 40 million sq.ft. of commercial space for sale, Rs. 9,000 crore (USD 2 billion) spent over seven years.[1]

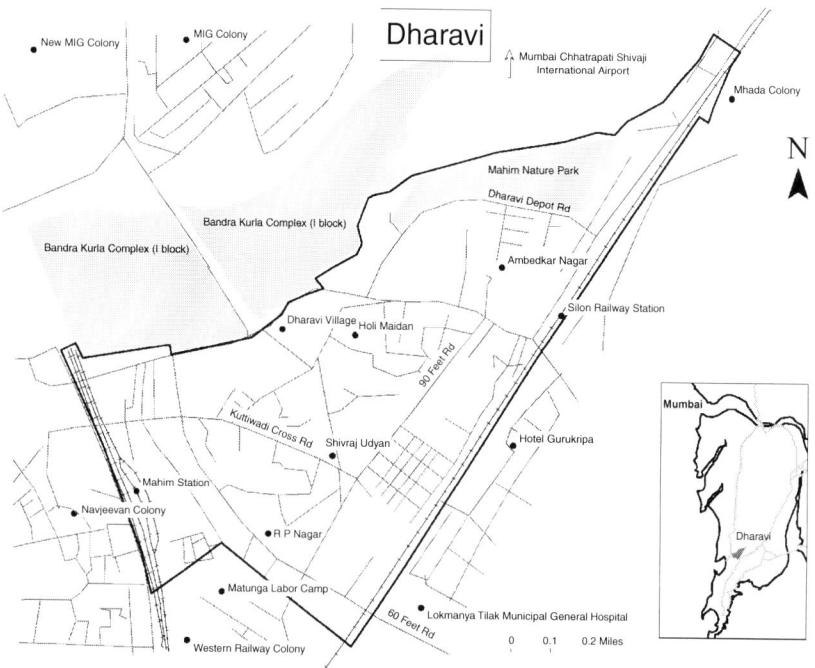

FIGURE 7.1 Dharavi: Location and Layout (credit: Kaushalya Herath).

FIGURE 7.2 Dharavi: A view (credit: Nihal Perera).

Unlike Colombo and Tashkent, where the inhabitants created spaces in relation to dominant spaces, Dharavi is created by its inhabitants (Figure 7.2). Our interest is in the debate surrounding its presence and redevelopment. The acceptance of Mehta's proposal by the state government of Maharashtra spurred a substantive debate on the future of the settlement. In the context of this redevelopment debate, this chapter examines the building of Dharavi, its interpretations, and the struggle to protect the space the inhabitants built and the achievements they made.

I will briefly map out the consultant's proposal and the positions of its contestants, especially Jockin Arputham, president of the National Slum Dwellers' Federation, and Sheela Patel, founder-director of the Society for the Promotion of Area Resources, an NGO that works closely with the Slum Dwellers' Federation. The discourse will be further examined by bringing in the views of journalists, academics, and planners. In so doing, I will investigate competing visions for Dharavi and how its presence is negotiated.[2]

Many opponents of the proposal questions whether there is adequate knowledge of the settlement on which to base any substantive intervention. As they employ different frameworks and vantage points, the participants of this debate see and prioritize different aspects in Dharavi and assign different meanings to them. A reluctant critic of *Shadow Cities* (Neuwirth 2005) asserted that living in Dharavi for a short period does not make the author knowledgeable of that community. At the same time, people who have never lived there have become experts by virtue of being residents of Mumbai and India. As this reveals, there is no comprehensive narrative of Dharavi: It is simultaneously a well-known and an unknown entity. Reconnecting to the issue of knowledge discussed in the Introduction, I will demonstrate that knowledge and legibility are central to this debate, and that illegibility has been the main defense of Dharavi.

Contextualizing Dharavi

As journalist Kalpana Sharma[3] learned right at the beginning of her research, Dharavi is not a single unified place even for its own inhabitants, but a complex network of spaces and connections. Spread over an area of 214 ha (535 acres) (Property Bites 2007), at the turn of the century it had a population of over 600,000 people and 57,000 dwelling units. All these are approximate figures; some estimates identify up to one million people in 100,000 dwelling units (projectdharavi.org 2008). Dharavi includes municipal land, private open land, and land leased to people under vacant land tenure (Menon 2007). It is a mixture of neighborhoods, some consisting solely of people from one region of India, and others with mixtures of northerners, southerners, Muslims, Hindus, and Christians. While most self-established settlements are mixtures of cultural groups, only a few, observes Sharma (2000), contain the extraordinary mix of Dharavi.

Its name and what it stands for in common circulation are culturally and politically stripped perception constructed by outsiders, including the state and developers. In perceiving Dharavi, the outsiders also project onto it social and cultural values.

They make the place and its inhabitants more uniform, orderly, and meaningful within structures. While symbolic of informal settlements in urban India, from Mumbai standards, Dharavi is a small settlement: 55 percent of Mumbai's population lives in designated "slums"; Dharavi houses only 4 percent of them. The observers tend to expand the gap between the lived settlement and its representation.

Dharavi was self-established. It is older than Bombay and existed when the city was seven islands around Mahim Creek. The *kolis* (fisher folk) are the earliest known inhabitants of the archipelago, and their settlements date back at least 400 years. In the *Gazetteer of Bombay City and Island* (1909), Dharavi is mentioned as one of the "six great *koliwadas* of Bombay" located at the edge of the creek that fell into the Arabian Sea (in Sharma 2000). The fishing communities in the region, about 38 in number, survived Hindu colonization at the end of the thirteenth century, the Muslim rule until the mid-sixteenth century, Portuguese and British colonization, and the explosive expansion of modern Mumbai (Savchuk 2009). Dharavi is much larger and more complex than its original *koliwada*.

Over 400 years, this settlement, first located in the margins of the city, moved to the center both physically and metaphorically. The economies based on fishing, pottery, and textiles are overlaid by a large recycling industry that processes garbage from various parts of Mumbai. Despite being deemed "illegal," with industries located unconventionally and working conditions that do not conform to official norms, the enterprises and industries flourish (Sharma 2000).

Dharavi is a unique, vibrant, and thriving "cottage-industrial" complex with an estimated 15,000 single-room factories (McDougall 2008) (Figure 7.3). Nearly two-thirds of the dwellings house family-owned cottage industries, making an astonishing range of products, from glass bangles and *bindis* to plastic buckets, toys, surgical sutures, *papads* (a thin biscuit used as an appetizer), and sweetmeats. The economic figures of these cottage industries are astounding: The annual turnover from its myriad enterprises is between Rs. 1,500 and 3,000 crores (USD 300–600

FIGURE 7.3 Industries: Pottery and Plastic (credit: Nihal Perera).

million). According to official sources, there are 4,902 industrial units in Dharavi distributed among textile manufacturing (1,036), pottery (932), leather (567), plastic processing (478), and *jari* stitching (498) (Menon 2004). Its 300 or more types of businesses provide more than 75,000 jobs. Eighty percent of the workforce lives in the settlement.

Ambiguous, Contested, and Illegible

Dharavi occupies an ambiguous position within Mumbai. As represented in the common phrase "city within a city," the mainstream society simultaneously accepts and rejects it; Dharavi is both central and marginal to the city. Yet, it is neither isolated nor independent. It is tightly enmeshed in the social and physical fabrics of the city. It is located between two of Mumbai's main commuter rail lines, Western and Central railways. Two major highways border it, and two major thoroughfares—the Sixty-Foot Road and the Ninety-Foot Road—traverse Dharavi. Adjacent to it is the fast-growing business district, Bandra Kurla. Henry Chu (2008) describes Bandra Kurla as

> [o]ne of Mumbai's swankiest new business parks ... a diorama of concrete and glass that shimmers in the tropical heat like a mirage of order and progress [it] looms just beyond a fetid bog of mangroves used by many of the slum dwellers as a toilet.

Dharavi is also close to Mumbai's domestic and international airports.

Despite its centrality, Dharavi is not legible to the outsider; most middle-class people do not dare enter, let alone engage. Unlike the French knowledge of Egypt that Napoleon's men developed as part of their conquest, which Edward Said (2004) highlights in *Orientalism*, the middle classes and the authorities have not been able to map Dharavi, nor has an outside agency been able to develop a hegemonic narrative that could overpower it. Dharavi has eluded such attempts, and there is very little government or mainstream knowledge about it.

This lack of knowledge is not limited to the physical environment. In spite of its contribution toward Mumbai's economy through production and recycling, hardly any (specific) data document its economic role within the city. Despite the desire to know the place, no outsider really knows how many people live in it, the kind of tenure they hold, or the tenure system in it. Its society, space, and culture also fall outside the mainstream cognitive frameworks.

Instead of acknowledging it, this illegibility is projected back on Dharavi by associating it with danger and filth, marginalizing attributes such as livelihood and production. The authorities and middle classes assume that the spatial layout of such settlements, and the density it represents, results in people literally living on top of each other, a layout that supposedly exacerbates social tensions (Sharma 2000). Jane Jacobs (1972) famously stressed that the connection between high densities and overcrowding is an obfuscation that planners inherited from Garden-Radiant City planning. Such a "slum" status makes the general populace presume that the site is a breeding ground for criminals and other "anti-social" elements. Entrepreneurs see the familiar: underutilized land; for planners, its uses are sub-prime despite being located next to a business district, and its social ills can be solved through physical upgrading.

Dharavi explodes these myths. For its inhabitants, Dharavi is a well-organized familiar space. It is not totally built up; the Holi Maidan (Figure 7.1), the largest open ground that has provided the setting for diverse social activities, dates back to the eighteenth century (Savchuk 2009). Despite the explosive mixture of different communities that live in crowded surroundings, there have been relatively few incidents of violence between them. Until riots in 1992 temporarily disrupted this stability, Dharavi was one place in Mumbai that had not witnessed a significant communal clash (Sharma 2000).

Dharavi is indeed an ingenious creation that no formal agency is able to reproduce, a phenomenon that echoes Jacobs' (1972) assertion that cities have the capability of providing something for everybody when everybody plays a role in creating them. It is a self-sustaining settlement. Despite its high level of production and precarious existence, its land-use distribution is quite efficient: 76 percent residential, 17 percent commercial, 2 percent industrial, and 5 percent other (On the Road to Mumbai 2008).

As James Scott (1998) argues, illegibility has been and remains a reliable resource of the powerless for political autonomy. Dharavi is no different. Dharavi's illegibility to the (middle-class) outsider is what has protected it from the outside world ever since it was established.

The authorities and businesses see what is familiar: land and land values. The development of Bandra Kurla has increased the land value of adjacent Dharavi. As Chu (2008) points out, "having what is possibly Asia's biggest slum [in this location] does not fit into ... [the] ideal, especially when the slum occupies premium property in the city where commercial rents can approach USD2,000 per sq.ft." The location of this unknown, illegible, illegitimate, "city within the city" is an anomaly.

Yet Dharavi is resilient and continues to negotiate its existence in the physical and imagined spaces of India. Not many people seriously complain about the kind of enterprises that operate there day and night because these small businesses provide employment to successive waves of migrants (Sharma 2000). The state turns a blind eye to the illegality of these enterprises because it knows they provide gainful employment to a large number of people (ibid.). Besides, the politicians do not want to antagonize the large pool of voters. Dharavi illustrates how a vibrant settlement continues to assert its existence, putting pressure on the state to endorse, even "encourage," what it deems illegal.

The "Slum" Redevelopment Proposal

Mehta, in Porus Cooper's (2008) words, is a self-styled "social entrepreneur" who had built luxury houses on Long Island, New York. After returning to a family business in India in 1995, he championed the ending of Dharavi's international distinction as a wretched community of filth, disease, and unsanitary conditions. Mehta cites strong personal, emotional, and social reasons for his "improvement" plan (Indian Environment Portal 2007). He convinced the government of Maharashtra to not only accept his USD 3 billion redevelopment plan, but also to make him an adviser to the project in February 2004.

His project aims to develop an area of about 144 ha in five sectors. It seeks to replace the maze of precarious brick structures with condominiums, cooperatives, schools, clinics, parks, and swanky shops (Cooper 2008). It opts to replace the old slum with residential towers, industrial parks, golf courses, a sports complex, and hotels. Out of 70 million sq.ft. of construction, 30 million is for residential use and amenities such as schools, parks, and roads for the current residents; the other 40 million sq.ft. of residential and commercial space is for sale. Each family in Dharavi will be provided with a 225 sq.ft. condominium in 7–14-story buildings, at the density of 650 families per hectare (Menon 2007). The project also includes five new roads and is expected to take 5–7 years to complete.

In what Mehta calls a "win–win" solution, the "slum dwellers" will receive "nice" apartments.[4] The amenities he proposes include state-of-the-art healthcare and entertainment facilities (ibid.). He propagates "sustainable" development in which both living and working occur in the same environment. This is achieved through "HIKES" standing for Health, Income, Knowledge, Environment, and Socio-cultural development.

Financially, the project is self-funded; Mehta employs a strategy of cross–subsidy in which all costs are borne by the developers who will eventually make handsome profits. The project is a private–civil society partnership, but its materialization requires the government's political power. According to this innovative business plan, for every 100 sq.ft. of pro bono construction of housing for current inhabitants, the developer is allowed to build an additional 133 sq.ft. of floor space for sale at market price (ibid.). The market price is expected to be very high, and the minimum opening bid is estimated at Rs. 1,000 crores (USD 200 million) (Menon 2007).

Mehta relates his personal attachment to the project to his own father's life journey and to the "American Dream." According to him, his father came to Mumbai from a small village in Gujarat with a few rupees and roomed for several years in a *chawl* (a single-room tenement building). Later, he built a sprawling mansion in Santa Cruz (Mumbai) with a swimming pool and tennis courts. This echoes the American Dream, which imagines that a person may lift himself up from rags to riches through hard work. The redevelopment plan is the instrument that removes the obstacles and fulfills the dream of Dharavi people to become middle class, in his eyes.

In this sense, Mehta believes in architectural modernism (Holston 1989), particularly its environmental determinism. He trusts that transforming the built environment can cause social change. As elaborated by his assistant: living in highrises will lift the slum dwellers up to the "middle class." The project takes—to quote Appadurai (1996: 182) from a different context—"the locality as ground [and] not figure, recognizing neither its fragility nor its ethos as a property of social life."

Mehta may not understand Dharavi from its inhabitants' vantage points, but he certainly knows the potential of his proposal. He has a different reading: He understands and utilizes the state and the market and timed his intervention well. He developed a pivotal knowledge and narrative, in essence an abstract space, for Dharavi. Everyone else involved in the debate, including the government, is reacting.

The State

The ambivalent name of the project—"Support Our Slums"—includes "support" but still retains the word "slum" and its associated undesirability. The central government, too, announced a grant of Rs. 500 crores (USD 100 million) allocated toward the infrastructure (Menon 2004). The project has been subject to repeated debate, delay, and negotiation. It has also changed in the process. Reservation for open space was increased from 8 to 15 percent, and space for amenities such as schools doubled to 10 percent (Menon 2007). In this, the government appropriated and reconstituted Mehta's proposal as its own project and opted to impose this abstract space on the lived space of Dharavi. With negotiations such as increasing public areas, however, it is unlikely that the cross-subsidy and the business plan can be fully materialized.

Yet Dharavi cannot be fully transformed unless the state carries out a ruthless project. There have been several historical moments when development in India was driven by utopian plans and an authoritarian disregard for the values, desires, and objections of the subjects, and, indeed, a mortal threat to human well-being. These include the massive city-building projects such as Chandigarh and infrastructure projects such as the Narmada Dam, built with little concern for people or attention to oppositional views, although compromised a little, in both cases.

Between intense projects, India has had a weaker state and an everyday democracy in which both the rich and the poor have exercised a lot of power in negotiating their own subjectivities and spaces. Each of the intense moments was supported by an "Orientalizing" of the target by incorporating it within a larger hegemonic narrative such as nationalism and development. At present, there is no agreed dominant narrative on Dharavi.

Nonetheless, the project has the clear objective of disciplining and incorporating Dharavi into the formal city of the middle classes. Mehta stresses that "I would like to integrate Dharavi with mainstream Mumbai and convert it into a cultural, knowledge and business centre. The main idea is to convert the whole population into a middle income community by 2010" (in Menon 2004). According to this perception, what is lacking in Dharavi is internal—an inability of its inhabitants to transform themselves into the middle class. The project claims to help this process.

The assumed trajectory of moving people to the middle class through the upgrading of the physical environment is flawed. Despite some successes, for the most part, transforming locales into middle-class domains has displaced their inhabitants. Increasing land values without increasing the inhabitants' income, which scholars call gentrification (Smith 1996), tends to push original dwellers out of the locale. The requirement on the existing industries to change to non-hazardous units—per the government definition—or move out, would exclude these too (Menon 2007). The project thus overlooks class differences, the political-economy that may have caused the inhabitants to choose a particular location and resort to self-building. Hence, the fragility of settlement the inhabitants have created is overlooked.

Despite the private–civil society partnership it propagates, the project adopts a developer perspective. In his work on gentrification in the USA, Neil Smith (1996) makes a compelling argument that capital—at the end of the twentieth century—has redirected its attention and energy into taming America's inner cities. Although it is not in the historic city center, Dharavi is the "run down" inner-city equivalent with "under-utilized" prime real-estate located near Bandra Kurla. Many middle class Mumbaikars see Dharavi as the "Other" that needs to be tamed and civilized. Mehta himself asserts: "You're talking of a location that's fantastic. This is the only location in Mumbai where I can bulldoze 500 acres of land and redesign" (in Chu 2008: np)

Contesting Voices

Concerned Locals

While the government envisions a future for them, Dharavi's inhabitants have their feet firmly planted in the present. Similar to outsiders who are unable to "read" Dharavi, its inhabitants, too, have a murky understanding of this external initiative crafted in an alien language. They too react to their own perceptions (see Chapters 8 and 9).

The inhabitants appreciate improvements to their environment, but most residents are skeptical about the plan's ability to improve their lives. Ravindra Keny, a native of Koliwada and an employee of the Customs Bureau, is one among many grassroots movement leaders. His 68-member family occupies a century-old building, and he would welcome any improvement to his living conditions. Dharavi Bachao Samiti, a neighborhood group formed around 2004, says it is not opposed to redevelopment (Menon 2007). Yet many residents with large houses cannot fathom how living in a 225 sq.ft. apartment several stories in the air could improve their lives (Bunsha 2004). Under the terms of the redevelopment project, which assumes that Dharavi is homogeneous, all families are entitled to a single 225 sq.ft.

flat (Dharavi.org 2008). The usual redevelopment practice is to award a unit per nuclear family, but the plan for Dharavi is unclear. Zuber Ahmed, 56, a railway worker who has lived in Dharavi for 31 years, is one of many who object. "We want 400 square feet of space," says the active member of the Save Dharavi Movement.

More important even than dwelling space, many residents fear losing their livelihoods. Raju Korade of the Bachao Samiti is afraid existing industries will have no place in a new Dharavi (in Menon 2007). In the words of Purshottam Bhanushali, a plastic and scrap dealer, "I know people are surveying the area, but they did not tell us anything about the project. There are about 1,200 plastic and scrap shops, and they are very old. My shop is about 4,000 square feet, and I doubt if I will get the same space" (Menon 2004).

Beyond living, carrying out their enterprises in a multistory building is unfathomable. Individual apartments do not have outdoor spaces or roofs, spaces central to the lives and economies of many. According to Shashikant Kawle, a local political-party worker, over 15,000 families in Dharavi depend on *papad*-making for their livelihoods. In Indira Gandhi Nagar and Shiv Shakti Nagar, rows of *papads* are briskly rolled by women. They dry these on large circular inverted cane baskets on rooftops and inside houses. "We don't want to stay in a [multistory] building," says Bhagobai Sherkare, who has rolled *papads* for 22 years. Sherkare has more questions: "Where will we dry our *papads*? They are asking us to take them to the terrace. How do you expect us to cart piles of *papads* up and down?" (in Menon 2004) The owner of a small shop, S. Ravindran, asks, "What arrangements have they made for our factories and godowns [warehouses]? Some people have large warehouses. What guarantees that they will get a plot [in] the same area? What about the people who work from home, making *papads*?" (in Bunsha 2004: np). Room is also a major concern for the 10,000 potters who inhabit the 2.5-acre Kumbharwada (pottery village). "We need space to keep the mud [clay], make the pots and then bake and dry," stresses Waljibhai Jethwa. Govindbhai Chitroda of the Potters Cooperative says: "We fear if the area gets developed, we may not get work" (in Menon 2004).

The eligibility for an apartment in redeveloped Dharavi is also contested. The criteria excludes people who settled or resided in Dharavi after 1 January 1995. Per the authorities, about 57,000 families are eligible. The locals dismiss this figure. In 1987, "when the prime minister's grant project was implemented, the number was 55,000 households. It is impossible to believe that the population remained static for a decade," says Sharma (Indian Environment Portal 2008). People are not prepared to trust one more promise to transform their lives without material evidence. They prefer to do it themselves. "Instead of giving land to builders, why doesn't the government give it to people? Then they can develop it the way they want. And the profits can go to people rather than to builders," says Selvaraj (in Bunsha 2004).

Clearly, the people's views are wide-ranging, and they do not speak the same language as developers and plan makers. They do not talk in terms of land use compatibility and land values, although the settlement they have produced is quite balanced in these terms and has high economic performance and livelihood.

"Slum Dwellers" Organization

Representing the voices of the people, Arputham has emerged as their main leader; he has found ways to directly contest the plan and represent the "slum dwellers." The leader of the Slum Dwellers' Federation is the central figure who enables the community to resist outsider intrusions and negotiate its present. The Magsaysay award winner and "slum-dweller" who represents the rights of the Dharavi residents is capable of speaking with and contesting the authorities and middle classes in their own territories.

He is skeptical about Mehta's plan.[5] Targeting Mehta, he takes an oppositional stand to the proposal and to its gentrification aspect. Arputham sees people instead of land. For him (ibid.), Dharavi is not empty land waiting to be exploited, but an economically vibrant community full of "social capital and self-employment." According to him:

> Dharavi is ... built by the people, and the community has always been involved.... Mehta is not rebuilding Dharavi, he is inventing Shanghai in Dharavi.... [People's building of Dharavi] is bottom-up planning, contrary to all international norms.... Mehta ... has to make a design based on people's needs and not the other way round.
>
> *(In Menon 2004: np)*

Arputham calls his vision "people-oriented" and claims to focus on people's rights. He sees the need to improve the living conditions of the inhabitants of Dharavi, but he feels they are short-changed by Mehta's plan. The problem, he says, is that the people do not have a voice in the process. "The government has made the plan in air-conditioned offices.... People have to just fit in. Earlier, people had a choice whether they wanted to opt for the SRS [Slum Rehabilitation Schemes]. With this new plan, they won't have an option" (in Bunsha 2004: np). As it was the implementing authority, the state did away with the consent clause for the DRP.

The lack of operational details, such as how people would be moved during rehabilitation, make him—and others in Dharavi—believe the plan is either flawed or a scam. The task of relocating more than 600,000 residents is unimaginable. "Where is the place to build transit camps?" asks Arputham. He believes that "In the process of redevelopment, you will create more slums" (ibid.).

Continuous debates against the proposal have, ironically, made Arputham appreciate aspects of redevelopment, even aspects of Mehta's plan. Arputham calls for global tenders and careful scrutiny. Instead of accepting or rejecting the proposal, he adopts a third position: Combining debates, protests, and discussions, he opts to negotiate the direction and details of the project. The state plans to remove some industries that it sees as polluting. Owners of large godowns and industries are likely to resist the move, says Arputham (in Bunsha 2004). Invoking the Geneva Convention, he calls for dwellings larger than 300 sq.ft. He also campaigned against investing in this project in several countries abroad. Protests were also staged in front of the project office at Bandra (Menon 2007).

The redevelopment of Dharavi is politicized. Dharavi is a vital vote bank. Its redevelopment has become an important issue in the formal political arena. Former Prime Minister A.B. Vajpayee visited Mumbai during the elections and promised Rs. 500 crores for infrastructure development. The newly elected local member of the parliament complains that the central government has not released this money. The government-appointed S.S. Tinaikar Committee, which investigated the issue, claims that "the geography of the area is such that it is virtually impossible to construct proper infrastructure" and concluded that projects relying on builders to construct houses for slum dwellers [sic] are doomed to fail.

In October 2008, Shiv Sena leaders opted to change the course of the project. Annoyed that the Congress Party government was gaining favors through promises of a new Dharavi, the right-wing Sena switched its role from conceiver of redevelopment to resister (Priyanka, nd). "How can we leave our old houses and resettle in these small flats?" asks Ramkrishna Keni, a local leader of Shiv Sena (ibid.). "The government should have at least informed us about the project. I don't want to oppose the project but we cannot be evicted from our ancestral lands," he said (in Menon 2004: np). Teresa Killekar, vice-president of the Koli Mahila Sangharsh Samiti, affiliated to the Shiv Sena, asks: "Why should we allow our land to be developed by someone else? We can sell it to the builder ourselves. Four generations have lived here—so why we should leave?" (in Menon 2004: np)

While political organizations have their own agendas, the political parties are compelled to deal with this politicized issue tactfully. Making the issue known to the public, subjecting it to public debate, and its resultant politicization provide layers of protection for Dharavi.

Schools

Design and planning professionals and academics also joined the debate over the future of Dharavi. The former director of the progressive TVB School for Habitat Studies, A.G.K. Menon, questions the basic planning values involved in the plan: "Planning is about dealing with people, not money ... [yet] Dharavi has a completely capital-driven strategy in which the architect is looking at land as an economic resource and trying to maximize on that" (Indian Environment Portal 2008). Utpal Sharma, the then dean of the School of Planning of the Centre for Environmental Planning and Technology in Ahmedabad does not question the redevelopment of Dharavi, but the norms.[6] In order to differentiate between Utpal and Kalpana Sharma, I use USharma and KSharma, respectively.

USharma engages the technical details of the plan. His approach is quantitative, with a focus on the physical, and calls for low-rise, high-density development. His students designed several projects to transform Dharavi. Based on measurements such as density, for him, the redevelopment project is impossible. "If the state adopts the original plan, the density will go beyond that of Hong Kong. . . . This is not sustainable," says USharma (JAI 2007: np). Dharavi has a density of 600–700 housing units per hectare. Town planners peg the tolerance ceiling at 500. "[Mehta's] proposal would have pushed density to 1,700," he added (in JAI 2007: np).

The government opted to treat Dharavi as a special case and allowed a floor space index of 4, FSI being the ratio of total space on all floors of a building to the lot area. The prevailing floor space index in the city is 1.33. Following town-planning procedures, the government invited objections and suggestions before this new floor space index is integrated into Development Control Rules (JAI 2007). The School of Planning of the Centre for Environmental Planning and Techno-logy and Kamala Raheja Vidyanidhi Institute of Architecture in Mumbai, with the help of the Society for the Promotion of Area Resources, developed an alternative plan. The low-rise, high-density rehabilitation project consists of buildings of four or five stories. Mehta was highly critical of this proposal when it was presented to a high-powered committee of secretaries in March 2007.

In USharma's proposal, the accommodations are closer to the ground, the build-ings have wide outer corridors connected by ramps or buildings on high stilts to provide space for work, community activities, and current functions. At the same time, builders are provided with the right to sell 40 percent of the floor area and make profit. It allows for 16-story buildings, selling 14 percent of Dharavi's land, and accommodates formal businesses.

Though the government promised to get back with USharma, it has not (Indian Environment Portal 2008). Ramanand Tiwari, additional chief secretary in charge of urban development, said the government has been considering the proposals made by the two schools of architecture and "We could . . . also have a mix of both the old plan developed by . . . Mehta and the new" (in JAI 2007: np). In this, the government has taken ownership of the project, but its ability to deliver seems limited.

Journalist's View

In *Rediscovering Dharavi* (2000), journalist Kalpana Sharma highlights Dharavi's resilience. According to her, Dharavi has been a place of change, from swampland, to tannery, to "slum," to a "mature" settlement. It is their belief in the future that keeps residents cautiously interested in the arguments others make about their land. The hope for legality and permanence continues to be a strong antidote to possible displacement. Where infrastructure was once non-existent, many households now have electricity and indoor water taps. There is also much that has not changed, and thousands of people live in untenable conditions in areas that are extremely difficult to upgrade because of their density and other environmental conditions. One of the central issues is the challenge of creating acceptable living conditions. *Rediscovering Dharavi* traces some of the many schemes that have been undertaken by a range of groups to redevelop various parts of Dharavi (ibid.). As she gets close to residents, her account is enriched by the many individual stories.

What distinguishes Dharavi is its amazing productivity (KSharma). The place is like a vast unregulated industrial estate, and almost everyone there is employed. Many of the leather factories, foundries, bakeries, garment factories, and soap-making shops grew from small home-based enterprises into major ventures. Although working conditions can be hazardous, unsanitary, and exploitative, thousands have prospered here (ibid.). Sharma also cites two other groups of people who visit Dharavi: business people (resellers) who purchase goods from the local craftsmen, and women and laborers who come to work in the recycling industry. In her opinion, it is doubtful whether the development proposal is based on any deep understanding of the life and livelihood of Dharavi residents. Sharma (ibid.) asserts that solutions to issues in a complex place like Dharavi are best arrived at by stopping, looking, and listening.

NGOs

Other organizations, especially NGOs, are taking on active roles in this debate turned struggle. Sheela Patel, the founder of the Society for the Promotion of Area Resources, adopts a social-justice-based politicized approach, somewhat empathic toward the inhabitants of Dharavi. Her struggle is not with Mehta, but with the government that now stands by the plan and has the power to implement.[7] "It is only when communities of those affected by this development get organized and develop capacity to negotiate what they want that some critical elements to ensure participation emerges in the process," stresses Patel (ibid.). She turns her words into deeds, working especially with Arputham and Kamla Raheja Vidyanidhi.

Patel's criticism focuses on Mehta's and the government's lack of knowledge of Dharavi. Dharavi, for her, is not a *tabula rasa* onto which outsiders can project their views, but a vast *terra incognita* that needs to be surveyed, mapped, and documented before it can be properly understood. She shares the view that Dharavi needs to be redeveloped to improve conditions, but before that, she says, it needs to be understood and mapped out in a formal sense. Without a proper base of understanding, there is no way to accurately plan for redevelopment.

The Society for the Promotion of Area Resources is building its own knowledge of Dharavi, but this might not be the knowledge that interventionists want. Patel focuses on the right to land, as a right of citizenship, and the underlying premise is empowerment. Any disruption of the area's built structures could spell disaster for the city's unemployment safety nets, she stresses. The need to know, for Patel (ibid.), is thus combined with the political position that land in Dharavi belongs to the people who live there.

Other Interventions

The debate over Dharavi's future opens up room for both people's voices and their objectification, ranging from slum tourism and films to conservative interventions. The timing of the movie *Slumdog Millionaire* in 2009 and its blockbuster reception may be a coincidence. Yet the interest in commercializing Dharavi has increased both with neo-liberalism and the redevelopment project; these are intertwined. The surge of interest has also given rise to slum tourism, which provides a different kind of objectification, story, and legibility.

An example is the Dharavi Slum Tours organized by Reality Tours and Travel. Instead of formal historic places such as the Taj Mahal or ecological locations, this tourism provides a look at the life and energy of the city (Mumbai) by walking through "chaos" in places such as Crawford Market, the bazaars of Kalbadevi and Bhuleshwar, and touching "peaceful havens" such as Jama Masjid (mosque) and Mumbadevi (Hindu) temple. The organizers claim to break down the negative image of Dharavi, India's slums, and their residents. They also claim that 80 percent of the profits (after tax) from these slum tours are donated to local charities; in May 2007, Reality Tours and Travel opened a Community and Education Centre in Dharavi.[8] This further objectifies and reinforces the stereotype of Dharavi residents as needy and that those who are willing to gaze at them for money can help them.

In a context where there is no comprehensive middle-class knowledge of Dharavi, its supporters keep extant quasi-views strong. The privileged position outsiders hold within this discourse depends on what Said (2004) calls the positional superiority. It places the outsiders in a whole series of possible relationships with Dharavi in which they do not lose their relative upper hand.

People's Agency

The lives and customs of Dharavi's inhabitants exist in a stark reality greater than most representations. Dharavi is not static and does not follow the paths mapped out in external interventions. First, external interventions have not succeeded in transforming Dharavi. Second, it has a history of subtly defeating outside interventions. Dharavi has demonstrated its ability to continue its existence through negotiations and localizing external influences. The most plausible outcome of the current redevelopment project is a compromise that depends on the strengths of the various actors.

Historically, the Kolis have numerous times defeated municipal redevelopment plans that threatened to erase or substantially transform their habitat. An early example is the Municipal Redevelopment Plan for Dharavi of 1944. In this, Koliwada was supposed to be divided in two, with two-thirds reserved for fishermen's residences and one-third for a fish market. The plan was never implemented (Savchuk 2009). In 1964, the Kolis defeated another plan proposed by the municipality under the Town Planning Act of 1954.

The inhabitants have also overcome the current redevelopment project. After many years of withstanding pressure, the Kolis won an exemption from the project. They argued that they occupied the area long before the government of Maharashtra was created. If they are squatters, then most villages in India are squatter settlements, they said. The community is in possession of many documents proving their claim, including early maps made by British surveyors (Dharavi.org 2008). Originally slated to be part of Sector V of the present project, the Kolis were granted an exemption by the government of Maharashtra in 2007. They have formed housing societies and are preparing their plan for improvement on their own (Savchuk 2009).

These victories were possible largely because of Dharavi's illegibility for the authorities and the middle classes; the lack of knowledge of this diverse settlement does not allow outside forces to subdue it without force. The participants of the debate keep crossing boundaries between inside and outside without being able to adopt a view from Dharavi itself. In this sense, they too contribute to making Dharavi illegible and invisible from external gazes.

Potential Outcomes

USharma is optimistic: "Projects get implemented in India, but slowly." In this scenario, Dharavi's landscape and the livelihoods will change, but not drastically, and not too fast. Hence, the most likely outcome is a partial implementation of the project. This is evident in the current landscape that is largely a sea of single-story, self-built dwellings dotted with clusters of flats (Figure 7.4). The tall buildings represent intermittent, half-hearted state interventions over a long period of time within the larger space created by the inhabitants.

FIGURE 7.4 Apartment Buildings Representing a Possible Future of the Project (credit: Nihal Perera).

Contrary to Mehta's projections, the beneficiaries of earlier projects have not become middle-class people. The current proposal is premised on two contesting models: the commercial model of Bandra Kurla and the people's model of Dharavi. The underlying assumption is that Dharavi belongs to an earlier time and will one day become like (modern) Bandra Kurla. As the state and entrepreneurs attempt to make headway into Dharavi by modernizing and making it legible, Bandra Kurla, which was built on a legible model for the middle class, is fast encroached by much-needed informal activities such as street vending and is acquiring Dharavi-like characteristics. According to a Japanese proverb, the capital (city) has its order; the village has its customs (in Scott 1998). As the state and capital try to order and commodify Dharavi, the people are expanding "Dharavi" into Bandra Kurla. The local standards of measurement, as seen in Dharavi, are tied to everyday practices. Formal schemes of order are untenable without some elements of the practical knowledge that the conceivers of abstract space tend to dismiss.

Anirudh Paul, director of Kamla Raheja Vidyanidhi, takes a more pragmatic middle path.[9] As the government has already accepted the plan, he thinks it is futile to simply oppose it and wonders how to best mediate this intervention. Instead of overhauling Dharavi, he wishes to convince the government to engage in some strategic interventions, making some substantial improvements. He critically adopts Patrick Geddes' idea of "conservative surgery."

As for the experienced urban planner Prakash M. Apte (2008), Dharavi's model of development has its own strengths. Despite its common depiction as a "slum," he sees it as a unique, vibrant, and thriving "cottage industry complex" (McDougall 2008). Productive activity takes place in nearly every home, and a unique characteristic is its close work–place relationship. As a result, Dharavi's economic activity is decentralized, home-based, low-tech, labor-intensive, and human in scale. This has created an organic and incrementally transforming urban form that is pedestrianized, community-centric, and network-based, with mixed use, high-density, low-rise streetscapes.

Apte (2008) is not blind to Dharavi's shortfalls and believes in providing adequate physical infrastructure. For him, this is a model most planners try to create in cities across the world. Hence, this model should be replicated with improvements. A simplistic re-zoning and segregation of activities would hurt this unique urban form.

The Strength of a People's Neighborhood

In sum, Dharavi is complex and illegible for the outsider. The lack of order and illegibility are relative: Except for particular infrastructure issues, Dharavi works well for its inhabitants, who continue to build it. It is a complex, "multicoded space" which is continually perceived and reinterpreted by the inhabitants as they carry out their everyday activities, creating different spaces and orders of space. Even from a standard land-use planning point of view, much of Dharavi is highly functional, efficient, and desirable.

There is no privileged discourse that can fully penetrate the meaning of spaces and spatial order of Dharavi. The debate is rich and includes a wide range of positions. Arputham represents people, but he is caught up in a discourse that is oppositional, albeit transforming. USharma explores a technically viable solution, and Menon wishes to reassert the larger mission of planning that is about people and the public good. Patel, who works closely with people, adds the right to land to the debate. From a storytelling standpoint, KSharma sees the significance of stopping, looking, and listening to understand Dharavi. Paul highlights the need to help the government engage in conservative surgery. Apte is bold about the significance of Dharavi's people-oriented development model and calls for its replication with improvements.

As it stands, it is difficult to arrive at a consensus on how to redevelop Dharavi, and the community cannot be fully transformed unless the state decides to carry out a ruthless project similar to Chandigarh. The democracy and the social power of the people in India is very different to the urban renewal of the USA in the 1960s and the urban transformation in China since the 1980s. Both were carried out with enormous power: the power of capital in the USA and the state power in China. Both marginalized less powerful people more easily.

Besides the model, illegibility for outsiders is Dharavi's strength. The mobility of the people and the change in the place have disrupted the middle class and the authorities' ability to read it. The fact that the state had taken over the project and the Koliwada received an exemption, among other developments, indicates that the project will take long and is headed toward a compromise. Like previous "slum redevelopment" projects, this one also will leave its mark, perhaps as few tall apartment complexes, within the larger landscape of Dharavi created by people.

Notes

1 1 crore = 10 million; 1 lakh = 100,000; 1 crore = 100 lakhs.
2 For an earlier version of this chapter, see Perera (2012).
3 Presentation of her work on Dharavi to CapAsia students at Rachna Sansad College of Architecture, Mumbai, March 6, 2008.
4 Presentation of "Dharavi Redevelopment Plan" by M. Mehta to CapAsia students at M.M. Consultants office, Mumbai, March 4, 2008.
5 Meeting with CapAsia participants. Dharavi, Mumbai, March 5, 2008.
6 Meeting with CapAsia participants. KRVIA, Mumbai, March 9, 2008.
7 Meeting with CapAsia participants. Mumbai, March 7, 2008.
8 For a discussion in the *New York Times*, see Weiner (2008).
9 Meeting with CapAsia participants. Dharavi, Mumbai, March 7, 2008.

References

Appadurai, A. (1996) *Modernity at Large: Cultural dimensions of globalization*, Minneapolis, MN: University of Minnesota Press.
Apte, P.M. (2008) "Dharavi: India's model slum," *Planetizen: The planning and development network*, September 29. Online. Available: http://planetizen.com/node/35269 (accessed November 16, 2008).

Bunsha, D. (2004) "Developing Doubts: A new plan is on to develop Dharavi, Asia's largest slum, but its residents are skeptical," *Frontline* 21, 12: 5–18.

Chu, H. (2008) "Dharavi, India's Largest Slum, Eyed by Mumbai Developers," *Los Angeles Times*, September 8. Online. Available: www.latimes.com/news/nationworld/world/la-fg-dharavi8-2008sep08,0,1830588.story (accessed December 1, 2008).

Cooper, P.P. (2008) "In India, Slum May Get Housing: A "social entrepreneur" plans to help Mumbai's industrious homeless," *The Philadelphia Inquirer*, September 22. Online. Available: www.philly.com/inquirer/front_page/20080922_In_India__slum_may_get_housing.html (accessed November 28, 2008).

Daily Star (2007) "Notorious Slum up for Sale," *Daily Star* 5, May 31. Online. Available: www.thedailystar.net/2007/05/31/d705311312131.htm (accessed November 28, 2008).

Dharavi.org (2008) "Koliwada," Online. Available: www.dharavi.org/index.php?title=B._Communities_%26_Nagars_of_Dharavi/Koliwada (accessed November 29, 2008).

Holston, J. (1989) *The Modernist City: An anthropological critique of Brasilia*, Chicago, IL: University of Chicago Press.

Indian Environment Portal (2008) "Dharavi's Real Estate Threat," *Down to Earth*, November 30. Online. Available: www.indiaenvironmentportal.org.in/node/25536 (accessed December 5, 2008).

Jacobs, J. (1972 [1961]) *The Death and Life of Great American Cities*, 2nd edn., Harmondsworth: Penguin.

JAI (2007) "[Forum thread] New Dharavi Redevelopment Plan in the Works!," *The SkyscraperPage Forum*, March 14. Online. Available: http://forum.skyscraperpage.com/showthread.php?t=126768 (accessed December 4, 2008).

McDougall, M. (2008) "Waste Not, Want Not in the £700m Slum," *Guardian*, March 4. Online. Available: www.guardian.co.uk/environment/2007/mar/04/india.recycling (accessed November 15, 2008).

Menon, M. (2004) "Dharavi Residents Wary of New Project," *The Hindu*, August 8. Online. Available: www.thehindu.com/2004/08/08/stories/2004080800101100.htm (accessed November 29, 2008).

Menon, M. (2007) "Rs. 9,000-Crore 'Slum-Free' Dharavi Redevelopment Project Runs into Roadblock," *The Hindu*, June 6. Online. Available: www.hinduonnet.com/2007/06/06/stories/2007060617161500.htm (accessed November 29, 2008).

Neuwirth, R. (2005) *Shadow Cities: A billion squatters, a new urban world*, New York: Routledge.

On the Road to Mumbai (2008). Online. Available: http://oladayooladunjoye.blogspot.com (accessed November 29, 2008).

Perera, Nihal (2012) "Competing Futures: Legibility, Resistance, and the Redevelopment of Dharavi," *Journal of Localitology* 8 (October): 113–44.

Priyanka, P. (no date) "Mumbai Makeover." Online. Available: www.karmayog.org/mumbai-projectsbygovt/mumbaiprojectsbygovt_14058.htm (accessed November 29, 2008).

ProjectDharavi (2008) Online. Available: http://projectdharavi.blogspot.com (accessed November 16, 2008).

Property Bites (2007) "Sobha-Puravankara Consortium Bids for Dharavi Project," September 10. Online. Available: http://propertybytes.indiaproperty.com/?p=1436 (accessed November 29, 2008).

Said, E.W. (2004 [1978]) *Orientalism*, New York: Vintage Books.

Savchuk, K. (2009) "About Koliwada: Dharavi—A Snapshot," October 30. Online. Available: www.dharavi.org/X._Urban_Typhoon_Workshop_Koliwada-Dharavi/*About_Koliwada_-_Dharavi:_A_Snapshot (accessed November 29, 2009).

Scott, J.C. (1998) *Seeing Like a State: How certain schemes to improve human condition have failed*, New Haven, CT: Yale University Press.

Sharma, K. (2000) *Rediscovering Dharavi: Stories from Asia's largest slum*, Australia: Penguin Books.

Simone, A. (2010) "On Intersections, Anticipations, and Provisional Publics: Remaking district life of Jakarta," *Urban Geography* 31, 3: 285–308.

Smith, N. (1996) *The New Urban Frontier: Gentrification and the Revanchist city*, London: Routledge.

Weiner, E. (2008), "Slum Visits: Tourism or Voyeurism?," *New York Times*, March 9.

8

SPACES OF MODERNITY

Daanchi between Vernacular and Modern

With Gaurab Kc

Daanchi is a beautiful village in the Himalayas. Once full of rural houses built with local materials, the vernacular environment seems to be giving way to modern residences. Almost all villagers, inhabitants in the area, and academics we interviewed shared the view that Daanchi is undergoing a natural transformation, from a traditional village to a modern neighborhood. For architectural modernists who welcome this change (Holston 1989), modern architecture (and environment) are capable of transforming traditional communities into modern societies. Admirers of disappearing vernacular architecture say it possesses a romantic form, strictly belonging to a place, and needs to be preserved. This chapter delves into the form and meaning of this change in Daanchi, examining these preservationist views which form the larger discourse that extends far beyond the physical and intellectual boundaries of Daanchi.

Daanchi is located about 8 km east of Kathmandu's ring road. In 1991 it had 1,082 households comprising 5,848 people (Census 1991). Originally a Newar town, Daanchi means a storage place. According to resident Kamal Prasad Poudel, Daanchi was a storehouse of treasure, grain, and ammunition in the seventeenth century. Later, Prithivi Narayan Shah's administration (1760–1775) established a large number of settlements in the fertile and irrigable Kathmandu Valley. *Kanths*, as they were called, consisted of 100–500 households and, population wise, fell between cities and villages. Since then, Brahman-Chettris formed the majority of Daanchi. Most families in Daanchi own 20–25 *ropanis* (2.5–3.1 acres) of agricultural land, estimates resident Sundar Poudel.

As Kathmandu expands, there is increasing pressure on *kanths* to urbanize, Westernize, and globalize, broadly understood as a need to modernize. Some *kanths*, particularly Lubhu, Nayapati, Bhimdhunga, Dadhikot, and Dhapakhel, have become suburbs of Kathmandu. The livelihoods of the people are shifting from subsistence to market-based activities. Instead of relying solely on farming, many of their residents also work in Kathmandu and nearby cities. The use of land in the settlements is changing from agricultural to residential, commercial, nursery, and poultry farming. The chapter examines the transformation of Daanchi, particularly how its dwelling environment is produced.

The key questions are: Where does the pressure to modernize come from? How do the inhabitants of Daanchi adapt to, resist, and/or negotiate the pressure to modernize? What spaces do they produce in the process? How can the changes be characterized? Following these questions, the study delves in between the vernacular–modern and global–local divides into the lived village and investigates the processes occurring behind the seemingly dichotomous façade(s). We will begin by exploring the transformation of houses and the residents' views about this change.

Changing Houses

Raj Bahadur Adhikari, 66, who retired as an army captain, has seen the village change. He belongs to the fifth generation of villagers. "When I was small, there were very few houses in the village, and I knew everyone," he says. "Now there are seven to eight people in each house, and there are people we don't know." The people have grown smarter but have become dishonest: "Earlier we could trust everyone, but, nowadays, we cannot trust anyone." In order to differentiate the people who feature in this discussion, I use their first initials before the family name.

RBAdhikari lives with his wife, son, daughter in-law, and two grandchildren in a traditional house. He has sufficient farmland (*khet*) to feed his family, but feels too old to work the ground. He hires farmers (labor) and pays in cash and kind.

The walls of his house are of sun-dried and kiln-baked clay bricks set in clay mortar on stone foundation. Baked bricks are used on the outside for better protection and appearance. The interiors are finished with clay plaster made up of cow dung, sand, clay, and saw dust. Some walls are finished with *bajra*, a mixture of beaten bricks, brick dust, black sticky oil, and lime. The house stays warm during winter and cool during summer.

The floor beams are of hardwood. These were bought in the market, hand-crafted, and transported in a *thela*, a three-wheeled push cart. Secondary beams and floor boards are of softwood. Built 30 years ago, the house cost between 30,000 and 40,000 Nepali rupees (approximately USD 400).[1] RBAdhikari is very proud of this achievement and evokes the Nepali saying, "You become a man only after you build a house."

The house was built by Newar builders (masons and carpenters) from Gorkarna. Unlike Newars, who live in close, compact settlements with houses attached to each other, Brahman-Chettris live in detached individual houses. Design and construction decisions are made by the owner in consultation with the builders.

For RBAdhikari, designing and building the house was a continuous, integrated process which engaged builders, helpers, and the community. Decision making, supervision, and building were not separate activities:

> We gave our input and kept designing as it was built. We changed [the design] and decided on it, while building.... We took advice from other people who had built, or were building houses. We also took advice from builders.

If the builder wished to introduce a different design or building element, he made a sample or showed the owner an example in another house. Once RBAdhikari's builder showed him a window and got his approval.

The building process was closely connected to the land and the surroundings. Building materials, mainly clay and wood, were from the site or the vicinity. The builders began by building an on-site kiln for baking bricks.

The building process was hardly smooth. RBAdhikari had ordered roofing tiles from a Harisiddhi factory, but his order of tiles was collected by someone else using his name fraudulently. He was powerless to get the factory manager to respect his order. So he used corrugated galvanized iron sheets. To accommodate this material, he had to change the design to a lean-to roof.

In regard to village life, RBAdhikari sees the loss of self-reliance that comes with modernization. "We never had to buy any food from outside; we even sold food to nearby villages," he reminisces. In times past, the village council (the *Panchayat*) and the village head (*mukhia*) solved most of the community's problems. This structure has now been replaced by the elected Village Development Council. Villagers used to be involved in organizations and engaged in village development. One person from each household volunteered labor, organized into the collective form of *shram daan* (self-help). They use this form of labor for activities such as repairing someone's roof or cleaning up the commons. They also donated money to help each other. Today, with declining incomes, many farmers need paid employment to survive. Such employment limits the time available for communal activities, and the monetization of work changes the attitudes toward helping others.

Some values have improved as modernization grew, RBAdhikari says. During his youth, education was meant for males. Females took care of the household. Today, both males and females go to school.

Farmer and Hindu priest *Kamal Prasad Poudel*, 73, also lives in a traditional house built with locally available material. The house is laid out along the east–west axis, facing south. This orientation provides effective sun exposure, and KPPoudel proudly claims that his house is warm in winter and cool in summer.

According to him, house is a culture that keeps changing: "Earlier the roofs were made out of *khar* [straw roof on *neem* tree branches], then tiles, and now corrugated sheets. Recently, people have begun to use reinforced concrete." He thinks people's lifestyles and their houses were integrated in times gone by. "Houses reflected farming practices," he says. For him, modern houses represent individualism, representing a "you do what you want, and I'll do what I want" mindset. Individualism is not a culture for KPPoudel, who prefers the older values.

Mukunda Subedi, 66, retired from the army and is now a farmer. He lives with his wife and son in a 60-year-old house. He senses the loss of cultural values.

Someone used to look after the house when the occupants were away, mainly in the field. Nowadays, the family locks the house. He thinks it is still safe in Daanchi because neighbors watch each other's property when one is away. The sense of security is still derived from the community.

MSubedi is critical of *pakki* (strong, usually equated with concrete) houses: "People are caught up in this practice to the degree that they even sell their land [a huge traditional asset] to build these. It is a fashion!" Some people say concrete houses better resist earthquakes and may last for two to three generations. He sees benefits such as comfort and better protection from rain. Yet for MSubedi, *pakki* houses are very cold.

For MSubedi, house-building is intertwined with community building, people helping each other. After a 1991 earthquake, he received help from family and friends, especially materials to repair his house. Yet this kind of support is decreasing.

Around 1997, *Ganesh Shrestha*, 53, built a *pakki* house and a shop on either side of his "traditional" house, built around 1970. He is a mechanic in the government factory but also has his own farm. He thus works in both the subsistence and market systems.

GShrestha differentiates between *kacchi* (weak, usually equated with "temporary" material) and *pakki* houses, calling the traditional homes *kacchi*. He sees many downsides to his *kacchi* house: "Its ceiling is low, the doors are small.... We face difficulties during rainy season, whether there is a storm or strong winds." The *kacchi* house is hardly romantic for him.

However, the *kacchi* house is warm and has better response to the climate. The *pakki* house is a social vice that destroys social and ecological harmony, he says. "People get sick.... My mother cannot live in it because it is very cold." The new culture is provocative, compulsive, and generates peer pressure: Even if one cannot afford, one feels the need to build a *pakki* house to be on par with others.

According to Huyssen (2008), urban transformation is the local result of the influx of transnational corporations and investments. As GShrestha and others reveal, spatial transformations are not simply imposed by corporations and investments or as a result of their action, but locally generated, embracing, rejecting, and adapting aspects of external trends and influences. People look out into the world and familiarize what academics see as global processes, developing their own perceptions and responses to them.

The local views are somewhat confusing to the outside observer and academic, not least because the locals use local worldviews and wisdom to make sense of external processes and develop their views. Hence, the local spaces which are part of this thinking are somewhat illegible to the outsider. Notions like ecological harmony are also influenced by local worldviews, the components of which include religious and medical knowledge.

Like GShrestha, retired army man *Kancha Dulal*, 63, is also building a *pakki* house next to his *kacchi* house. The biggest difference, he laments, is the cost. The old house cost Rs. 14,000 (USD 140), but he has already spent over a million rupees

(USD 10,000) on the new house, which is not yet finished. Nowadays, "The income from a job is insufficient to build a house," says KDulal. He shared the Nepali proverb: "One should know the size of the throat before swallowing a bone."

A major drawback to building a *pakki* house today is the lack of knowledge of the new construction technology in Daanchi. In KDulal's words: "We solely trust the contractors. For the old house, I carried wood myself and was familiar with construction. In this new method, there is a great chance of getting cheated." The old house was faster to build, too. "We began in November, laid the foundations in December, and moved in in February," he recalls. "The new house is taking much longer to complete."

He feels helpless due to the knowledge gap between new building methods and local needs and culture. "The house is failing to meet our needs, but we have to move according to the time. Today's time has brought about a change in the building culture." The building materials are imported, causing the whole nation to depend on other countries. The government regulations reinforce this dependency by requiring *pakki* buildings with concrete pillars. While he is also constructing this trend, in his mind, he is dragged into it.

According to MSubedi, instead of using houses to create a future for themselves, people are creating a future of the house. The house has become individualized and a personal property, no longer a community asset. He does not resist technology, but he feels this technology is a leap too far from the current society. He desires to acquire (or develop) a knowledge of a house that everybody can build.

Sundar Poudel, 64, has both a traditional and a concrete house. He says, "People are always in a state of progression according to their capabilities." This relates to what academics call local- or hybrid-modernity (Hosagrahar 2005). The residents of Daanchi are becoming more inclined to sell a piece of land, build a house, buy a motorcycle, and/or establish a shop front, restaurant, nursery, and/or poultry farm. They are shifting from traditional, agricultural lifestyles to more commercial modes of living, looking for new ways to make money.

Echoing MSubedi, SPoudel says land selling has become a fashion. City people buy land in the village and resell the land later at higher prices. They do not intend to build on the land or add to the community, but instead to sell land for profit. The commodification of land and speculation are diluting the sense of place, and the turnover of inhabitants destabilizes the population in the village.

Badri Bogati, 64, who was visiting SPoudel at the time of this interview, confirmed that city people buying agricultural land is the main external intervention into Daanchi. According to this retired driver from the Nepal Electricity Authority, there are many land subdivisions in the village with streets, sanitation pipe lines, and electrical poles. Daanchi is being "developed," but for the benefit of outsiders. In this sense Daanchi and its land have become objects of speculation. Daanchi's transformation does not bring much economic gain to the community.

The above interviews highlight a complex struggle characterized by the adapting of external influences by both changing themselves and localizing change, thus becoming partners of the larger change and creating their own modernity at the same time. The people also employ their own worldviews and wisdom that informs them; for example, the house is a social relation, and building a house is a collective exercise that also transforms the village. They see the need to better coordinate between the social values of the inhabitants, the physical space of the village, and incremental progression, rather than leaping into a future.

Change and Continuity of Domestic Spaces

The transformation of Daanchi is complex: It is not the simple embracing of a new (Modern) house type, nor can all houses be neatly categorized as vernacular or Modern. A detailed examination of domestic spaces reveals that "traditional" houses are also modernized, and modern houses—for which we use lower case—incorporate traditional elements, pointing to (adapted) continuities within change.

Kitchens and *puja* (shrine) rooms are the most sacred and significant spaces in a Nepalese house. Chettri-Brahmans in Nepal usually locate the kitchen at ground level, and the kitchen and dining areas form the entry to the *puja* room. While some houses have separate rooms for cooking, eating, and *puja*, in others, these functions are still largely carried out in one room, mostly on the floor, in a sitting posture.

The use of modern materials like cement plaster and plastics has substantively transformed the kitchen. In his new house, SPoudel has placed the kitchen at the back end, accessed by a corridor and from a back door. In this modern arrangement, both the kitchen and the women who manage it have lost centrality within the house. Women increasingly use tables for cooking and enjoy standing positions. Most families have replaced the hearth and firewood with gas stoves. Dining tables have replaced hay mats on the floor in many homes.

The *puja* space ranges from a room to a stone outside the house devoted to praying and offering to gods. While a separate room for *puja* is traditional, wall niches are more common today because of the expense of a room in a *pakki* house and perhaps due to the influence of Christianity. Most new *puja* rooms are much smaller in size and placed on the landing of the staircase or the roof terrace. BBogati's house has a box-like niche for praying.

Aagan, the terrace in front of the house, is a defining space. It is used for washing, cleaning, drying food, sitting in the sun in winter, and drinking tea with guests. Washing, whether hands before meals, utensils, food items, or the body is central to the culture, and the *aagan* has a water tank and washing area. This enables the people returning from fields to wash mud away before entering the house. Washing has not changed much, nor have the functions of the *aagan*; even *pakki* houses have an area in front of them for washing dishes, clothes, and hands. Internal bathrooms and kitchens have areas for washing in a sitting or squatting posture (Figure 8.1).

Instead of a single threshold, the transition from outside to inside and public to private goes through several spaces (Perera 2013). The *aagan* transitions into the interior through *pidi*, a semi open space (veranda) (Figure 8.2). *Pidi* is bound by a

FIGURE 8.1 Socializing in *Pidi*, *Aagan*, and the Washing Area (credit: Gaurab Kc).

FIGURE 8.2 *Pidi* in a *Pakki* House (credit: Gaurab Kc).

colonnade that supports the projecting roof and the front wall of the house and is separated from the *aagan* by a raised floor. Providing maximum sun exposure, the *aagan* and *pidi* are usually on the south or southeast side of a house. Although people still wash, dry, and socialize on *pidis*, both materials and activities have changed; cement plaster and steel pipes now feature in old *pidis*. New houses have balconies which substitute and expand the *pidi* functions. In the process, some uses like hanging objects such as tools, clothes, ropes, and sometimes utensils on the wall and the roof have been reduced.

There is no specific living room in older houses, but in newer ones it is the largest and perhaps most significant room. Many owners of older homes have converted a bedroom into a living room to meet this new style. Along with the television stand/show case, a sofa is introduced to this room, thus transforming it into a living room. The sofa represents a modern gesture for greeting guests and seating respectable people. The living room is a space to entertain, within the house, the guests who were received in the *hiti*, the community meeting place.

The living room is the showpiece of the house. When it was used as a bedroom clothing might have been hung on the walls (Figure 8.3). Now this converted room displays family photos, photos of major events like weddings and retirements, honoring ceremonies, certificates that mark the greatness of the family, and pictures of the former king and queen. This exhibition space represents the greatness of the family to outsiders.

This modernized living room continues to be used for sleeping, but the furniture, especially beds and dressing tables, is modern. Along with these, the room has also seen the presence of computers, television, and telephones. For the most part, it is the television and the sofa that define its modernity, supported by carpet and flooring mats.

In every home, food grains are the major storage item stocked in large quantities. The most common storage spaces are boxes, niches, and rooms on the upper floors or attics. As refrigerators are uncommon, there are smaller storage spaces like niches in walls where porous windows allow airflow to maintain the freshness of the food. An attic, which typically stores hay, wood, boxes, utensils and tools, may have a separate area for food grain storage.

In new houses, storage is mainly in boxes and under the staircase and beds. Separate unused rooms are also used for storage. They use kitchen cupboards for storing everyday food items. Foods that need ventilation are also hung from the ceiling.

The circulation areas are minimal in old houses; the stairs usually have one flight and are located along a wall, near the entrance. There is a lobby at the upper-floor landing which provides access to other rooms. The lobby is used to store shoes in a rack or bags of grain. There is a window on the inside to light the lobby. In

FIGURE 8.3 The Use of Walls (credit: Gaurab Kc).

KPPoudel's house there is a horizontal door—cut out of the floor—separating the kitchen (lower) and the upper floor; it provides security for the grain storage. The villagers may leave their kitchens open, but not the grain stores.

The entry to the toilet—another modern feature—radically changed the houses. The villagers used to defecate in the fields; later toilets were built outside the houses. Today, most modern houses have internal toilets, and people's habits are changing. However, most families are yet to figure out the new relationships between the toilet and various rooms such as the *puja* room and kitchen. In all, while Nepali domestic spaces and their relationships are being restructured, these changes do not represent a separation from the past, but change and continuity of different spaces and a negotiation between older and newer practices mediated by aspirations, desires, and financial and other possibilities and constraints.

New Building Culture

The building processes in Nepal are not separate from the house and living. Nepali architects and engineers trained in India and the West have brought new technology associated with Modern architecture. Both the new building technology, which entered Nepal in the 1950s and 1960s, and the desire for modernity have spread throughout the country, mainly in urban areas. Places like Daanchi began to feel the wave at the turn of the twentieth century.

House-building in Daanchi has been a collective process with the owners, too, participating in construction. The owner is knowledgeable of what is being built, how it is built, and the conditions of various elements of the house. The owners know the performance of their houses and how to maintain them.

The collaboration goes beyond the builder and the owner, involving friends, relatives, and neighbors who provide suggestions, thus making design and building a collective affair. While the villagers believe that many people can seldom go wrong, the owner relies on other house-builders' experiences.

The new building methods have minimized the owner's involvement in crafting his own domicile. First, there is heavy use of industrially produced material (Chapter 9). High-quality concrete depends on high-quality aggregates, fine-grain sand, and their cleanliness. The method of construction is also radically different: Reinforcement rods should be bound precisely, concrete should be well mixed, set in good form work, and well cured. Building has thus become a technical practice, the work of specialists. Yet the knowledge-bearers of such construction do not reach places like Daanchi. Architects and engineers are beyond the affordability of these owners. This limits the homeowners' creativity and involvement in building activity; most houses become standardized.

The building process has distanced the owner and the builder, and their understanding has become contractual. The owner provides materials, and the builder manages labor. Work is itemized, and each item is rated, or an overall amount for the whole project is negotiated between the owner and builder. The completed items are measured for payment. Most of this is beyond the owners' understanding. As the building language is esoteric, there is a knowledge gap between what is being built and what the owner knows, or thinks, is being built. This gap places the owner at a disadvantage; s/he is unable to monitor and guide the building process and guarantee a desirable space and product. The homeowner is thus vulnerable to cheating by the builders.

Modernization is expensive. The skills are expensive, and most building materials are foreign and expensive. Daanchi has neither a big bazaar, nor hardware stores. Transportation further increases the cost of materials by 20–30 percent.

Non-availability of funds also slows down modernization. Banks have not reached Daanchi. City banks provide loans, but against collateral. The villagers' asset is land, but that has no high market value in the eyes of banks. Most people feel the banks only serve the rich who already own a lot of property. New to this market game, people think it is risky to mortgage their only asset.

The building of new *pakki* houses is largely limited to those with capital. Others make amendments to their vernacular houses, and small sums of money may be borrowed within the village from particular individuals at a high interest rate. Hence modernization has spawned a new unevenness based on the ability to engage in market activity. With the lack of resources, space has been minimized, but the use has been maximized. This is evident in the intense use of space, especially those spaces above and below the landings of staircases.

The Social Change

The transformation of the village is large and is not limited to building new houses, nor is it limited to physical changes. For Navraj Subedi:

> Changes [in the village] are evident in the passage from cycles to cars, from greeting *namaste* [bringing the hands together] to handshake, and the orientation towards the West and English.... Some changes are good: There were no toilets in people's houses, but with the changes in toilet habits, people have slowly learned hygiene within the new paradigm.

In BBogati's house, the toilet is below the landing, and the *puja* room is above it. In forging these new spatial proximities, relationships, and organizations, the family has been compelled to redefine and find new relationships and balances between sacred and secular, between purity and filth.

During marriage ceremonies, for example, neighbors and relatives used to cook together, but the villagers increasingly use catering services. Responding to this need, new businesses have emerged in the city fringes, especially in Chabahil and Gaushala, to not only serve cooked food, but also to erect tents and arrange the venue for the ceremony. As the villagers emulate urban practices, they become dependent on urban services.

After building, SPoudel thinks differently than he did before. "The new house is more hygienic and better lit," he says. "The old house was hard to clean and to re-plaster [with clay] for every big occasion." However, he thinks the modern house breeds poverty. Because of the expense of building a *pakki* house, many ordinary people must sell a piece of land to afford it. Today, according to NSubedi, selling a plot of land to build a *pakki* house has become a status symbol. People sell land because they cannot earn enough through salaries for the modernizations they desire.

Part of the change in Daanchi is caused by external actors. This is evident in land pooling. In this cooperative activity, people in a contiguous area donate their land to the government which "develops" it through the provision of infrastructure. Newly blocked-out lots are then redistributed among the donors of land. The new lots are smaller, but they have infrastructure and higher market and utility values. In Daanchi, land pooling is carried out by private developers who commodify farmland and transform it into housing lots.

Outside sources and local developments such as land subdivisions generate the local desire to modernize. The villagers are exposed to outside ideas through travel and media. BBogati incorporated a perforated *jali*-like element on his wall which he saw in South India. Most villagers have not traveled far, but they also receive ideas through the schools, television, and other media.

There is a strong external influence for spatial change and a fast-paced life. The younger generation believes in this culture and representation. Umesh Subedi, who sold land to build a new house, identifies modern technology and education as causes of change. GShrestha sees the new culture as provocative and compulsive: Even if one cannot afford, one feels the need to build a *pakki* house to keep up with others.

Despite external influences, the desires and directions of the change are shaped from within the village, by families and individuals. SPoudel was a subject of pressure; his family urged him to keep up with changing times and not to be left out. The views of family members may depend on others; relatives and friends living in the city are likely to enjoy modern amenities and facilities.

According to SPoudel's wife, the old *kacchi home* cost her daughter a marriage proposal. After a visit, a potential suitor from the city saw the family as traditional and gave up on the proposal. Since then, the mother wanted a *pakki* house that represents modernity.

For the mother, the immediate concern of getting her daughter married was more important than any global discourse. Yet the materialization of her desire for the daughter, i.e., to marry an educated modern boy, depends on the worldviews of desired partners. Hence she had developed a dependency on such a view which requires her—and the daughter—to match the social status, or the perception, of the boy. While a substantive transformation may not be possible, especially within a short period, she opted to change the representation, the most crucial of which was the house.

Beyond a simple desire for the new, villagers also see the need to escape the shortcomings of their traditional homes. KDulal shares:

> During a stormy evening in the month of May,... in addition to rain, the front yard was filled up to knee level with hail. The roof began to leak, and

I felt like the house was falling apart. That night I felt miserable living in this house … I wanted to build a new house. Even though it is way beyond my affordability, I decided to build bit by bit.

Like KDulal, many villagers see the comforts afforded by the *pakki* house. NSubedi recalls other benefits of the Modern: "There was a television in one house and the others joined. We received electricity and telephone connections about 10 years ago. Cable connections reached the nearby village Thali three years ago." He hopes that it will reach Daanchi soon.

This desire for a "modern" life has taken the villagers to various jobs and places. According to USubedi, people work in real-estate businesses, the building industry, and in sales, dealing in bricks, sand, aggregate, and cement. Despite this "urbanization," there are no offices, factories, or job-oriented work-places in Daanchi. Those who do not want to, or cannot farm, have to travel to work. Some go to the city, but many go abroad, contributing to a national trend: 12 percent of the national income of Nepal is from remittances from overseas workers. People have emigrated to India, Dubai, Japan, Malaysia, Qatar, and the UK for work.

With little substance, but a representation and lifestyle, according to USubedi, the villagers have become subjects of bigger city dealers. Spatially, Daanchi is transforming into a dependent suburb of Kathmandu: The people depend on city services, particularly from the fringe, profits flow to these service providers, and the village-land is gradually occupied by outsiders.

Unlike classical suburbs of the USA, Daanchi still has a bazaar, but with simple goods; for higher-order goods, villagers must travel. According to USubedi: "We can buy vegetables and goods for daily use in Daanchi, but for goods related to *puja* (offerings) and festivities, we have to go to Kathmandu." The villagers have historically stocked food such as rice, wheat, potatoes, and corn which come from the fields and are durable for up to six months or so. Vegetables for daily use, including onions, garlic, cauliflower, pumpkin, and other greens, are grown in the *bari*, the kitchen garden.

Globally Connected Local Modernity

As evident, the Modernization of Daanchi is not complete, perhaps it will never fit in with any outside definition. While older practices have continued into new houses, new elements have been introduced into old houses. Combining these, the people in Daanchi are constructing a translocality, a locality connected to other localities across national and other boundaries and a present for themselves within their own potential and constraints. Although selling land will change the demography, and the dependency may erase Daanchi as we know it today, so far it is Daanchi that negotiates between the traditional and modern as well as between continuity and change. The design of houses still continues to be an inside-out process, with the owners making choices, although they must now listen to others' suggestions as they lack the in-depth knowledge necessary to describe and understand all aspects of the new building processes.

People like *Prem Bahadur* are adopting technology quickly, but their lives are not totally changed. PBahadur's house has television, a gas stove, a computer, and a telephone. The new life developed through the adoption of technology is nestled with farming. At times, he talks with his relatives in Kathmandu while drying potatoes in the dining area and grains in the *aagan*.

PBahadur and many others have moved on from a *chulho* (wooden fuel burner) to gas stoves, and the dining areas now speak in a foreign language of tables and chairs, replacing the seating on the floor on hay mats. Yet the modern house greets the familiar way via the *namaste roof*, a replica of the pitched roof attached to the façade, indicating the continuity of Nepaleseness.

This represents a mixture of tradition and modern, Nepali and Western, local and foreign, but the locals do not think this way. We neither have the words, nor concepts, or frameworks to fully fathom the lives they live and the spaces they conceive. Hence, we call it a hybrid or a third space within dualities familiar to us. It is better "understood" as a new life, a time-space confluence which incorporates from the past and distant places. PBahadur lives his "modern" life in good old Daanchi, but this translocality is connected to a multitude of other localities within and outside the nation without which his locality would not be the same (see Chapter 7).

Despite "modernization," the village is still organized around particular social values and culture. The most respected people in Daanchi are the priests and the elderly. The community respects "good" people "who do not harm others, those who do good to others, and who can think and act for the good of the others. Such people are invited to meetings to resolve social problems," says USubedi.

Residents have a sense of pride and attachment to Daanchi. Although he is building a "modern" life for himself, USubedi thinks his life would be better if he could work in the village itself. While there is a sense of loss, Daanchi still holds onto its "own" values. According to USubedi, the villagers usually do not buy much; they sell the extras such as rice, milk, and yogurt. There are very few freezers in the village. The new culture is transforming these producers into consumers. Although this is not the same self-reliance that RBAdhikari highlights, the use of freezers is resisted, even now, because people believe in eating fresh food.

Some amenities like water are still maintained at a higher quality. All 25 households in Daanchi receive water. The pipeline provided by the government comes from Sundarijal into a reservoir built by the government. Yet, people do not totally trust "government water" which they use for washing dishes, clothes, and bathing. For drinking, villagers use water from a small stream and an underground water source collected in another reservoir. USubedi prefers the provision of amenities through community efforts.

Despite modernization, much of what takes place in SPoudels' house has not changed. Outsiders visit and drink tea with the hosts in *aagan*, while the hosts continue with their household tasks.

BBogati feels the advantage of this village over the city is clear: "We have electricity, telephone, drinking water, and sanitation. We also have a better environment."

This sounds like Ebenezer Howard's dream come true, but created in the rural. With no end to the urbanizing tend, the environment may not remain the same.

Gari Khane, Dekha Sikhi, and Adaptation

The house in Daanchi still epitomizes a *gari khane*: A bowl to cook your own food. *Gari khane* also means do it yourself, to feed yourself, and/or to make a livelihood by yourself. A house is not simply a physical object but a space that supports daily activities and is shaped by the latter. It embodies an event cascade that supports and is affected by both the livelihood of the inhabitants and its representations. Using the new freedom, the inhabitants use rooms in multiple ways: Most houses have unconventional spaces for livestock, shops, and renting. People use these rooms to make extra income, support themselves, and achieve a better life. The income helps them maintain and enhance the house.

This relates to the commonly practiced *dekha sikhi*, or learning/borrowing by looking/observing pedagogy. If we may refer to Confucius, there are three ways of learning: (1) learning by imitation, which is easy; (2) learning by reflection, which is noble; and (3) learning by experience, which is bitter. *Dekha sikhi* fits into the first category. More than simple mimicry, it encourages everyone to learn from each other and be at par with others. It encourages individuals to strive for higher goals, to push one's limits to that of successful members of the community.

In the context of change and continuity of building practices, *dekha sikhi* marks a significant continuity. The builders first learned the technique through imitation and further developed it by trial and error. The older building practices were primarily built upon the collective memory of people and their skills. The ideas were spread by word of mouth. In this way, the language of building keeps circulating and is used in different forms but changes as it is used in different buildings.

While the building process has multiple roots, including in tradition and colonialism, the latest trend is to adopt "modern" dwellings from the city. This is similar to the postcolonial Indonesian architects adopting colonial architecture as a present (Kusno 2000). For builders in Daanchi, adopting modernity involves the learning of new construction techniques. In the city, the keepers of these techniques are engineers and architects. Yet these techniques are now practiced by builders in Daanchi who have adapted the new methods to suit the conditions of the village and their own skills. As authorities of this knowledge, the builders have developed superiority over their clients.

It is an upward movement derived from outside. Although copied, this knowledge has become local and adapted to economic and technological conditions and constraints of Daanchi. There is also ample debate about what is best, and the practices and knowledge are adapted and transformed through learning by doing. The knowledge is now resident in the community and flows horizontally. It is not only applied in new construction, but also used to transform older buildings through additions and changes within. Material such as cement plaster, steel pipes, concrete columns, and concrete roofs now feature in old *pidi*s. At the same time, the balconies of new houses adapt and expand *pidi* functions.

The house and the household change together, in small increments. In older houses, beginning with two rooms or so, the villagers keep adding spaces such as rooms, attics, washing areas, and/or widening the access as and when the need arises and finances allow. Changes also involve removing parts of buildings and maintenance such as reinstalling the thatched roof, or "upgrading" to tiles or corrugated sheets. Building a new house is also a sign of this change, and new buildings, too, grow incrementally, referring to extant culture.

People work on their houses continuously. A house is never finished; it is a work in progress. Recently, KPoudel painted his walls blue. RBAdhikari has plastered the wall with cement. This shows their desire to add new materials and elements when affordable.

The financial situation of inhabitants supports small-scale, incremental changes. While large banks are not helpful, local banking methods exist for small lending and borrowing. Lately, cooperatives, small financial institutions which lend microcredits on a personal basis, have become popular in Daanchi. The loans are usually small, ranging from Rs. 100,000 to Rs. 300,000 (USD 1,000–3,000). This system is popular among farmers and villagers who have been using the same for buying fertilizer and storage material. Overall, the village economy is made up of the circulation of small money; the investment in house-building is also small, and growth is slow and incremental.

The process of building a house is an engaged one. Unlike Western environments, where the buildings are fully built before occupation and deteriorate from then on, in Daanchi, even *pakki* houses grow. There are very few houses in Daanchi that were fully built before occupation. The landscape is marked with steel rods protruding upwards from columns, above the buildings, indicating that the building is waiting to grow. The village thus grows incrementally.

Locally Produced Modernity

Besides defining the shells of houses and styles, the concepts of vernacular and Modern, and their opposition, are unable to explain much of the built environment of Daanchi and its transformations. The explanation of the built environment and its transformations requires alternative concepts and approaches. Regardless of the house type, the inhabitants' spatial practices represent both continuity and change. This is evident in modern buildings paying gestures to tradition (namaste roof) and the introduction of the (modern) living room in older buildings.

The urge to become "modern" is exerted from outside, especially the West, the city, and relatives who live in other places. Those who travel like BBogati may develop desires for the modern. Foreign ideas are also brought to the living room by the media, especially television.

In regard to the building process, the builders and owners have learned a foreign building method, but they practice it in a local cultural setting without the aid of formal professionals and many components of this modern practice. They have restructured the methods to suit the setting. The borrowed knowledge is localized by first subjecting it to debate and then gradually practicalizing it. By learning and adapting new technology, many of the builders have reestablished their authority over the building process. Although they were disadvantaged at first, the owners still decide what they want, continue to learn from others, and adapt the buildings to their needs.

People of Daanchi have substantially changed (modernized), but still adhere to some core Nepali beliefs and practices. While aspects of new construction and socio-cultural practices are clearly different from the past, most practices from the past are continued but are adapted and combined with the new and other borrowed and newly developed aspects, creating a present. Most people have given up the use of firewood to cook; they not only use gas stoves, but they have also changed the posture of cooking from sitting on the floor to standing. While aspects of cooking and eating have changed, the people of Daanchi largely eat the same kind of food, with their fingers, and wash their hands before and after meals, mostly outdoors. While their domestic spaces and their relationships are being restructured, the inhabitants of Daanchi have neither separated themselves from the past, nor totally absolved in modernity. Daanchi represents the change and continuity of different spaces and a negotiation between older and newer practices mediated by aspirations, desires, and financial and other possibilities and constraints.

Although responding to external "forces" such as globalization and modernization, the pressure to transform comes from within families and the community, and new practices are conceived within households. The idea of transformation is a combination of people's desire to escape from particular conditions like poor weather performance and achieve dreams that come from other places. In practice, these ideas are mediated by the capacity of the subject and the potential and constraints in the immediate environment. In short, spatial transformation in Daanchi is locally generated, embracing, rejecting, and adapting aspects of external trends, impositions, and influences, combined with local aspects of life and space, also adapted to the contemporary, thus developing their own perceptions and responses to outside influences.

Note

1 It is normal for people in this region to give ranges instead of exact figures.

References

Census. (1991) *Census 1991*, Kathmandu: Census Department.

Holston, J. (1989) *The Modernist City: An anthropological critique of Brasilia*, Chicago, IL: University of Chicago Press.

Hosagrahar, J. (2005) *Indigenous Modernities: Negotiating architecture and urbanism*, London: Routledge.

Huyssen, A. (2008) "Introduction: World Cultures, World Cities" in A. Huyssen (ed.) *Other Cities, Other Worlds: Urban imaginaries in a globalizing age*, Durham, NC: Duke University Press, 1–26.

Kusno, A. (2000) *Behind the Postcolonial: Architecture, urban space and political culture in Indonesia*, London and New York: Routledge.

Perera, N. (2013) "Critical Vernacularism: A view of architecture from the places of production," in N. Perera and W.-S. Tang (eds.) *Transforming Asian Cities: Intellectual impasse, Asianizing space, and emerging translocalities*, New York: Routledge, 78–93.

9

EVERYDAY BUILDING

The Production of the Middle-Class Built-Environment in Gangtok, India

With Sweata Pradhan

The everyday environment of Gangtok, India, has failed to impress the professionals. Although the city is set in the beautiful foothills of the Himalayas, professionals call its built environment unsightly and disorganized. Public buildings and spaces do have admirers: Most upper-middle-class people and professionals are proud of how well, for example, the main market square is designed and maintained. This chapter focuses on (ordinary) private buildings. The city government has laws aimed at directing the growth of the city toward its ideals, although these hardly address the natural setting. With the high volume of new construction of private buildings, the city continues to maintain its informal (lived) character.

For ordinary people, especially the "owner-builders" who have crafted the existing built environment, architects and planners are involved in abstract thinking, impersonal strategies, and expensive projects. As in Daanchi, the modern building forms and techniques arrive in Gangtok without the experts and the infrastructure really needed (Chapter 8). The standardized building regulations of the city have little meaning for Dilip, Dorji, Kamal, and others (discussed below) who operate at the level of individual buildings, immediate surroundings, and local knowledge. The relationships between their buildings and the surroundings are shaped by their individual needs and the requirements of those who are directly affected by these spaces. This chapter focuses on the conflict between the standardized norms and everyday individual building that produces localities.

Small property owners are expected to build according to policies and live in the abstract city, in "assigned" spaces within the city conceived by its authorities. Ordinary citizens hire architects and engineers, but only to comply with the law on paper to satisfy the authorities, not when they actually build their houses fulfilling their own needs and wants. They build "by themselves," with the help of local builders (contractors). These owner-builders introduced in this chapter are not squatters with no legal rights to their land, but belong to a middle-income group.

They are not traditionalists who reject Westernization; rather, they share middle-class values and build their own local modernity. They operate through and outside the high-end, the low-end, and the traditional areas of the city which are the foci of mainstream knowledge (Perera and Tang 2013). The "builders" neither totally adopt, nor totally reject dominant perceptions; they exercise their agency in the "room for maneuvering" between adopting and rejecting. They see opportunities for widening these cracks in the system into real changes and achieve their life goals (see Healey 1997). They adopt various tactics to negotiate rules and regulations, adapting them to suit their own needs and wants while remaining "legal" (de Certaeu 1984).

Gangtok

Gangtok is the capital of Sikkim, an independent kingdom incorporated into India in 1975 (Figure 9.1). Since incorporation, Gangtok has grown considerably. The city's establishment as an administrative center is complemented by its economic growth; the best hospitals, schools, colleges, big businesses, and banks in the state are located in and around the city. Employment opportunities and the relatively higher standard of living[1] they espouse draw migrants from Sikkim and neighboring states, especially West Bengal and Bihar.

Tourists add to the population: In 2000, 154,680 tourists visited the city of 188,517 people (Department of Tourism, Government of Sikkim 2004). While the city itself is a tourist destination, those who travel to other parts of the state also stop in Gangtok because of its hotels and travel agencies. It is the gateway to tourism in the region: In addition to the physical access it provides, permits to visit many restricted areas of the state can only be obtained in Gangtok.

Sikkim's economy largely depends on tourism. Although tourism is seasonal, the industry takes up a large proportion of the land in Gangtok. Many prime locations are occupied by hotels, restaurants, travel agencies, and parking. While the city population is rapidly increasing, the amount of land available for housing and local needs is decreasing.

Gangtok has a very steep eastern slope. As this restricts expansion, the city grows along the national highway. However, most inhabitants prefer to live close to the city center; commuting long distances on less-sturdy mountainous roads susceptible to landslides is neither safe nor desirable. New buildings quickly take up spaces left between old ones, and existing structures grow vertically.

In the 1960s, under King (Chogyal) Tashi Namgyal, the state began to lease crown land to people who would then build using their own means. The policy still continues, but the Urban Development and Housing Department (UDHD) is now responsible for the allocation of land for housing. In 2007, more than 2,000 applications were filed for "virtually non-existent housing lots."[2] Under immense pressure from the public, UDHD allots a few very small lots (20 × 30 ft. to 20 × 25 ft.) every year. Increasingly, land deemed unsuitable for building is also allotted. Private land has also been subdivided over generations into small lots.

FIGURE 9.1 Locations (credit: Sweata Pradhan) (source: adapted from Google Maps).

As a result, Gangtok is dense; the hillside is covered with buildings. Public access between residential buildings is often narrow, with steep staircases.[3] It is not uncommon to see buildings encroaching onto public pathways or built very close to each other, heavily restricting light and ventilation. Most buildings along the road lack garages, have small setbacks, and use street parking, congesting the narrow streets. We wish to examine how and why this physical environment is created.

Delving into the building culture in the following pages, we investigate the building processes of four individuals in Gangtok: Kamal, Dorji, Dilip, and Bimal. Their houses are diverse and were built under different circumstances. Kamal, Dorji, and Dilip are property owners who constructed new buildings; Bimal lives in a distinct house built several years ago. This chapter investigates individual building processes, highlighting the building culture, its specificities, and how these individual practices shape the environment of Gangtok.

The Owner-Builders

Kamal Tamang shares ownership of a four-story building with his sister and brother. (We have not included images to protect the privacy of the builders; for a general street scene, see Figure 9.2.) As the Tamangs have the same family name, we use the first names for effective differentiation. Kamal co-owns a successful travel agency and an economy-class hotel with his brother, Vinay. His sister Madhu is a government employee. Kamal is married to Aarati, and they have a four-year-old son. Between his family, constant telephone calls from customers and travel agents, and managing white-water rafting and trekking trips that last for over a week, Kamal leads a busy life.

Penangla, where the property is located, is a prime area within a 15-minute walking distance from downtown (Figure 9.2). Penangla is a thriving business and residential district that accommodates two of the best schools in the city, a few

FIGURE 9.2 General Streetscape (credit: Sweata Pradhan).

banks, and prestigious hotels. The bus terminus is across the street from the property, taxis are easily available, and the hospital is within half a kilometer. Properties in this neighborhood are much sought after.

The Tamangs' building, like most other buildings in Gangtok, is made up of a concrete structure and cement-plastered brick walls. As is common with buildings in the hills, two floors are built below the road level. The third floor, facing Penangla Road, is divided into five rooms, four of which are rented for shops. The fifth is the travel agency and hotel reception. Madhu and Vinay have their apartments on the first floor; the second and fourth floors have hotel rooms. Kamal's family lives two doors away, in an apartment owned by his father-in-law.

News about the small lot on the northwestern side of the Tamangs' property disturbed the stability. The surrounding community used this government land for informal gatherings and idle chatter. It was also the children's playground and a point of exchange for local news and stories by adults. The Tamangs and neighbors also used it for drying clothes and basking food items in the winter sun. They felt this space would always be there.

The Tamangs heard from a neighbor that UDHD was in the process of allotting this land to a person with significant (local) political standing. Practically, the 600 sq. ft. trapezoidal lot bordering Dichiling Road was too small for a building. As over 90 percent of the people in Gangtok build four- or five-story buildings and do not follow rules, Kamal feared that a massive structure might block his property. He decided to preempt this by acquiring the land himself.

Yet Kamal was ineligible: Property owners in Gangtok are not eligible to buy government land. Being from a "respectable" family, Kamal would not think of appropriating the land illegally. Although he can apply for legal sanction later, squatting on government land is below his status. Kamal relied on social capital. His father-in-law, a man with political standing, wielded sufficient influence to have an exception made; he got the land allotted to Aarati. It is fairly common in Gangtok, and India, for people who have "contacts" with high-ranking government officials and politicians to be granted such favors.

After obtaining property papers from UDHD, Kamal paid an undisclosed amount of money to the former beneficiary, eradicating any potential problems caused by him. Kamal left the land vacant but with a boundary wall around it.

The life of this lot took another sharp turn. A friend told him that if nothing was built on UDHD-allotted land within six months, the government would reclaim it. There is no written rule as such, but Kamal did not want to verify it with any authority as that would make him/her aware of the situation and his anxiety. He reinforced his entitlement by investing in a building that he did not need.

Every building in Gangtok is legally required to have a permit, but Kamal was not concerned. Permit drawings must be made by an architect, but, in his opinion, architects are impractical, idealistic, and more concerned with the visual appearance of a building than with functionality. He was also reluctant to ask a professional to design such a small building; he felt the job would be below the professional's dignity.

He wanted a simple reinforced-cement-concrete structure which he could build by himself. He intended to sub-divide it, when needed, into rooms. Since he had been involved in the design and construction of the building where he lives, he was confident of his basic knowledge and ability. He still needed a building permit.

Getting a permit from UDHD could take years, but Kamal had neither the time nor the patience. Expediently for him, draftsmen at UDHD not only drew plans, but also obtained permits for a much smaller amount than an architect's fee for drawings. Once drawn, they got the signature of a government-recognized architect who works with UDHD for a fraction of an architect's fee. Draftsmen also made sure the file moved quickly through the sanctioning process and that site examination was carried out without delay.

As Kamal had no intention of following the drawing, the draftsman was free to make decisions. The permit was issued within a month, and Kamal paid only two visits to the UDHD office.

The sanctioned drawing is for a 3.5-story structure with a 160 sq.ft. footprint, set back seven feet from Dichiling Road and six feet from all other boundaries. Yet Kamal's addition of three-foot projections on two sides enlarged the upper floors to 300 sq.ft. each. The first floor has a garage and a shop; other floors consist of a lounge, room, and a toilet. Providing a garage, a legal requirement that no one follows, is the draftsman's strategy to please the sanctioning officer.

Although the drawing was for a taller building, only two floors were sanctioned for construction. According to the submitted stability report, the lot is unsuitable for taller structures. A two-story building does not need a concrete framework, but Kamal preferred concrete and bricks. The other option, vernacular building materials such as wood and stone, would have been more expensive. Concrete offered the possibility of vertical expansion and was more appealing.

While building materials such as sand and wood were delivered by private suppliers in Gangtok, Kamal bought factory-manufactured products such as cement, steel, and plumbing fixtures in Siliguri, 114 km from Gangtok (Figure 9.1). Along with new materials, design ideas were also imported.

The construction was organized by Kamal. He hired a mason—a *de facto* contractor—from Islampur, a small town in West Bengal (Figure 9.1). While Kamal supplied material, the mason provided labor, mainly bricklayers, carpenters, and helpers all from Islampur. In Kamal's opinion, local masons are weak at calculations and therefore more prone to making construction errors. He expected good-quality work.

Kamal and the mason negotiated the overall sum for the job; the mason received a predetermined weekly amount for maintenance. In the absence of "precise" drawings, the verbal contract enables the easy incorporation of changes to what the mason is building, even as construction progresses. If new suggestions add more work, the men negotiate a price for it.

The drawings and the actual building have very little connection. Kamal trusted the mason more than anyone else. All decisions regarding construction were made by Kamal, but in consultation with the mason. Kamal once invited a civil-engineer friend to visit his site with the hope of obtaining advice. The engineer proposed smaller columns and beams, with fewer reinforcement bars. Despite his friend's expertise, Kamal accepted the mason's call. Construction workers, he and most people in Gangtok believe, use time-tested methods that can be better trusted than those of engineers (and architects) who, he believes, hardly possess a practical knowledge of construction.

As Gangtok is geologically fragile, the strength and stability of the structure are of utmost importance to Kamal; larger columns represent strength and stability for him. He points to how two buildings in Gangtok, presumably designed by engineers, recently collapsed. Kamal is open to new ideas: On his mason's behest he agreed to use a special and more expensive aggregate which was supposed to make the concrete structure stronger.

This difference is more spatial than temporal. The mason's wisdom is not necessarily "traditional." It is that engineers' and architects' knowledge is located in more urbanized upper-middle-class domains. It is also temporal as these middle classes believe they are Modern. As in Daanchi (Chapter 8), people in Gangtok adopt "Modern" technology within their own environments, (building) cultures, and subjectivities. This is precisely what is unfathomable and illegible to the authorities and professionals and upper-middle classes.

Kamal is considerate of his neighbors, and they have influenced his building activity. As he installed plenty of windows on the roadside, he opted to build a shared wall with Chettri, who owns the adjacent building. Chettri agreed but did not want the wall to block his window. Kamal built an ingenious extension touching Chettri's wall, but a few inches short of the window, creating room for a toilet in his building.

Kamal reduced the roadside setback to three feet. As he is used to shops opening directly to the street, the seven-foot setback on the drawing appeared wasteful. Chettri had not left that much room either. As Chettri was not troubled by the authorities, Kamal considered it safe to have the same setback.

The smaller setback does not allow for a ramp to the garage. Kamal is not concerned; he parks his car on the street. Free parking is allowed on Dichiling Road and available where the road is wide enough. It is sometimes difficult to find a parking spot, but Kamal would rather rent out the garage space for a shop. Income from it is worth the occasional discomfort of searching for a parking spot.

Kamal exercised his freedom to build on the eastern side, where his older property is located. First, the (sanctioned) six-foot gap between the structures was reduced to a three-foot passage. With the three-foot cantilever, the new slab projects over the passage, connecting to the floor of the older building. Evidently, Kamal's intention was to connect the two buildings. The extended slab, however, blocks most of the daylight that reached the ground floor of the older building where Madhu and Vinay live. Kamal believes he did not have a choice. Madhu and Vinay do not seem to care about daylight either; they simply turn on electric lights.

In contrast to the other three sides where Kamal used "every possible inch," on the northern side he left some open space. Kamal felt that the triangular piece of land was too small and irregular to build anything usable. Usability was, therefore, a key criterion. Moreover, he needed some room to store building materials and mix concrete during construction. The leftover space that had little value for incorporating into the building was ideal for these purposes.

As illustrated, it was a "spontaneous" building process that was instigated by external factors but conducted through a process conceived by Kamal based on his own worldviews that many outsiders may not share. He is happy with the building which is "straightforward" with no frills except for a small section of brick-bond design on the front wall. He expected to rent the shops on the first floor soon, but he had no plans for the second floor, except not wanting to rent it. The naked reinforcement rods protruding from the columns indicate that the building process continues, and he intends to build more than the sanctioned two floors.

Dorji Bhutia was a government contractor until he retired in 2005. His (extended) family, made up of his wife, son, daughter-in-law, daughter, son-in-law, and four grandchildren live in his apartment in Nayagaon.

Nayagaon is a residential community located 1.5 km from Gangtok city center. With no building regulations, its growth was guided by the market. In 1985, Nayagaon was incorporated into the Notified Town Area of Gangtok and brought its building activities under the purview of UDHD, also formed the same year. Reflecting its historical development, Nayagaon has the character of an organically built, densely inhabited "Indian" urban environment. Its buildings line the narrow Nayagaon Road as it winds down the slope. About 95 percent of buildings house multiple uses, with a variety of shops at road level run by grocers, fishmongers, and tailors.

The road forms a community space, as does the *handiya* discussed in Chapter 10. Vehicular access is limited to about 25 percent of the buildings; the structures beyond the roadside properties are accessed via a labyrinth of footpaths. Some paths were built by the government, but most of these were built by property owners (Figure 9.3). The result is a mixture of passages and stairways of various widths and types.

Built in 1984, Dorji's four-story building is on his ancestral property, with Nayagaon Road on the northwest side. Three floors built in concrete and bricks are rented: the first floor for shops, the second and third for apartments. His apartment, made of *ekra* (wattle and daub) walls and a sloping corrugated galvanized iron roof, sits on this concrete structure. It consists of three rooms, a kitchen, and two bathrooms.

Dorji is constructing a new building on the vacant part of his property. The main reason for the project is economic: He wants to invest his savings for retired life. This is especially needed since no one in his household has a regular source of income: His son and son-in-law undertake small building contracts as they come; all women in the household are housewives, and the children study in a government school. The rent from the shops and apartments in his older building would be insufficient for the whole family in the long run.

Dorji's savings are insufficient for the multistory structure he envisions; hence, he builds one floor at a time, renting each floor to raise money for the next.

FIGURE 9.3 Labyrinth of Footpaths (source: Sweata Pradhan).

He made good use of his social connections to obtain drawings and approvals. His permit drawing was made by a civil engineer. Like Kamal, Dorji did not discuss his requirements with the engineer. He provided site dimensions and the stability report and let the engineer do the rest.

The approved 5.5-story building is similar to other roadside properties in Naya-gaon. The first floor of the concrete and brick structure is divided into a shop and garage; second through fifth floors are single-family residences, the sixth being a penthouse with a sloping roof. The floors extend on the northeastern side over a set of columns, projecting 3.5 ft. toward the road. The upper floors are accessed directly from the road via a staircase which cantilevers to the southwestern side.

According to Dorji, he got his permit in two days. The drawings lack required information such as site dimensions, waste-water drainage, and sewage disposal plans. He must have known someone in the sanctioning department. The lack of dimensions on the plan afforded Dorji some flexibility regarding the setbacks.

Construction began in 2002, and, at the time of study, he was finishing the interiors of the fifth floor where he intended to move with his family. As the builder, he ensured the quality of construction he wants, balanced the budget, and maintained business aspects. Dorji feels that daily wages make employees work slowly to earn more money for the task, so he hires laborers on a task basis. He tries to retain the same laborers as they get better trained and get used to each other's working methods and styles over time. Most of them live in the same neighborhood, and Dorji knows them personally. He can recall them after breaks in construction.

Like Kamal, Dorji buys most of his building materials in Siliguri. He also prefers to choose materials such as tiles, bathroom fixtures, and door and window fixtures.

Sanctioned drawings are not much followed in Nayagaon. Builders believe they are entitled to what everyone else was allowed during the time before regulations. The regulations particularly refer to the extant setbacks, heights, and number of floors. The inhabitants have been successful in achieving what they want in these areas.

Dorji, too, follows his needs and desires. As he does not own a car, he did away with the garage and rented the first floor for two shops. The inhabitants of Nayagaon often park their vehicles on the street, not least because most houses are not directly accessible by road; older buildings adjoining the road rarely have garages. People complain about the lack of parking spaces, but they do not want to use rentable commercial space for a garage. Dorji's building has a three-foot setback on the roadside which is half the legal requirement, but is the same as his old building.

Dorji began constructing a flight of steps from the road to the second floor level in the legally required gap between his two buildings. Serving as a public pathway, these steps were to connect to an existing public stairway. The internal staircase begins at the second floor, saving more space for shops on the first floor.

He abruptly stopped construction, and now the public staircase leads into a narrow passage with an open rainwater drain in the center. Dorji's daughter, Chewang, believes that enough room to complete the stairway was not left because her father made a construction mistake. A neighbor thinks that Dorji decided not to allow access to the rear building through his property when his relations with the owner of that building went sour. Regardless, the second floor and the internal staircase to the upper floors can only be approached through this passage with a drain or a set of irregular steps at the back of the building. These steps are connected to an existing pathway, and there is a two-foot height difference between the last step and the second floor level. Since there is no room to extend the staircase, Dorji has placed a few bags of earth as a stopgap measure.

Dorji's building may not comply with all state regulations, but his investment responds well to the market. According to a survey conducted by UDHD, 79 percent of the total households in the area are tenant households (JNNURM and Urban Development and Housing Department, Government of Sikkim 2006). A large majority belong to the lower-middle-income group who work as drivers, waiters, and construction workers. Many of them are migrants from neighboring states such as West Bengal and Bihar. The price and size of small apartments built by Dorji perfectly correspond to the needs and affordability of potential renters; he uses basic finishes to keep the construction costs low. In this, people like Dorji are far ahead of formal political and economic analysis and interventions.

However, Dorji used more expensive finishes on his own residence than on the rental property. Tiles on the last flight of steps leading to the fifth floor distinguish his house from rentable apartments. In contrast to concrete counters in rental apartments, he has a "modern kitchen" with granite counter tops and wooden cabinets and shelves. His bathroom has tiled floors and walls; and the door shutters and fixtures are also of higher quality. His apartment also has a verandah, a space not available to his tenants.

Dilip Basnet wanted land to build a house. Unlike Kamal and Dorji, he was eventually allotted a parcel of government land 300 m from his rented apartment, after waiting for 13 years.

Originally from a small town in Sikkim, Dilip is a fireman. His wife, Nina, a school teacher, is from a village in West Bengal. They both moved to Gangtok for employment. The couple has twin daughters who began kindergarten at a private school in 2007. Dilip's daughter from his earlier marriage is in college and visits during holidays. Dilip and Nina had lived in a two-bedroom apartment for six years, since their marriage. They were yearning for a house of their own.

Dichiling, where they live, is a residential community favored by professionals. As in Kamal's and Dorji's neighborhoods, amenities such as grocery stores, taxis, buses, and medical facilities are easily accessible in Dichiling. The workplaces of the couple and the children's school are within 15 minutes' walking distance.

Because of the neighborhood amenities and their friendships, the couple were keen to build their house in the same area, but land is extremely expensive and difficult to find. Dilip reopened his pending petition in 2004 and received a housing lot from the government in 2005.

Here, too, social capital was at work: Dilip knows a town planner who recently joined UDHD. With his intervention, Dilip's was the first application to get approved. Prior to that, Dilip "offered tea"—a local euphemism for offering money to get work done—to a draftsman at UDHD and received information on possible building sites in Dichiling. Dilip was therefore able to request a lot within the same block where he lived.

Besides being inadequate for building, the 350 sq.ft. lot is too steep for construction, with a roughly 70 percent slope. Retaining walls would take up much of the land. Moreover, the site does not have vehicular access. Dilip does not own a car, and pedestrian access does not bother him. Almost everything the family needs is available within walking distance from the site. Public transportation is dependable in Gangtok, and Dilip is comfortable using it for commuting long distances when needed.

The concrete sidewalk that provides access from Dichiling Road runs along an open storm-water drain. The drain runs along the boundary, making the geologically fragile land more susceptible to landslides. Unaffected, Dilip feels fortunate to have a lot that many other applicants desired. Since the lot is close to his apartment, he expects the management of construction to be easy.

He plans to secure the drain by strengthening side walls along his property line, thus preventing erosion of his land. Dilip will spend his own money, but he is hopeful that the State Public Works Department will assist him financially as the drain is public property.

Like many others in Gangtok, Dilip believes that concrete can help him make up for the lack of land stability and that a strong house with sturdy concrete foundation and retaining walls will withstand landslides. He takes solace in the fact that many others before him have built houses, especially the two houses directly below his, on lots with similar conditions.

Dilip is particular about legal issues. Although architects undertake projects involving complete design, he got an acquaintance to draw a permit drawing. He did not discuss his requirements with the architect and planned to build the house according to his own needs. He provided the architect with a site plan prepared for official records and the geological report.

The official drawing is for a 4.5-story structure built from concrete and bricks. After leaving an eight-foot setback on the storm-water drain side and five-foot gaps on other sides, the ground coverage of the building is 274 sq.ft. The house was thus designed vertically with the living room on the ground floor, one room and toilet each on first and second floors, and a kitchen on the top. Even within that small space, the architect had squeezed in a rentable apartment in the basement with a 10 × 10 ft. room, kitchenette, and toilet.

To shorten the sanctioning process, Dilip paid the draftsman and made a few visits to the town planner he knew. The draftsman carried out all other formalities. At the end of the fieldwork, Dilip was about to begin construction. He was not planning to use the architect's design since that house is too small for him.

Bimal Magar is a lower-division clerk in a government office who rents an apartment in a building diagonally opposite to Dorji's property. His 14-year-old daughter and nine-year-old son attend a government school. His wife stays at home but makes pickles and special food items to order. They found their apartment eight years ago, when Bimal was searching for a dwelling closer to the business district, possibly within walking distance of his children's school. It belongs to a person from Bimal's home village.

The building is atypical: It is a single-story building with substantial open space around it in a district where almost all structures are multistory and every possible inch is built upon. *Karma*, the owner, built this house in the early 1980s when Sikkim had just been incorporated into India. He often visited Gangtok for official work and personal needs such as consulting a doctor or buying something not available in the village. Gangtok was both the only large town and the "happening place" in the state. Owning a house in the city was also a status symbol. As he had land in Gangtok, Karma built a house for him and other family members to stay in when they visited the town.

A vacant home is susceptible to theft, vandalism, and encroachment. Besides these concerns, Karma thought the building would be better maintained if it was occupied. He therefore built a rentable house with a small apartment for himself.

Since there were no housing regulations at the time, Karma's building project was guided by his needs, wants, financial constraints, and social norms. Perhaps from a rural point of reference, he wanted the house to be far from the road and have a front yard and a garden. Instead of excavating down to the road level, Karma leveled an L-shaped site for the house halfway between the road and the highest point of his lot. He located the house away from the road, leaving plenty of open space all around the building

Karma used his own money to build the house. Obtaining bank loans for construction was not common then. He also chose concrete and bricks; at the time of building, people had already begun to use these materials, giving up on *ekra*. The incorporation into India made these materials more available. Karma wanted his building to be modern, on par with those of other owners. Concrete gave him the choice of adding more floors if and when he chose. Despite the use of "urban" materials for the house, Karma used rustic materials and building methods for the steps leading to the house.

The house is relatively simple, and Karma created the plan with his mason. The building consists of a long corridor with three rooms on one side; two kitchens, a bathroom, a water closet, and a toilet on the other; and a room at the end. Three rooms, the bathroom, water closet, and a kitchen make up the rental unit; the rest is for his use. Karma's idea was to rent out the space to bachelors or young couples who formed the majority of tenants. The tenants were to share the kitchen, bathroom, and the water closet.

Unlike Kamal, Dorji, and Dilip, Karma was not caught up in the urban process. His property remains unaffected by the growth pressure, largely because he does not live in Gangtok, but in his native village. He never saw the need to add more floors. The naked reinforcement rods protruding from the columns on the terrace have simply become a feature. He has less use for the house now because he no longer visits Gangtok frequently. Many of the facilities once found only in Gangtok are now available in other towns close to his village. The new road has made going to Siliguri much easier. He prefers Siliguri because goods and services are cheaper and more varied there.

Karma therefore rents his entire Gangtok building. Bimal is the caretaker; he occupies the rooms that were saved for Karma, collects rent from others, pays bills, and takes care of maintenance.

The building is in a state of disrepair. Concrete flooring is peeling; the external walls have mildew and fungus growing on them; the internal walls have patches of these caused by dampness; and the paint on walls, doors, and windows has faded. It seems that Karma does not care much about the building.

Furthermore, his property has been subject to encroachment. The building in front has been built so close to the boundary that its wall almost touches the roof slab of Karma's building. In the absence of the owner, Bimal does not have much control over his neighbors' actions. Children in the neighborhood use the open space in front as their playground. Bimal does not complain: He knows there are no playgrounds for children in the neighborhood, and his children also play there.

Bimal has adapted himself to the condition of the house because that is what he can afford in close proximity to downtown. He does not have any intention of buying property in Gangtok. Like many other residents of Gangtok who are in the city to earn a living, Bimal intends to return to his village upon retirement.

It is, however, uncommon to find properties like Karma's in Gangtok. Only a few such properties have not succumbed to urban pressures. These properties are dispersed throughout the city, with buildings like those of Kamal and Dorji forming the fabric of Gangtok's environment.

Shaping the Built Environment

Kamal, Dorji, Dilip, Bimal, and Karma are ordinary people and individual actors working within their own capacities to make life better for themselves. In the process, they transform their environment. They are bound by the formal/legal system, but the power to control building activity within their territory largely rests in the hands of individuals and the government officials in charge of building regulations (Chapter 4). At the immediate level, the built environment of Gangtok is negotiated between the abstract space envisioned by the authorities and the people's efforts to build spaces for their daily uses and cultural practices. The larger environment so created constitutes the confluence of intentionalities, influences, activities, and conflicts.

The authorities try to bring a sense of formality (abstract organization) into the built environment and have succeeded in some areas: Public spaces and buildings are built through a formal process where plans and designs are made by architects and planners, and construction is carried out by contractors within written legal contracts. The main market area, Mahatma Gandhi Marg, for instance, has undergone many facelifts since the early 1960s to give it a formal, Westernized character (Figure 9.4)

However, the informal character of the built environment is fully pronounced outside the designed and built government areas, especially the residential and commercial areas. The housing area is dominated by individual builders. Government or public housing is minimal; the State Housing Development Board, which was partly responsible for government housing, is presently defunct. In many Indian cities, real-estate developers are responsible for providing housing, particularly for

FIGURE 9.4 The Main Formal Area of Gangtok (credit: Sweata Pradhan).

middle- to higher-income groups. In Gangtok, the government policy is not con-
ducive to large-scale real-estate development by private actors. Individual builders
fill this gap. As housing constitutes 69 percent of the buildings in urban areas of
Sikkim, with another 6.8 percent being residences combined with commercial and
other uses (Data Dissemination Wing 2003), the overwhelming majority of the
built environment is shaped by the people.

The builders meet the government at UDHD. The government is represented
by the rules and those who implement these. The rules are not followed for several,
interrelated social, cultural, and practical reasons. Most significantly, the abstract
imaginations within which the rules and institutions are made and the "practical"
worldviews within which people build do not match; they are mostly in conflict.
The rules oversimplify issues concerning complex processes of city building and are
based on generalizations and standardizations that do not work in individuals' favor.
Many of the rules, especially the planning and management perceptions behind
these, are imported. In their application, instead of adapting the rules, the authorities tend to transform their imagined "ground conditions" to fit the abstraction (see
Perera 2005). In result, even those who are supposed to implement the rules do not
have a high regard for them; they make additional income out of this conflict.

All above, builders—except Karma who built before formalization—have dis-
regarded the rules. The key document of interaction for the authorities is the permit
drawing. The builders neither communicated their needs to the professionals who
prepared plans, nor did they intend to follow the drawings. The drawing is not a
part of the builders' worldviews. They neither draw and build, nor think of abiding

by a permit. As most prevalent in India, but also most other countries, while legislators negotiate laws and regulations before their approval, people negotiate these on the ground, when implemented. This is amply evident in the building processes and stories documented in this volume.

Every builder/inhabitant has a different set of needs, requirements, constraints, and potentials with which to work. Maximizing space and materializing the potential of impossible sites are far more important than following some standardized rules viewed as universally valid. Providing a garage for one's own vehicle is considered beneficial to all. Yet this imported notion is not valid for Dorji, who does not own a car; building a parking garage is a waste of space and money for him.

The rules hardly take account of the social and economic condition of owner-builders. The abstract numbers and maps the data-hungry professionals use somehow miss these realities. Moreover, the conditions implied in the rules and procedures are not abstract in the sense of the term; they are abstracted from the concrete elsewhere, especially Western contexts and sometimes from middle-class environments in India. Hiring an architect is not economically viable for most people, who use their life-time savings—either in cash or bank loans—to build a house. For Kamal it is an expensive luxury. He shares a common sentiment: "Rather than use my hard-earned money to pay an architect, I would use that to construct a floor slab." Dilip, who is acquainted with an architect, used his services free of charge.

For many of the people, architects, planners, and officials belong to a social group distinct from their own. In their minds, this "elite group" does not understand the needs of ordinary people. Kamal, Dorji, and Dilip do not have the power to flagrantly oppose the authority represented by UDHD, and that is not their intent, either. Instead, they follow the rules on paper. They all have permits to build. They view the sanctioning process as lengthy, cumbersome, and unnecessary. Hence they find ways to bypass it.

Permits are important for people for the same reason as for the government. In addition to making the building legal, sanctioned drawings are also necessary for procuring water, power supply, and bank loans which are imposed by the formal world. Thus, for most people, obtaining a building permit is an integral part of the building process. However, their need for formal approval does not extend to the physical construction of the building. Despite the public transcript of obtaining a permit, behind the scenes, Kamal, Dorji, Dilip, and others follow their own more practical needs and standards.

People also know they can avoid the rules. The government the builders encounter is represented in people such as sanctioning officers, town planners, and draftsmen. This is where social capital becomes a significant asset rather than some informal thing. Builders have access to the government through draftsmen and other lower-level staff members.

Formal is also highly informal at the local level; there is hardly a threshold separating these. They interpenetrate each other. In addition to the extension of the state and the market into everyday life, everyday spaces also seep into government offices, structures, and the legal systems and the formal economy. This includes how public spaces flow into private, and private flow out into the public (Perera 2013; Chapters 4 and 10). Many people are able to find "connections," "offer tea," and/or "formally" pay the officers for their services, including private work as in preparing permit drawings and extra work such as pushing the application through the permit process.

Hence, the government is also a part of this "informal space." According to a draftsman at UDHD, he and his colleagues make as many as ten approval drawings each month. An architect, on the other hand, may get only one or two residential consignments in the same period. This is like the UNESCO consultants earning money from the residents of Galle Fort (Chapter 4). In Gangtok, site inspections are rarely made, and sanctioning mostly takes place within the office, if the papers are in order and the building is safe. The safety of the buildings is determined by the use of professional knowledge.

In the rare case of getting caught, the "perpetrators" have ways to avoid legal action. Just as Kamal used his father-in-law's authority to acquire land, which is formally impossible; some use their contacts with politicians and high-ranking officials to avoid penalization. Others fake ignorance: According to an assistant town planner at UDHD, people often ask for forgiveness citing ignorance of rules. Officials, too, feel emotionally blackmailed into conceding and letting them go with a warning.

The municipality itself has offered the possibility of negotiation by allowing the payment of fines. Any built space that goes beyond the approved plan, but within the owner's property, can be legally sanctioned for a small fine of five Rupees per square foot and an application for "regularization." Buildings without prior permission can also be similarly approved. In this, the municipality struggles to formalize the built environment within its frames of operation.

People are not simply selfish, nor are the negotiations one-sided, or even two-way. Once we are able to see beyond the government-people (or civil society) binary, people are influenced by a multitude of factors, including history and neighbors, in addition to the state and capital. People are more inclined to adhere to social norms than laws because the former are locally grounded and based on the interests of particular communities.

As all studies illustrate, rules are not rigid in most places, most of the time; if a particular action fits the interest of the individual without negatively affecting the community, the rules can be negotiated between neighbors or altered with the consent of an elder member of the community. Hence, social rules—more than state laws—have a better standing among people. Kamal did not find it necessary to follow the sanctioned drawing, but he met his neighbor's request and built the common wall without obstructing Chettri's window. In this, social concern took care of what the law is supposed to, but is incapable of fulfilling.

Conversely, people tend to see what others have as entitlements, within a "fairness" discourse, which the law may not respect. Where Kamal and Dorji live, the shops directly open to the street. Their buildings disregard the law but respect this customary practice.

FIGURE 9.5 Terrace: A Place for Meeting and Basking in the Sun (credit: Sweata Pradhan).

Evidently, in addition to the state and the market accepted in social sciences, "culture" is a regulator of society. The difference is that the latter is unrecognized and marginalized in mainstream scholarship; they have been unable to theorize it the way the state and the market has been. Hence it is illegible within data-hungry, serial thinking.

While there is no need to romanticize, the resulting building culture has led to the creation of a distinct built environment: a dense and seemingly haphazard environment which serves both the material and psychological needs of the people (see Turner and Fichter 1972; Lang 1994). In comparison to formal, designed environments that have often lost their human appeal in the pursuit of abstract spaces and monumentality, environments built by individuals, piece by piece, are human in scale, feel, and function. The residential communities in Gangtok are lively, dynamic, and animated, and the people who live and work in these environments inject life into these. They have a sense of place and belonging. Even the terraces of buildings become meeting places where men and women come to bask in the sun, dry clothes, read a book, or play a musical instrument (Figure 9.5).

Notes

1 Sikkim has the second highest per capita income in India at Rs. 142,625 (Sikkim First Bureau 2013).
2 Interview with town planner, UDHD, by Pradhan, Gangtok, December 27, 2007.
3 Public buildings have good access; most people of Gangtok are proud of how well maintained the main market square is.

References

City Population. (2007) *City Population 2007*, Gangtok: Census Department.

Data Dissemination Wing, Office of the Registrar General (2003) *Census of India 2001: Housing Profile: Sikkim*. Online. Available: www.censusindia.gov.in/Census_Data_2001/States_at_glance/State_Links/11_sik.pdf (accessed April 21, 2007).

de Certeau, M. (1984) *The Practice of Everyday Life*, Trans. S.F. Rendell, Berkeley, CA: University of California Press.

Department of Tourism, Government of Sikkim (2004) *Annual Report for 2003–2004*, Gangtok: Department of Tourism, Government of Sikkim.

Healey, P. (1997) *Collaborative Planning: Shaping places in fragmented societies*, Vancouver: UBC Press.

JNNURM and Urban Development and Housing Department, Government of Sikkim (2006) *City Development Plan, Gangtok*. Online. Available: http://jnnurm.nic.in/cdp-of-gangtok.html (accessed December 28, 2007).

Lang, J. (1994) *Urban Design: The American experience*, New York: Van Nostrand Reinhold.

Perera, N. (2005) "Importing Problems: The impact of a housing ordinance on Colombo," *Arab World Geographer* 8, 1–2: 61–76.

Perera, N. (2013) "Critical Vernacularism: A view of architecture from the places of production" in N. Perera and W.S. Tang (eds.) *Transforming Asian Cities: Intellectual impasse, Asianizing space, and emerging translocalities*, New York: Routledge, 78–93.

Perera, N. and Tang, W.S. (2013) *Transforming Asian Cities: Intellectual impasse, Asianizing space, and emerging translocalities*, New York: Routledge.

Sikkim First Bureau (2013) "Sikkim has the Second Highest Per Capita Income in the Country." Online. Available: http://sikkimfirst.in/2013/12/18/sikkim-has-the-second-highest-per-capita-income-in-the-country (accessed March 4, 2015).

Turner, J.F.C and Fichter, R. (1972) *Freedom to Build: Dweller control of the housing process*, New York: Macmillan.

10

PEOPLE'S NEIGHBORHOOD CENTER

Handiya in Sri Lanka

With Nirmani Liyanage

One morning, out of the blue appeared a jackfruit stall made of two boxes built from timber palettes (Figure 10.1). Located near the busiest place at Moratumulla Handiya (i.e., the *pola*), its middle-aged vendor was trying to sell three bags of jackfruit. Similar to a farmers' market, *pola* is an informal (farmers') market for vegetables; Moratumulla *pola* also has fish. The vendor was, in fact, launching a new business with some jackfruit he plucked from a neighbor's tree (with permission) after losing his previous means of income. For him, *handiya* is a place of opportunity; that is where he opted to rebuild his livelihood. His stall grew into a family business within two years (Figure 10.1)

FIGURE 10.1 A Self-Starter at Moratumulla Handiya: Then and Now (credit: Nirmani Liyanage).

Handiya is an ordinary space formed around the intersection of streets in Sri Lanka. Most people's lived spaces are defined by one or more *handiya*s. Most residential areas in Sri Lanka are organized around *handiya*s where people carry out many non-residential daily activities.

Unregulated, and also regulated in some ways, *handiya* both supports and challenges—accommodates and rejects—individual efforts. It constitutes bloomed emergences developed through successful inside-out processes, negotiating external forces and influences. It is also a people's laboratory to try out small-scale ventures.

Such spaces are not limited to *handiya* or to Sri Lanka (Deden and Purbadi 2013; Janz 2013; Hamdi 2004). Informal settlements like Dharavi, Daanchi, and the middle-class environments in Gangtok are also largely produced by the inhabitants (Chapters 7–9). Yet there is very little understanding of such people's spaces. As Perera and Tang (2013: 17) have highlighted:

> In the professional world, people's everyday language and spaces have not entered policies, plans, planning reports, and management discourses. In Sri Lanka, people define space in terms of *handi, malu*, and *adavi*, in India they use *chowks*; in Kathmandu space is organized around *durbars, hitis*, and *chautaras*, whereas *longtangs* are important in Shanghai. The activities and practices associated with these "publics" have hardly entered those urban perceptions employed in professional discourses whose explicit objective is [to serve the public]. In making simple translations of these words into their technical languages, [some] practitioners transform and, in most cases, marginalize the spaces and activities familiar to the user.

Both the disability of mainstream intellectual frameworks and the illegibility of people's spaces through mainstream frameworks are evident in Jagath Munasinghe's (2007: 95) apt study of small towns in Sri Lanka. He documents the towns' transformations in abstract language and incorporates their histories into a single evolutionary process related to the nation: "these townships act as the nodal points of Sri Lanka's spatial structure [and] ... reference points [in the] cognitive map of the national space." Yet his unit of analysis is borrowed from the United Nations classification of urban areas, overlooking the local organizers of space such as the *handiya*. He discusses the transactions between planning agencies and local agents/ elements; in particular, how the powerful actors like the élite and merchants' associations reproduce their power by negotiating national-level projects such as road and bridge construction. This narrative, which filters out people's agency in the name of phenomenology and "transactions," overlooks small actors, the creation of lived spaces, and their political economy. Critically addressing these shortcomings, this study attempts to investigate the *handiya*, particularly how it is produced and reproduced by people through daily practices, using their agency.

Handiya is not merely a physical entity, but a social space defined by a set of activities and processes. The myriad activities that makes it include: buying, selling, eating, drinking, walking, waiting, meeting, chatting, sharing information, learning, teaching, criticizing, gathering, protesting, fighting, and celebrating. Intense activity areas include a local taxi park, a few shops, and a *pola*. As a place, it organizes the larger surrounding space and particular core activities. It is a local, inside-out creation that makes the state and capital negotiate their own spaces for projects such as road widening. *Handiya* has never been successfully replicated by outsiders, whether professionals, policy makers, or politicians. It is illegible to the middle classes. In addition to the social and physical, *handiya* is a product of the discourses that take place there. These are impossible to understand within formal approaches to concepts of gossip and rumors that marginalizes some core processes that form the *handiya*, below the radar of the authorities. This chapter investigates Moratumulla Handiya located on Soyza Road off Galle Road (Figure 10.2), but will draw on our findings at Radampola, Mavi-Ela, and Mullaitivu *handiyas* (see Figure 10.7).

The original fieldwork was carried out by Nirmani Liyanage in 2012, followed up by both authors. In addition to her observations and interviews, Liyanage also lived there for four years with local families which depend on Moratumulla Handiya for their daily needs. Her landlord's weekly visits to the *handiya* on Sundays supplied enough food and information—including gossip—for a week. We also draw on our own experiences growing up in Sri Lanka relating to *handiya*s.

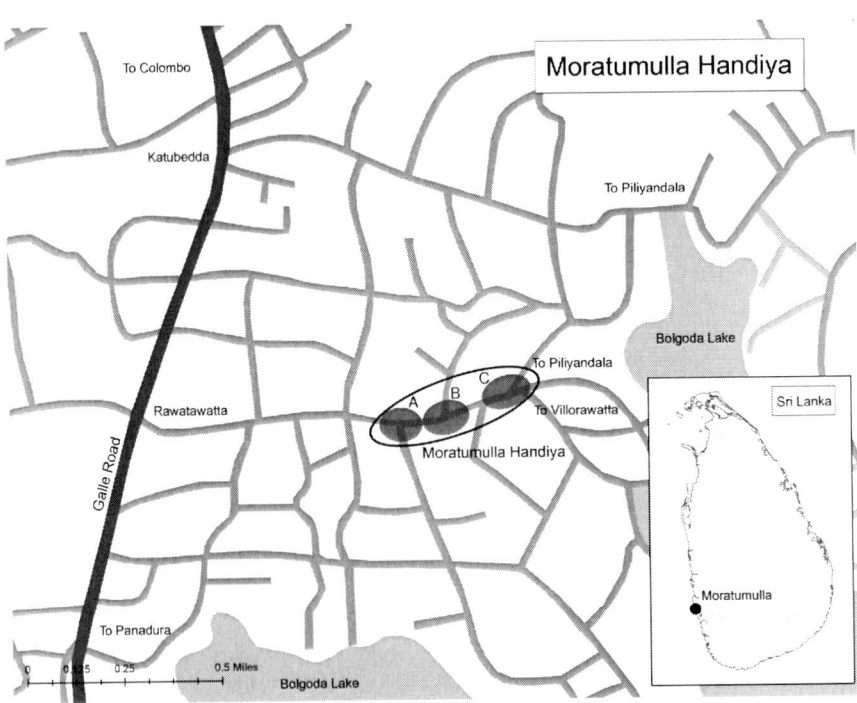

FIGURE 10.2 Moratumulla Handiya (credit: Nirmani Liyanage).

Defying Definition

Handiya defies precise definition. In Sinhala, *handiya* means an intersection, connection, or a joint that refers to a place where two (or more) physical elements join, like an elbow. It can be a connection of moving parts like a wrist or a universal joint. Physically, *handiya* is where roads and/or streets cross, join, and/or branch off. The roads that connect to form a *handiya* can be similar or different from each other in scale, function, and capacity for transport.

Unlike an Indian *chowk*, a road/street intersection is a necessary condition for a *handiya*, but not sufficient. While every (physical) road/street intersection can be called a *handiya*, and affords the so-identified social space, not all materialize this potential. For example, the famous Kalagedihena Handiya in Gampaha District, which had great potential, was hardly a *handiya* until recently. It was adjoined by large lands whose owners were not interested in developing or selling. According to resident Pradeep Dissanayake, the *handiya* began to bloom in the late 1990s, only after the land was subdivided and used for new activities by new owners. At Moratumulla, out of all roads off Soyza Road, only A, B, and C have materialized the potential (Figure 10.2). Referred to as west, middle, and east confluences, they together make Moratumulla Handiya. The road intersections that have not developed into *handiyas* are viewed by people as entrances or turning points.

The connection between physical and socio-spatial *handiyas* is similar to the body and the self that make people or the hardware and software that make computers. A pile of hardware is not a computer until it is assembled in a working combination and life is infused through software. *Handiya*, too, requires more elements than physical, such as a working combination of functions and willing actors to perform relevant tasks. More than the street intersection, the *handiya* is defined by the activities on each side and the connections across the streets/roads. Gunasena Sinhala-Sinhala dictionary identifies a road intersection as *mansandhiya* and the place where people gather as *handiya*.

Most *handiyas* have a sense of branching off a smaller road that connects a more "remote" area. The people who use the branch road, for the most part, transfer from their main transportation to the secondary, a daily activity for most of them. *Handiya* provides services that are not available in the "interiors." Hence it is better identified as a social-spatial confluence where a branch meets the main artery, although there are many variations, including confluences of two equally important connections.

Ideally, *handiya* is defined by its functions and character. The roads, too, change their character at *handiya*: It is place where the road is both a thoroughfare and a place, serves both vehicular and foot traffic, and sees traffic move in multiple directions. It is more festive and slow than other places. The people have dominance over vehicles which are slowed down by foot traffic, especially if there is a *pola*. The roads become more of connectors of their sides than dividers as roads usually do. There is also a lot of noise and interaction among people, colloquially called hustle and bustle. It is a people's place.

The physical definition, particularly the center and boundaries of *handiya*, vary according to the user, particularly how and for what s/he uses it. The *handiya* is not only used, but also reproduced and (re)shaped by the user. Also its definition can change over time: When she was a schoolgirl, Jasintha, 52, thought of the bookshops and street-food stalls as the *handiya*. Now, as a mother, her center of Moratumulla Handiya is the market and the church.

Padma, 55, who grew up in nearby Puwakaramba, visited Moratumulla every week with her mother. Now, as a mother and resident of Moratumulla, she commutes daily to Piliyandala for work in a garment factory. Every morning, during fieldwork, Liyanage saw Padma waiting for the 7:35 a.m. bus at the east confluence. On her way home, Padma gets off at the middle confluence to buy vegetables and other culinary needs for the next two or three meals. These complex processes make *handiya* an area with multiple soft and hard boundaries.

Handiya is better understood from *handiya* itself: Understanding it from an outside-in perspective, as a road intersection, node, central place, or small town transforms it into an element of the cognitive framework. *Handiya*s are "central places," but neither evenly distributed nor hierarchical enough to acknowledge the assumptions of central place theory. *Handiya* is a node, but all nodes are not *handiya*s. Kevin Lynch (1960: 47) defines nodes as "strategic spots in a city into which an observer can enter." Colombo Fort, Maradana, and Kandy railway stations are main nodes in Colombo and Kandy, but they are not *handiya*s. Nor is *handiya* a simple node: It is a transportation node, but transportation alone is insufficient to make a *handiya*.

Handiya is integrated with the lives of the people associated with it. The more formal Sinhala word *sandhisthana* refers to "crossroads," a point in one's life where the life-journey is paused and one is presented with alternatives. It provides the possibility of redefining and/or reshaping the rest of the life. This is the idea pursued in the famous Sri-Lankan novel *Thun-Mang Handiya* (Three-Way Handiya), in which the main character's life choices depend on the direction he picks to go from the three-way *handiya* that connects his village to three different places (Sekara 2000).

Moratumulla Handiya

Unlike most common single-intersection *handiya*s, Moratumulla Handiya is made up of three significant streets branching off the main street within half a kilometer. In addition, there are nearly 20 small-to-medium-size paths connected to the main street. All these connect the *handiya* to surrounding neighborhoods that identify with it. Users apply the term Moratumulla Handiya to the ensemble of all three confluences and the strip of road that connects these. While respecting the functional interdependence, users employ descriptive names to differentiate each confluence. The west confluence is called the "*handiya* near the police station." The middle intersection is both "*pola*" and "the *handiya* near the church." Intersection C (east) is known as "*kanda uda handiya*" (*handiya* on the hill). Despite their broad usage, these identifications are not formal and are not found on the signboards of shops. The locals use the term "*handiya*" interchangeably to identify each confluence, the physical intersections, and the ensemble of intersections as one social space: Moratumulla Handiya, the name we use here.

To identify specific places, users employ physical and non-physical references. "Ruwan Bookshop," a famous bookshop that closed 30 years ago, is one reference point that is used even today. Unlike Lynch's (1960) elements, which are visible to the outsider, these are not physically visible. They may be simply known by the users of *handiya* or be memories. The name and image of the bookstore still exist in the mental map of the users.

Moratuwa city is well known in the nation for its furniture industry, and Moratumulla is one of the main neighborhoods that provides this reputation; other neighborhoods include Egoda Uyana, Katukurunda, and Koralawella. Most spaces in Moratumulla are directly or indirectly related to the industry and, through it, to various places in the country. However, Moratumulla is not totally defined by carpentry and does not bear the characteristics of Lynch's (1960) districts.

The activity strip that connects the three confluences also defies conventional (Western) definitions: It is a *para* which is neither a road nor a street, but in between and both. It is like a main street of a small town in the USA with smaller streets directly connecting over eight (Sri Lankan-type) neighborhoods, Moratumulla being one, but other than a police station, it has no government buildings to identify it as a town.

Moratumulla can be viewed as a (large) neighborhood center organized around three closely located and interrelated confluences and an activity strip that connects these. Ramesh, a 32-year-old taxi driver, differentiates between a *handiya* and a town:

> A *handiya* consists of an intersection, a local taxi park, a few shops, and a *pola*. This is where people meet others from the neighborhood. A town should have petrol [gasoline] stations and big institutions like post office and hospital. *Handiyas* do not have these, but there are exceptions.

This strip of Moratumulla Handiya is lined by a wall of buildings on either side. Although not obvious, there is a second row of sparsely located buildings, mostly residential. These are accessed through the "solid" front row, between and through buildings. The space in front of buildings—between the front wall and the carriageway of the road—plays a vital role (Figure 10.3). The multitude of functions of these "side strips" includes six bus stops located on both sides of the strip. None of these has a shelter or another demarcation. Located at specific places known to locals, they work efficiently without blocking the pedestrian flow on either side of the street.

The side-strips used by pedestrians are not paved; the functions are negotiated between pedestrians, shop owners, and vehicle drivers (Figure 10.4). The side-strips allow people to window shop or inquire about prices and check the quality of items. The level of inspection and time invested depends on the durability and

FIGURE 10.3 Open Spaces (credit: Nirmani Liyanage).

FIGURE 10.4 Solids and Voids (credit: Nirmani Liyanage).

value of the item. The sides are also where people stop at the sight of an acquaintance to share informal stories, both serious and gossip (*opadupa*). Bus stops bring this activity to a peak. When people wait for buses—and other purposes—the conversations take the form of entertainment.

A solid–void analysis does (Figure 10.4) not do justice either. Street vending places are inseparable from the static/solid environment; the softer elements intermingle and interpenetrate with the hardscape, creating an integrated environment. The row of static structures lining the strip and the intersections is complemented by myriad kinetic elements (see Mehrotra 2008) such as mobile stores. There are more than 20 mobile shops at Moratumulla, but not all kinetic elements are mobile or completely ephemeral. Some *pola* structures are kinetic elements that are static. Although "mobile," belongs to the softscape and ephemeral, these are defining elements of the *handiya* and they make the *handiya* somewhat dynamic and "informal." The mobile snack vendors who appear near the bar every evening are one such connection between soft- and hardscape.

The "voids" or soft spaces are not public; they are private. Only the cross-hatched areas on Figure 10.3 are public; most unspecified activities occur on the sides. This space—which the solid–void and open-space maps are unable to capture—affords hundreds of undefined (smaller) spaces for a range of uses from walking to opening a business; the space is negotiated among the users (Figure 10.5).

Handiya is diverse, and its activities are uneven. It gets more active at confluences, with the middle one being most intense. It is the geographical center, the busiest confluence, and the place for everyday needs. With four large grocery stores, the *pola*, and many other small shops specialized in different daily goods and services, it sets the tone for the larger *handiya*. The *pola*, which is the most substantive space created and operated by people, is the core of activity (further elaborated below). In addition, there are small shops specialized in particular items such as coconut, meat, tea, and stationery. Categorizing these as shops oversimplifies their uses.

Ranjith, 55, who owns the tallest structure (three floors) on the middle confluence, describes a normal day:

> I live with my daughter's family on the second and third floors. The shop spaces on the ground floor are rented to different people. My daughter now owns this coconut shop [which Ranjith used to run and located among rented shops]. She wakes up early and sends kids to school and husband to work. Hence, I open her shop in the morning; she takes over by 9 a.m. I then hang out in and around the shop. This is where I meet my friends. They stop by almost every day, and we discuss politics. We drink tea and buy the newspaper from a nearby shop. We take a break after lunch and reopen in the evening, operating until 8–9 p.m. That is when we get most customers who

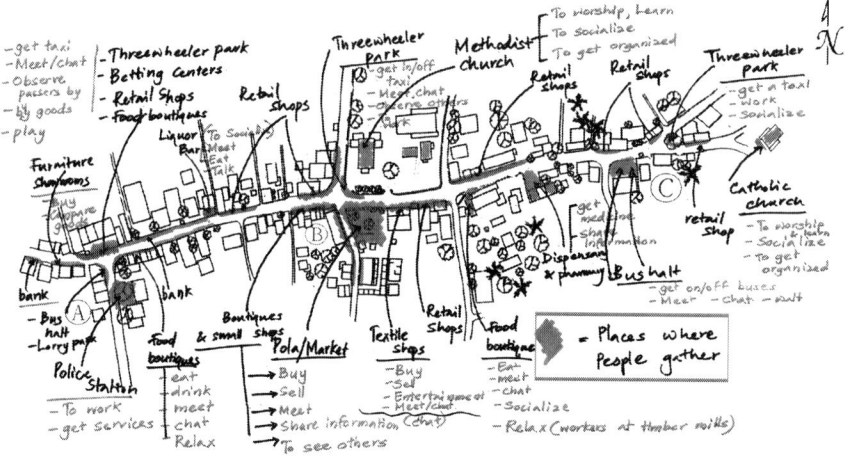

FIGURE 10.5 Gathering Spaces and Reasons (credit: Nirmani Liyanage).

are on their way home after work. I take care of the shop in the evening session because my daughter gets busy after kids return from school. She has to be in the house [upstairs].

Ranjith's building is a mine of activities: His shop is also the place where he meets friends; when he checks the maintenance of rental units, he spends time with the tenants. His family also lives in the same building. A whole range of social relations take place in it, including mother–child, landlord–tenant, customer–shop owner/keeper, and friend–friend.

The social meaning of the place changes across time. Ranjith's coconut shop turns into a place where he teaches business to his daughter and where he hangs out with friends. The role of space depends on the relation he shares with others present in the building at a given time. The physical space is not static either: He sometimes extends it onto the street by adding a few chairs for his friends to sit. This flexibility and creativity make it impossible for anyone to capture its meaning in terms of pure categories and fixed physical entities. Such complexity is found in almost every space in *handiya*; not only the *handiya* comprises a large number of uses, but each space is also made up of a multitude of activities.

Developed by people, it is a messy lived space. Most of the users are customers of the *pola* (market), mobile shops, and formal shops including Ranjith's. They are not mere customers, but also friends who meet other friends during their daily or weekly visits to *handiya*. They exchange news with old friends and new acquaintances, shop owners, and vendors, and buy what they need until the next visit. For this, they visit a number of shops and stalls during each visit.

There are different types of customers; class, type of work, and status are key differences. First, the housewives from the immediate surroundings and men who work in and around *handiya* form the largest group of users. They rarely refer to a shop by the product it sells, but by the name of the owner or his/her spouse, whoever is closer to them. Second, those who live around the *handiya* but work somewhere else, pass the *handiya* every day, and stop quickly to buy specific items. They come early in the morning and/or late in the evening, on the way to and from work and have little time to socialize. So their relationships are less with shop owners, more with the products they buy at *handiya*. They refer to shops by product names. Some customers pay quick visits during the week but hang out a longer time with the shop owners during the weekend. Others simply visit during the weekend. They have close relationships with shop owners and other users, but the duration of socialization depends on work schedules and locations that govern their time.

The third group is those who live and work in the *handiya*, such as carpenters (discussed below). A fourth group is made up of migrants. Being a suburb of Colombo, greater Moratuwa attracts many young people who work and/or study in Colombo but cannot afford to live in the capital. Some of them live around Moratumulla Handiya. The University of Moratuwa also attracts a large number of students who live in Moratumulla and adjacent neighborhoods. These groups do not have long-term friendships with shop owners but develop a certain level of acquaintance with select shop owners.

Vimukthi, 26, who was a student at the University of Moratuwa, settled in Molpe area near Moratumulla after her marriage. As a student, she only knew the area as a *handiya*, understood through her prior engagements with *handiyas* where she grew up. After marriage, she made weekly visits to Moratumulla Handiya for fresh vegetables and meat. During the first few visits she learned about vendors and shop owners, including who cheats and who does not. This trust then developed into relationships: She learned about them; they learned about her.

Before we examine other confluences, it is pertinent to investigate the historical production of Moratumulla Handiya.

A People's Creation

Moratumulla Handiya is a unique people's creation: It even has its own daily schedule and rhythm. Although not formally recorded, Moratumulla has a long history. The local informants have their own stories of how the *handiya* transformed over the last 100 years. Justin, 83, and Ranjith are two key knowledge-keepers who shared their memories with us. The histories we learned from the older generation confirm and complement each other

In 1920, Moratumulla Handiya was largely limited to the middle confluence. It had two tea shops, two grocery stores, two churches, an Ayurvedic medical store, and some products such as furniture and dairy items produced and sold in individual houses. Moratumulla was connected to other places by gravel roads. As there were no telephone connections until 1978, merchants, when they had a big enough load, brought timber to Moratumulla by themselves on bullock carts. The merchants came in groups from places such as Horana, Polgasowita, and Kottawa. They camped at *galawatta*, meaning parking space for bullock carts, for weeks until they sold the stock. The campers used water from a nearby well and cooked their own food.

The local élite later used motorized vehicles and telephones to completely transform the structure of furniture businesses and Moratumulla; a few merchants became very rich. In the 1960s the élite bought trucks and drove to the source points of wood. They established the first large-scale timber mills and furniture showrooms at Moratumulla in the early 1970s. These were named after the owners: Siripathi Medura, Sri Anura, and E.S. Cooray. Symbolizing the change, *galawatta* was turned into a furniture showroom and carpentry workshop. Challenging the monopoly of a few rich people, a few businessmen became richer and a substantial number of medium- and small-scale shops emerged in the 1980s. This is when the middle class in Sri Lanka began to cash in on the benefits of the "open-economy" initiated in 1977.

The arrival of a police station in 1982 indicates conflict and represents the power the rich furniture capitalists were able to acquire. According to shop-owner Sarath, 70, robberies at *handiya* rose, and the poor locals became suspects. The Timber Merchants Association, established in 1965 to negotiate with the government, had enough influence to get a police station. The police station was built in 1979 on the land adjacent to *galawatta*. This land is where the Indian-Tamil municipal laborers (pejoratively called *sakkili*) who cleaned toilets lived. They were evicted. The police station changed the image of Moratumulla Handiya. Ramesh shares his meaning: "Sri Lankan *handiyas* normally do not have police stations, but Moratumulla has; people there must be unruly."

Moreover, the new structure further impoverished the carpenters. They had to either buy timber at high prices determined by local timber merchants and mill owners or work in their mills or carpentry shops. This widened the gap between the rich and the poor both in regard to social power and economy. Independent carpenters have always been in debt. There are local poems about the poverty among skilled carpenters.

> *Sikuradata hithe* (dreaming of money on Fridays)
> *Senasuradata athe* (money in the hand on Saturdays)
> *Iridata hithumathe* (freely celebrating on Sundays)
> *Sandudata hamathe* (back to starvation on Mondays)

The poem refers to the weekly financial cycle of a poor carpenter who borrows a piece of timber from a rich merchant at the beginning of the week and spends Monday through Friday creating a piece of furniture. On Friday he dreams of receiving money, but when he is paid on Saturday, he receives less than what he expected. He then spends all of it on Sunday. Broke and hungry, on Monday, he borrows timber again from the same merchant.

Lucian, 69, asserts that carpenters are never paid in full. Yet there is no one to complain to. Some poor carpenters resort to betting as a means to increase their income. Twenty years ago there were two small betting centers at the middle and west confluences. As the demand for betting increased, a larger company called Sporting Star opened a branch in Moratumulla in the early 2000s. With the arrival of its competitor, Sporting Times, within a few years, it opened another branch, symbolizing the gap between the need and the actual earnings of poor carpenters.

According to Jayasena, 45, the cycle of poverty has gotten worse due to the timber merchants' decision to impose a minimum load of timber that can be purchased from them. While the merchants association has a voice in regional politics, the carpenters association does not. Therefore the issues of carpenters, mostly about the way they are treated by employer-merchants, go unheard.

However, in July 2013, the two associations collaborated for the first time and organized a protest against the change in national policy on timber transportation permits. The insurgency of the carpenters and merchants of Moratumulla grabbed national attention largely because Moratumulla has a large economic image in the country. In the locality, however, people's everyday struggles shape *handiya*. They deserve equal attention.

In Sri Lanka, essential food items had been subsidized and rationed by the government and were distributed at the neighborhood level by multipurpose cooperative societies (*samupakara* until 1977). In Moratuwa, 18 smaller cooperative societies formed the Moratuwa Samupakara Association. The Molpe branch was located at the center confluence in front of the Methodist church. A few local entrepreneurs soon recognized that the people who collect/buy their dry-food rations might like to buy fresh produce too around the same place. Beginning with a few stalls, the market grew into an informal fish and vegetable market: *pola*. The activities and spaces created in the process strengthened the market and the centrality of the center confluence.

The trajectory of the market was marked by many imaginations, conflicts, and changes. The officials' attempts to remove the market began in 1985. Blaming the vendors for blocking road traffic, the municipality tried to evict them and expand the road. The functioning of the *handiya*, particularly the market, and the slow traffic are complementary. Shantha, 58, questions the need for expanding the road:

> The roads are narrow and busy, no pedestrian crossings, but the *handiya* has no records of road accidents. (We later learned that there was one accident within the last 10 years.) The middle confluence is busy during the peak hours of the market, but drivers do not pick Soyza Road if they want to go fast. Some people buy vegetables by simply slowing down their motor bicycles as they pass the *pola*. Why does it [the local government] want to make the main street wide and fast like a highway when the function requires the traffic to slow down? There are many alternative paths to reach places around the *handiya* if anyone needs to bypass the middle confluence.

Pola is not the only institution that was challenged; when the private sector was granted the freedom of importing goods and the government subsidies for poorer people were curtailed, the cooperative store lost its significance. In 1998, the Cooperative Society of Moratuwa decided to downsize the Moratumulla retail outlet and shifted the remaining functions such as loan services to a small room constructed nearby.

In view of shifting the *pola* from the street, the local government constructed a few vending spaces behind the new building. The space was not enough for all vendors, nor could it attract enough customers. Within a year, all vendors moved back to their original places. As the *pola* issue became politicized, politicians began to use the *handiya* to make political statements; holding political rallies, they promised to allocate a permanent space for the *pola*. In 2001, under the United National Party rule, Moratumulla Cooperative Society removed the boundary wall. The *pola* gained more space, but it was subjected to a daily ground rent, charged by the cooperative.

To build a formal *pola* space, the old cooperative building was demolished in 2004. Aligning with a local politician, some directors of the Moratuwa Cooperative Society decided to build a *pola* structure. The Moratumulla people who were suspicious of the political intentions of this move used a parliamentarian to convince the mayor of Moratuwa who forcefully stopped the construction of the new market in 2009.

While the trajectory of the *pola* is contested and politicized, the *pola* continues to function at the same place, but now with dual road frontage to the main street and the perpendicular Jana Asiri Mawatha. Currently 38 vendors operate in self-built structures, paying a daily ground rent to the Moratumulla Cooperative Society. Dina Pola Velandunge Subasadaka Samithiya, the welfare society of daily market vendors founded in 1998, continues to negotiate with the Moratuwa Cooperative and the municipal council for a new *pola* structure with sanitary facilities. Karunaratne, chairman of the vendors' welfare association, concluded his interview with the following statement:

> We will somehow maintain the *pola* until we can get a structure and [infrastructure] facilities for it. The most recent promise is about the big grant the cooperative society is likely to receive from the government to build the structure. The issue is we are never consulted when they [both cooperative society and the local authority] plan for us ... the vendors' association is disappointed!

The significance of the daily market (*pola*) has increased with the recent changes at the middle confluence. A Sathosa Co-op City outlet was introduced in 2013 on the other side of the strip. Sathosa, a dry-food store like the former cooperative, recontextualized the *pola* that again plays the complementary role of providing perishable fresh-food items.

The middle confluence is not limited to the *pola* and commercial functions; it is simultaneously commercial, residential, political, and religious. The house and coconut shop building is also located in the heart of the confluence. The intersection is also used by politicians for meetings during election times. As a people's creation, this *handiya* is well grounded. Perera's (2010: 163) account of people's activities in a town center well matches its activities:

> Sri Lankan people visit the nearest urban center frequently—daily if possible—to buy fresh vegetables and food ... towns are filled with pedestrians. As people carry out a multitude of tasks while in town, walking from one facility to the other, each town is compact and made up of various (mixed) land uses and functions that are not separated out in the way that cities are understood in the Western land-use discourse.

The middle confluence has its own routine: Vendors take two breaks during the day, completely shutting the market, and setting a pattern. They open the market early at 7 a.m., but close from 10:00–11:30 a.m. After another busy period, vendors take another break at 2 p.m. and reopen the stalls at 5 p.m. The last work shift goes on until 9 p.m. *Handiya* has its own rhythm.

This ingenious organization has shaped the routine of almost the entire middle confluence. The formal stores in and around the intersection mostly follow the same schedule; a few operate throughout the day with no breaks, perhaps responding to the customer base. The bookshop near the market is open during the second break because that is when schoolchildren return home.

This is an inside-out construction of space through the negotiation between vendors of informal and formal stores, the customers and the users of the confluence, and the mobile stalls, over a long period of time. The time schedule has grown from an arrangement between the vendors of the market and the customers to one that defines the rhythm and activities of the whole center confluence.

The transformation of the *handiya* is neither natural nor evolutionary; it is driven by conscious human interventions and negotiations. The change is more like an "event cascade": "an action sequence which gathers momentum, reverses course, changes direction, stalls, and resumes anew" (see Roseneau 1990). Since the *handiya* is an inside-out creation, its creators do not have to transform planned or provided (abstract) spaces into lived spaces. It is the power actors, including timber merchants and politicians, who try to transform the people-created *handiya* to insert their needs and wishes.

It is impossible for outside-in processes to create a place like *handiya*. As Jane Jacobs (1972) argues, the way land uses are separated and/or categorized—techniques used in urban development—has made secondary and tertiary land uses disappear. Even "mixed use" cannot recover these. Created by people, Moratumulla is a lived space of the highest quality.

Moratumulla Handiya at Large

Moratumulla Handiya is diverse. The "A" confluence, closest to the Colombo–Galle Road, has a concentration of furniture showrooms, workshops, and other services that support the carpentry industry. "Confluence A" is like a large workshop. Most alleyways around it are mini furniture factories consisting of hundreds of small carpentry shops, usually attached to each other and served by small alleyways (Figure 10.6). Some workshops are of medium size with five to ten carpenters working in each.

The immediate row of buildings along the strip is made up of well-maintained furniture showrooms. The area thus resembles an assembly line where the process begins at timber mills, and furniture ends up in these showrooms facing the main street. One such alley we visited in 2013 has now (2015) become a small commercial alley. As they do not have road frontage to attract passers-by, furniture makers keep agents at the west confluence to bring customers to their furniture shops. Thus, smaller investors have created more variety and a greater number of spaces compared to larger actors such as merchants and the cooperative society.

Institutions that serve the carpentry industry are represented in banks, leasing companies that lease vehicles and heavy machines, nicer restaurants serving visitors/ clients, and chemical and other material suppliers for the furniture industry. The wage laborers employed by timber mills are also served by restaurants and kiosks at the confluence, with lunch menus different from the restaurants but affordable to them. There are snack and tea shops, both fixed and mobile. Some households prepare food and use front rooms as kiosks.

FIGURE 10.6 Furniture-Making Alleyways (credit: Nirmani Liyanage).

The Y-shaped confluence-C divides the flow of buses in two directions: toward Piliyandala or Villorawatte. In the mornings, the east confluence is busy with passengers who switch between the two bus routes. The confluence is more residential and has no restaurants. It consists of a few timber mills and carpentry shops; in some houses, a road-side room is converted into a small shop. Serving mostly the laborers in the carpentry industry and commuters, these small shops sell takeaway food items, snacks, and grocery items. During the church feast in November, this confluence has a few seasonal shops.

The distribution of mobile shops reveals much about the *handiya* and raises many questions about the way the space is categorized and understood by professionals and scholars. The mobile shops and food-vending carts by the road strategically coincide with pedestrian flows. Most mobile shops are parked at the same place every day and have acquired a sense of fixity. Specialized according to the needs and/or business potential at different times of the day, these stalls are similar to stores operating through more static/solid structures; they have a well-defined customer base which shows up at the particular place, at the same time, expecting the same vendor.

Handiya's dynamism is enhanced by mobile shops. The same mobile shop was found in two locations along the strip at different times of the day serving/targeting different groups of customers. In the morning, the vendor sells breakfast and lunch packets to office workers and school children who take the bus from the middle confluence. In the evening, the same vendor sells snacks to male carpentry workers who visit the bar, closer to the west confluence.

Mobile shops and food-vending carts are very sensitive to changes in pedestrian flows. They have different constellations during different times of the day. The bar area, between the bar and the busiest bus stop of the *handiya* (between the middle and west confluences), becomes very busy from 5 p.m. to 9:30 p.m. Mobile shops are responsive to these changes. Several vendors sell spicy snacks for the drinkers and dinner packets for those who arrive by bus.

Public and private spaces at Moratumulla Handiya are neither oppositional nor totally exclusive. As in Galle Fort (Chapter 4) and teahouses in Chengdu (Wang

2003), public and private spaces meet, overlap, and interpenetrate at the side-strip. Mobile shops, which are private spaces for owner-vendors, mediate between these.

While the static environment houses private spaces, the kinetic environment extends the same into the public space in the form of an archipelago of private spaces. Conversely, public space seeps into the static component of the built environment through and between the front row of buildings, into the second row, gradually disappearing into private space. Instead of a threshold, there is a huge liminal and hybrid space where the houses move out into the street in the form of stores, restaurants, stalls, and seating spaces attached to them (see Perera 2013). Many of these structures are not so separate in regard to functions. They are lived-in businesses open to outsiders who are not allowed to go into interior rooms, as with Ranjith's coconut shop and the house. The proportion of clearly defined public and private spaces is much smaller than that of these hybrid spaces.

The *handiya* is not defined by a boundary or a threshold; whatever defines it is a frontier, at best. In its place, there is a long and uneven transition space around the core of the *handiya*. The function, meaning, and feeling of the *handiya* begin long before one enters the strip. It depends on the ways people reach and leave the *handiya*. Jasintha usually feels the *handiya* atmosphere when she joins her sister who lives nearby to walk to the market. The *handiya* flows outwards along small paths where the two women can buy snacks or have tea from a stall.

Each confluence has its own three-wheeler park (local taxi service) to serve those who live a bit interior or wish not to walk, but for a price. The "three-wheelers"—motorized lightweight taxis known as auto-rickshaws—became popular in Sri Lanka after 1994. Almost in every rural and suburban settlement a few entrepreneurs have bought three-wheelers and park these at the last bus stop (usually a *handiya*) where many people exit the public transport system and begin the walk home. By the end of the 1990s, Moratumulla Handiya had two three-wheeler parks at the middle and west confluences; a third was established at the east confluence in the late 2000s.

The three-wheeler drivers normally rest on the more-comfortable back seat of their vehicles, waiting for customers. When someone gets off the bus or is walking from the market side carrying a big bag or a child, the driver comes out and greets the potential customer, planting the idea of an easier ride home. The drivers further serve visitors as information providers as they are experts of local addresses and street names. The three-wheeler park is not merely a transportation hub, it is a hangout for some boys. The association of three-wheeler drivers and owners plays a significant role in organizing community events such as New Year or religious celebrations.

The daily work schedule extends into the week. The market functions on Sundays but does not open until after mass ends at the Catholic church. Even though nearly 70 percent of the area population is Buddhist (SCCAP 2002), the customer flow after the Sunday services of the two main churches—the Methodist church at the middle confluence and the Catholic church along Villorawatte Road, east of the east confluence—seems more important on Sundays. Most churchgoers pass the market on their way home. They are relaxed and buy items to meet their weekly or daily needs, and socialize.

According to Sarath, despite being the minority (25.8 percent), the Catholics and Christians have a greater impact on the market and the overall image of the place than their numbers would suggest. The two main churches physically complement the strong Christian presence. Built in 1814, the Methodist church is one of the oldest in Sri Lanka. The large church with walls around it takes half of the middle confluence, somewhat limiting its expansion. The Methodist church has provided education support for underprivileged children since 1979, serving more than 4,500 students from the area. Currently, the program is funded by a Sri Lankan who lives in New Zealand. Many such connections are not visible from outside.

The work pattern also varies across the year, according to ethnic and religious calendars. The *handiya* is invigorated during the Catholic church feast in November and other annual events such as Sinhala-Tamil New Year in April.

Challenges, Familiarizations, Changes

The élite and business owners kept improving their community during last two decades, pushing for an efficient and safe environment for businesses, access to credit, and better transportation through road widening. They brought the police. At every step, ordinary people also have expanded their businesses, activities, and their presence. Making and selling food for the workers at large furniture workshops, providing accommodation, and operating small shops are among those many creative endeavors.

The arrival of new formal businesses like banks in the 1980s was a huge change. According to Ranjith,

> When the use of cash decreased due to the arrival of banks, the élite and their businesses were further strengthened; but all citizens [at *handiya*] benefited by services like banking. Some learned the habit of saving money; some learned the possibility of using bank loans to start small businesses.

As the *handiya* continues its "journey" through challenges, influences, and familiarizations, over time, the kind and flow of goods and the type of activities in it have also changed. In this, the *handiya* exhibits the local taste, its choice of imported goods or practices, and their familiarizations by the setting up of new shops and/or functions. There is a huge flow of imported goods to Moratumulla—and other places in Sri Lanka—since the shift toward a liberalized economy in 1977. The consumerist environment so-produced enhanced the furniture business and expanded the daily-goods market. It took a few years for ordinary people to benefit from the policy shift; by 1980, most of the houses along the strip were converted into various stores. Some residents moved into the second row of buildings, turning the houses along the strip into shops.

Since then, the *handiya* has changed much faster than its landscape. While telecommunication centers/shops with multiple telephone booths became prominent in the 1990s, they now have given way to video game centers. When many people began to use mobile phones, people went to *handiya* to see and buy these. The *handiya* has never failed to introduce new global and national trends to the locality and to modernize it. Yet what the vendors bring to the *handiya* is influenced by the changing tastes and the desires of the customers.

Handiya is gendered: Women try to avoid the bar, the three-wheeler park, the betting center, and odd gathering places. Women do not like to walk in the bar area after 5–6 p.m. due to the possibility of confronting drunken men. The three-wheeler park is a hangout for boys. Walking through one with no intention of hiring a driver can make a woman a target of teasing. Yet women have familiarized the *handiya* their own way. Women mostly visit the *pola* and churches. The *pola* at the center confluence is mostly used by middle-aged women from adjacent communities. Some women use *handiya* to empower themselves without even physically being there through endeavors like cooking snacks for restaurants from home.

Currently the three-wheeler parks at the middle, west, and east confluences have 30, 25, and 20 three-wheelers, respectively. These parks operate on their own rules and limitations; for instance only the drivers/owners from Fernando Mawatha (avenue) can join the west confluence's three-wheeler park. The other two also have their own rules to reduce conflicts and expand opportunities. People are creative in identifying different markets and social opportunities to achieve individual goals, especially to distribute the business more evenly.

The incorporation and familiarization of new elements and the adaption of the *handiya* to evolve is a continuous process. The most recent addition to Moratumulla Handiya is two key supermarket chains in 2012–2013; one is located near the east confluence and the other between the middle and west confluences. While these intruders threaten to suck the life out of *handiya*, *handiya* also offers them the choice to naturalize and become a part of it. So far, the new stores have not caused any negative effects on existing businesses or the *pola*. Instead, the *pola* is expanding along roadsides. The new trend is facilitated by shop owners renting parts of store fronts to vegetable and fish vendors. The *pola* vendors association does not like the practice, but does not intend to control the trend. As is evident, abstract space is not as strong or dominant as projected in mainstream discourses. The authorities or the élite hardly developed the *handiya*. Ordinary people have created and reproduced their own *handiya*s and continue to reproduce these on their own terms. The informal vendors getting the support of politicians and the jackfruit vendor beginning his business are quite normal in *handiya*s. People use politics and social capital when needed and create limited new social, economic, and cultural opportunities in the cracks of the formal polity, economy, and space (see also Wajahat 2013).

Learning from Handiyas

It is hard to replicate a *handiya*. Radampola in Matara was included in a nationwide Mini-Town Development Plan series by a cabinet minister from the area (Figure 10.7). The feasibility study failed, yet the project was implemented, replacing the

FIGURE 10.7 Study Locations (credit: Nirmani Liyanage).

original *handiya* with a shopping complex that has no resemblance to what people created according to their needs (Figure 10.8). The media unit of the ministry publicized the creation of the new mini town by the Urban Development Authority as setting a new trend to develop *handiya*s. This plan considers that *handiya*s are undeveloped, that they lack something, that the cause is internal, and that the development authority can fix it.

Handiyas created by people have narrow roads where all sides of an intersection are functionally connected; also, people use space outside structures to create the social meaning of *handiya*. By contrast, the authoritatively planned "*handiya*" is

FIGURE 10.8 Radampola: Original *Handiya* vs. Planned (credit: UDA 2009).

almost a building that restricts most uses of outside space such as chatting, relaxing, observing others, and playing (Figure 10.8). *Handiya* is more of an outdoor environment that is supported by static built elements. Unlike in a natural *handiya*, at Radampola, there is a manager of the place, a huge supporter of the cabinet minister, who makes sure that no betel-chewer spits on the newly paved sidewalks or sits on the walls. Alterations to shop spaces are strictly prohibited, and the people in general are not welcome to their own "*handiya*." Wide roads further restrict the interactions between uses and users on both sides of the road.

Identifying *handiya* as a significant social space and wanting to make a planning contribution is valuable. The thinking of the politician is one step ahead of the intellectual incapacity of planning scholars in Sri Lanka who are yet to see the *handiya*. Yet, as evident, in Radampola, the planners who designed this project have no real understanding of *handiya*. The re-planned *handiya* exhibits the "illegibility" of socially produced spaces to professionals. A planning intervention that abandons all the spaces and space-making processes initiated and carried out by locals is a bigger threat than not identifying *handiya* as a prime social space. The architect-planner himself stated that the mini town would take more than 20 years to function.

Mullaitivu Handiya confirmed that resilience and location are keys to *handiya*s. In 2004, Mullaitivu Handiya was washed away by the Indian Ocean tsunami and was later bombed many times during the three-decade civil war. After each destruction, the *handiya* was rebuilt by people to better suit their new conditions. It served the locals as a space that supported their daily lives in the midst of a war, and also as a place for the exchange of goods, services, and ideas with other areas of the country and among themselves.

Unfortunately, the end of the war brought the end of Mullaitivu Handiya, too. *Handiya* is a delicate product of the people; it cannot be randomly moved without destroying it. The new plans created by the planners in Colombo—who came from a totally different cultural and environmental background—separated and relocated the major functions of the *handiya* to relatively distant places, challenging the people to conduct their daily lives accordingly, irrespective of local climatic (heat and dust) conditions and social relationships.

A much smaller *handiya* at Mavi-Ela confirms that personal relationships, competition, and negotiations among residents and shop-owners shape *handiya*s. At Mavi-Ela, the competition between the two main grocery stores is largely settled through the shop-owners' family relationships with residents; the friendlier one gets more customers.

The stories in this chapter are not meant to romanticize the *handiya*. *Handiya*s are ordinary places and have their own vices and failures. Locals at Mavi-Ela used to complain about an outsider (*pitagam-karaya*) running a store successfully at their *handiya*. Yet one morning that shop had turned into a pile of ash, and no one knew who set the fire or why. Two Tamil shop-owners had to leave Moratumulla during the 1983 riots. Unlike in Moratumulla, the *pola* land in Mavi-Ela is owned and managed by a family, and their inability to facilitate the market resulted in losing many vendors. A new *pola* opened in a nearby *handiya* and has attracted many vendors and customers. The first *pola* then failed to maintain its customer base and is hardly surviving. The main issue is large property at the physical intersection, as in Kalagedihena, prevents the physical intersection from becoming an active *handiya*.

The powerful actions at *handiya* are carried out through consensus. At Mavi-Ela, a bus shelter was once demolished because the family whose land was behind it did not want a permanent structure to block their view. They were able to convince a group of youth to demolish it. One tea and grocery shop owner who rented a building was evicted because a powerful person in the area wanted to open a gas station on that land. Yet the villagers offered a place along the same road to the shop-owner as they wanted the shop to continue.

At Moratumulla, the catchment is dense and larger than any of the above *handi-ya*s. At least 23 neighborhoods (villages) are organized around it, locals say. Across this catchment area are small teashops and grocery stores, mostly located in homes where one room has been converted for the business. They serve specific smaller catchments such as a residential street around the university. Yet none has become a *handiya* of Moratumulla caliber.

Handiya is also a place of negotiation and emergence. The timber merchants of Moratumulla Handiya seek more clients in other cities and countries by appropriating the latest (cyber) technology, while a nearby locality named Indibadda competes with Moratumulla by reducing its furniture prices. At the same time, plastic furniture produced by multinational companies (Damro, Nilkamal) reduces the demand for wooden furniture. Some carpenters who have had not been happy with their income and achievement now take sub contracts from these companies to produce cheaper furniture. Overall, the inside-out processes that shapes and reshape keeps the *handiya* competitive.

People's *Handiya*

This study helped us develop a grounded understanding of the *handiya* and its production. Clearly, *handiya* is not physical, and all road/street confluences are not *handiya*s. *Handiya* is a social space created through the materialization of the social potential of a physical road/street confluence. It is a place where a road confluence is developed into a square of sorts through small interventions. Hence, road/street confluence is a necessary condition, but is not sufficient.

Handiya is not an outcome of people's reaction to abstract space. As a people's creation, at *handiya*, lived spaces become the reference. It is the authorities and the élite who try to reshape and assert their power by nibbling into this high-quality, unruly lived space. In this, people's (lived) spaces condition any intervention (abstract space) by the authorities or other powerful actors.

The authorities are unable to curtail the power of *handiya*. The complexity of the form, the function and the meaning makes *handiya* an illegible place for planners, policy makers, and scholars. Our lack of knowledge of *handiya* has little to do with the *handiya* itself; it is the poverty of the intellectual frameworks. External, particularly Western, theories and concepts cannot capture the *handiya*. Instead of large, abstract, "measurable" categories that professionals and scholars depend on, *handiya* is produced and reproduced through highly flexible, small space-making processes. Theory-driven, data-hungry, serial-thinking social science, planning, or policy making are thus unable to capture the social reality of *handiya*. These constructs see land, land values, and road widths which can only capture the "body" of the *handiya* and not its "self." Instead of defining and/or capturing, these intellectual tools transform ground conditions to fulfill the expectations of the tools. Such imposition of meaning and identity destroys the *handiya*, revealing the poverty of professional and academic discourses of social space.

Handiya is an inside-out creation par excellence (Figure 10.9). It is the most significant pivot around which people's spaces are organized across Sri Lanka. People's orientation largely hinges on the *handiya*; it is the unit through

FIGURE 10.9 Cartoon View of a Handiya (credit: Hasantha Wijenayake).

which space is read, understood, used, and communicated. The *handiya* is the main conduit through which people from neighboring communities physically, socially, economically, and culturally connect themselves to the larger world. People also use *handiya*s to traverse across larger formal territories such as provinces and districts.

Handiya is an ongoing people's process that achieves and/or materializes the potential of space for the community. It is never stagnant, but goes through dynamic changes caused by the users. Produced by people, it continues to absorb new external interventions and influences, familiarizing these within its organizational principles, simultaneously adjusting and/or restructuring itself to accommodate these.

References

Deden, R. and Purbadi, D. (2013) "Street Vending in Indonesian Cities: Their characteristics and activities in Yogyakarta" in N. Perera and W.S. Tang (eds.) *The Transforming Asian Cities: Intellectual impasse, Asianizing space, and emerging translocalities*, New York: Routledge, 123–36.

Hamdi, N. (2004) *Small Change: About the art of practice and the limits of planning in cities*, Sterling, VA: Earthscan.

Jacobs, J. (1972 [1961]) *The Death and Life of Great American Cities*, 2nd edn, Harmondsworth: Penguin.

Janz, W. (2013) *Leftover Rightunder: Finding architectural potential in found materials*, Chicago, IL: Half Letter Press.

Lynch, K. (1960) *The Image of the City*, Cambridge, MA: MIT Press.

Mehrotra, R. (2008) Negotiating the Static and Kinetic Cities: The emergent urbanism of Mumbai" in A. Huyssen (ed.) *Other Cities, Other Worlds: Urban imagineries in a globalizing age*, Durham, NC: Duke University Press, 205–18.

Munasinghe, J.N. (2007) "Self Organizing and Planning: The Case of Small Towns in Sri Lanka" in N. Perera and W.S. Tang (eds.) *The Transforming Asian City: Innovative urban and planning practice*, HongKong: Hong Kong Baptist University, 93–102.

Perera, N. (2010) "When Planning Ideas Land: Mahaweli's people-centered approach" in P. Healey and R. Upton (eds.) *Crossing Borders: International exchanges and planning practices*, New York: Routledge, 141–72.

Perera, N. (2013) "Critical Vernacularism: A view of architecture from the places of production" in N. Perera and W.S. Tang (eds.) *Transforming Asian Cities: Intellectual impasse, Asianizing space, and emerging translocalities*, New York: Routledge, 78–93.

Perera, N. and Tang, W.S. (2013) *Transforming Asian Cities: Intellectual impasse, Asianizing space, and emerging translocalities*, New York: Routledge.

Roseneau, J.N. (1990) *Turbulence in World Politics: A theory of change and continuity*, Princeton, NJ: Princeton University Press, 303.

SCCAP (2002) "Profile: Moratuwa Municipal Council." Online. Available: www.unhabitat. lk/downloads/SCP/Moratuwa.pdf, (accessed February 2, 2015).

Sekara, M. (2000 [1967]) *Thunman Handiya*, Colombo: Godage Publishers (in Sinhala).

Wajahat, F. (2013) "Perceptions of Tenure Security in a Squatter Settlement in Lahore, Pakistan" in N. Perera and W.S. Tang (eds.) *Transforming Asian Cities: Intellectual impasse, Asianizing space, and emerging translocalities*, New York: Routledge, 137–47.

Wang, D. (2003) *Street Culture in Chengdu: Public space, urban commoners, and local politics, 1870–1930*, Stanford, CA: Stanford University Press.

11

CONCLUSIONS

Production of Social Space: From Coping with Provided and Imposed Spaces to Creating Their Own

Studies in this volume reveal that even the spatial structures, processes, and spaces created by the most powerful actors are not complete. They are unable to create fully complying subjects. Even those who volunteered to be subjects have adapted these spaces, functions, and their envisaged meanings within their frameworks. People were heavily affected by the war in northern Sri Lanka, the tsunami and the post-tsunami reconstruction process in the south, the establishment of a World Heritage site in Galle, and a stagnant housing stock in Tashkent. People have been resilient. After an initial setback, beginning with spaces of basic survival, most subjects built their lives and spaces necessary for their new life trajectories, instead of recovering the life they previously had. They refused to be victims; they are survivors.

We see in the example of colonial Colombo how ordinary people may first resist a change, then find ways to survive in the midst of their new reality, adapting to new spaces as necessary (Chapter 1). In the early sixteenth century, the Portuguese established Colombo as a White male Christian city. Beginning with creating third spaces nestled in private ones, women in Colombo not only bifurcated and con-tested the formal public sphere, but over centuries, laid claims to it (Chapter 2). The colonial authorities subjected Colombo to a massive change in the late nine-teenth century. The process of Ceylonese becoming subjects within colonial society and space caused an even greater transformation in the city (Chapter 1). In the process, by bringing a power institution to the indigenous side, the Ceylonese subverted—at least weakened—the structure of the colonial city. The examples in this volume show how ordinary people shape and develop their own subjectivities and spaces to a degree that has not been acknowledged in scholarly and professional work.

Contemporary social space is largely defined by the conflict between (abstract) spaces created by powerful actors, especially for their subjects and (lived) spaces that ordinary people opt to create for their livelihoods, and how the differences between these are reconciled. The negotiations range from the subjects trying to cope with spaces such as colonial and World Heritage sites imposed on them by the state and capital, to the latter attempting to find accommodation in spaces created by people such as self-built settlements and in *handiyas* (Figure 11.1).

Formal spaces are provided and/or imposed by the authorities and powerful actors. The subjects' responses vary from voluntary subjugation to subversion, yet the differences are blurry. In nineteenth-century Colombo and the 60-Houses project in Galle, the subjects went along with the imposed structures. Yet the

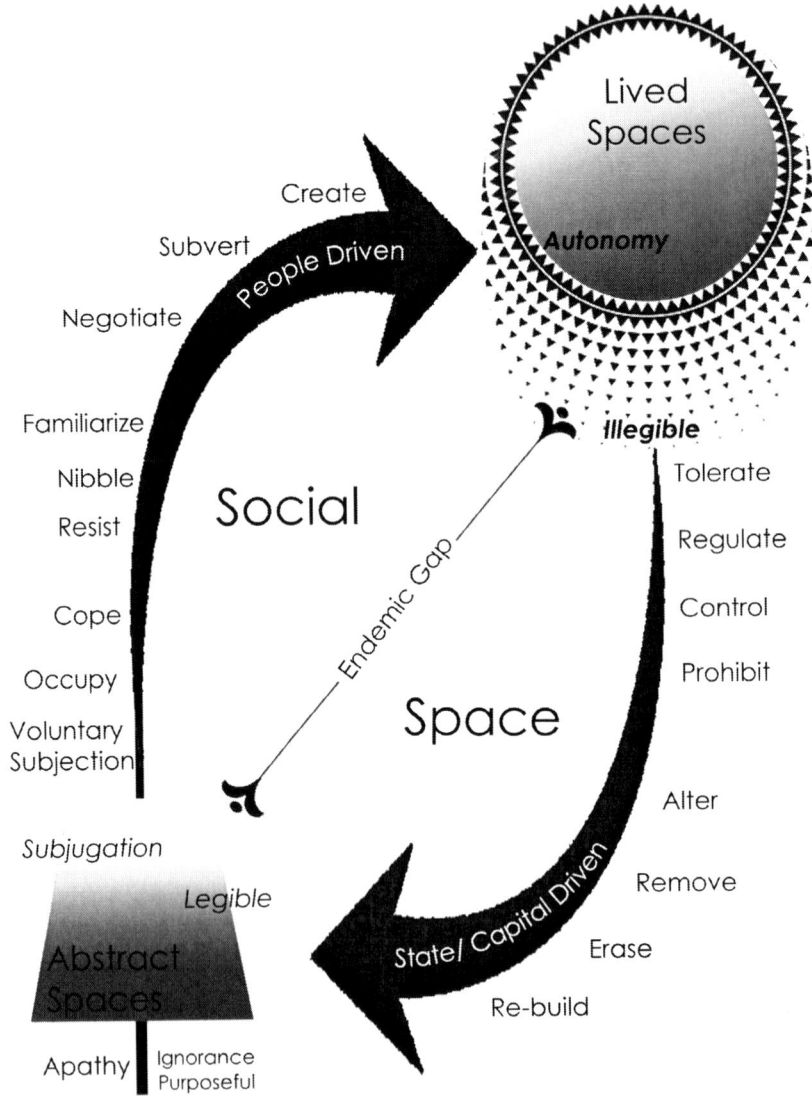

FIGURE 11.1 Production of People's Spaces (Schematic) (credit: Nirmani Liyanage).

occupation itself disrupted their mapping, demonstrating the incompleteness of abstract spaces and the differences in spatial perceptions and practices of the creators/ providers and subjects of these spaces.

Some people may initially practice apathy, but most subjects are not passive recipients, not even those who accept subjectivity. When resistance fails, as in Colombo and Galle, people cope with impositions. Yet in most cases, beginning with finding accommodation for their activities, the subjects familiarize the strange as in Jaffna and Galle, negotiate space as in Kalametiya, and subvert as in nineteenth-century Colombo. People produce their lived spaces by carving out room for their daily activities and cultural practices (within constraints) and decentering the meaning of imposed and/or provided spaces.

People employ the provided and/or imposed spaces as both the point of departure and the raw material for creating their livelihoods and lived spaces. The inhabitants of Daanchi redefined outside influences (globalization and Westernization) from their standpoints, and the inhabitants of Kalametiya used aid to build the lives they desired. Almost all of Gangtok is built by people, but through the very formal system to which they are subject. Despite the rules and sanctioning procedures, most planning and building in Gangtok occurs along unwritten (informal) processes developed by people. Between and outside the successive spatial ordering of society by the state and the market, ordinary people and small organizations produce a greater quantity and variety of spaces.

Most places, especially in the "global south," are developed by people. Historically, lived spaces predate contemporary abstract ones, even in the West. In regard to Dharavi and Moratumulla Handiya, people initiated the production and transformation of space on their own terms. Gangtok predates regulations. In these places, the conflict between abstract and lived spaces is reversed: The state and capital are compelled to negotiate their needs through formalizing public areas and/or infrastructure, by resizing, reshaping, or restructuring elements such as roads, public areas and infrastructure.

Abstract Spaces: Incomplete, Contradictory, Paradoxical

Abstract spaces provided and/or imposed by powerful actors are incomplete. They have cracks, fissures, and fuzzy boundaries. Whether created by a colonial regime, state policy, warring parties, the disaster-response machine, or a World Heritage designation, abstract spaces hardly create subjects the way authorities, planners, and policy makers envisage. Rather, the spaces are contradictory, paradoxical, and easily disrupted by simple occupation.

Despite the strong pretensions and influence they have, modern social systems, particularly states and their constituent discourses, are never complete. Partha Chatterjee (2006) argues that even industrial workers have not fully internalized the work-discipline of capitalism. Even when they do, they do not do so in ways anticipated by the authorities. Scott (1990) says compelling evidence suggests subordinate classes under feudalism and capitalism have not been ideologically incorporated to the extent claimed by analysts.

As evident in the chapters, contemporary abstract spaces created by the state and capital do not fully operate the way these are perceived by their creators and enforcers. The World Heritage project itself is flawed: It is a bundle of different projects conceived and carried out by UNESCO, the national government, and the Galle Heritage Foundation, with gaps between them (Chapter 4). None of these projects has produced complete abstract spaces. Even Colombo at the height of colonialism had fissures, cracks, and gaps.

Abstract spaces are instruments of order designed and established with subjects and subjectivity in mind. The successful performance of these spaces depends on subjects' compliant occupation. Ironically, the simple occupation disrupts the map. Abstract space is conceived in terms of large-scale abstract notions and categories, and the culture of its construction is camouflaged. In contrast, the act of occupation is "concrete," and the subjects rely on their cultural perceptions (Figure 11.2): Even voluntary subjects in nineteenth-century Colombo and the 60-Houses project perceived spaces using their cognitive frameworks, within their worldviews, and occupied at individual and/or small-group scale. With such contradictions, even mimicry produces alternatives (see Bhabha 1994).

Abstract thinking of academics and professionals is also developed in particular times and spaces, and almost always derived from times and spaces different to those of ordinary people. Such abstract thinking privileges and builds on Western and middle-class experiences. While there is no specific West these days, Euro-centrism in intellectual activity is the dominant form of thinking: London, New York, and Singapore are more valued at the Centre for Environment, Planning and Technology (Ahmedabad) as examples to study than Chharanagar. *Handiya* is hardly mentioned in planning documents, scholarly work, or the curricula in Sri Lanka as a significant organizer of space (Chapter 10). They miss the locals and the locality.

In short, abstract spaces are incomplete and contradictory. Abstract spaces are neither capable of fully subjugating the inhabitants, nor preventing them from creating alternatives. Ordinary people could hardly occupy abstract spaces, whether these are intended to subjugate a population or created as the spaces of the Other. Even if the ideas of space and subjectivity are well transmitted from the creator to the recipient, these are bound to change as they cross cultural boundaries, even from an upper class to a lower one. At least as rapidly as new influences and ideas are brought into a community, people localize these in one way or another (see Appadurai 1996; Goh 2002; Perera 2009; Vidyarthi 2015). War, tsunami, globalization, and Westernization caused external influences and impositions, but the people in Jaffna, Daanchi, and Kalametiya responded to their own perceptions of these influences. In this, they produced their own globalization, Westernization, and modernity.

Ordinary people's understanding of a norm at local levels is quite different where the local standards of measurement are largely tied to "practical" needs (Scott 1998). The ordered and totalized notions of space conceived by authorities and professionals are largely alien to their subjects. People do not think in terms of pure categories and oppositions, but employ a mixed bag of resources that may be Western,

Modern, traditional, and vernacular. Instead of discriminating between these aspects that scholars and practitioners see as separate, people create new pertinent ideas using the necessary combination of these. The officials they deal with in government offices are the government for people.

In de Certeau's (1984) terms, there is a gap between the spatial language used by regulated operations and that enunciated in daily activities by ordinary people. Despite the "formal order," Kamal Tamang in Gangtok (Chapter 9) responded to a rumor that someone is planning to build a structure on the lot adjacent to his and usurped this project. Owner-builders in Gangtok obtain building permits, but they do not follow the drawings. Even when he had the free services of an engineer, Tamang valued his mason's advice. Most cities in the world are built like this. Ordinary people's small space-making is urbanization, and these efforts *en masse* create urbanity. What is lacking is a vocabulary to understand these.

This foregrounds a significant paradox: The success of a norm, abstract space, or subjectivity depends on its failure (Perera 2009). The successful transmission of an idea depends on the ability of its "recipients" to grasp it precisely and practice it fully. Yet the grasping depends on the interpretation within recipients' worldviews, cultural contexts, local languages, and practical norms. People cannot use space the way it is intended, but using space for a different purpose is viewed as failure. Hence, the intended occupation by the subjects cannot be achieved without the allowance of this "play." As evident in the studies, larger norms that define abstract spaces hardly survive the transmission process, but instead get modified one way or another. Abstract spaces simultaneously fail and succeed, leaving a gap between the intended purpose and the actual use. The gap may be small, but this highlights the inherent contradiction (i.e., a paradox) in abstract spaces.

The incongruence and conflict between abstract spaces and lived spaces (i.e., between the way authorities intend for a space to be used and the way the space is ultimately used) is endemic. Hence, abstract space is in continuous crisis. The authorities and the powerful opt to resolve the crisis by closing what they see as loopholes in the formal system, thus perfecting their spaces through new plans, policies, laws, and policing. In this they keep suppressing the lived spaces of the subordinates. Yet, the brilliant work of Di Wang (2003), which focuses on Chengdu, China, highlights how the authorities were unable to control the way people used streets. Galle Fort, Gangtok, Daanchi, and Tashkent have all been redefined by their subjects. In order to save abstract space—with modifications—authorities have allowed select exceptions. In Gangtok, the municipality accepts a fine for the extra floor area built by the permit holder.

In regard to modern social systems and their rules, Chatterjee (2007) highlights that exceptions are as important as rules for their functioning. Most rules are bound to fail without exceptions, even the one-child policy in China. All studies in this volume highlight the significance of paying attention to exceptions and not discarding them as in theory-driven, data-hungry, serial-thinking type analyses. At times, exception may be the most important piece of information. Understanding people's spaces requires us to pay special attention to the "messy" spaces they produce.

The crisis is much deeper, and, as the stories in this volume indicate, the authorities fight a losing battle but spend enormous resources and energy to maintain power, reap financial benefits, and reproduce the discourse for various benefits. There is no evidence to believe in a natural progression from a "slum" to a middle-class environment, as conceived by the state, capital, and mainstream professionals and scholars. Neuwirth's (2005) findings refute this possibility. My observations in Mumbai cannot confirm that Dharavi will one day become like Bandra Kurla. The evidence supports the opposite: Teashops and street vending are emerging in Bandra Kurla as if Dharavi is expanding in that direction. In reality, Bandra Kurla and Dharavi are in conflict, but exist side by side, complementing each other.

Under formal (abstract) notions of "progress," even when people improve their living conditions, the environments they produce may not be accepted by authorities and planners. Although people moved to Colombo for work, following colonial dreams, the authorities were discontent with the environments the migrants created, which the authorities saw as overcrowded and pathological. Similarly, tsunami survivors continued their life journeys but did not follow the plans of the government or the NGOs. This mismatch hardly represents any poverty of the people; it discloses the poverty of formal urban spatial discourses and analytical frameworks: our inability to read and understand. More likely, spaces like Dharavi are an integral part, or a product, of urbanization caused by linear thinking that privileges spaces of capital such as Bandra Kurla and Pudong.

Although abstract space depends on its occupation, none of the authorities who created the abstract spaces discussed in this volume asked for the consent of their intended subjects. While public participation was practiced in places like Hambantota District, the effort was to get people involved in the planning and development processes, not to understand them as real people, selves with agency. Hegemony, a necessary condition for the "success" of abstract spaces, is missing from its practice. In this, while bodies were distributed in space, they were hardly transformed into subjects.

Per authorities' and professionals' views, people's reactions to formal space are caused by the "lack of knowledge" among them where professional knowledge is expected to be applied. As Chatterjee (2007: np) argues, "It is only by recognizing [the] norm at the local level that the larger structure will survive." Yet the professionals fail to view that their own lack causes this gap. Academics, for the most part, hardly see this issue. They overlook a great learning opportunity: Instead of turning the critical lens on themselves, they are quick to educate people to the "professional" way of doing things. Most planning workshops and public hearings are directed at educating the people rather than learning *from* them. When plans and policies face obstructions, most of the time in regard to the planned entitlements for the powerless, planners and policy makers are quick to think that the issue is with the plan or the policy (Verma 2002). Instead of fulfilling those entitlements, the professionals are quick to create new plans and policies. Instead of developing knowledge from the ground, professionals and academics look to transform the ground according to their views (Perera 2005).

Authorities also attempt soft efforts and compromises. As Michel Foucault (1980) demonstrates in regard to governmentality, large governance structures depend on the infusion of formal norms into the day-to-day culture. Projects, especially large ones, depend on a host of informal practices and improvisations that can never be codified and are "parasitic on informal processes that, alone, they could not create or maintain" (Scott 1998: 6). Businesses based on today's information technology, too, depend on the various informal mechanisms to expand their markets (see Neuwirth 2005). The informal mechanisms are thus essential for the functioning of formal social structures, systems, and processes.

The dependence of the formal on the informal is extensive. The whole building permit system in Gangtok is informal; even the local state depends on it (Chapter 9). The reliance on the informal is hardly unique to Gangtok or to the building permit process. In South Asian cities, the middle classes rely on cheap taxi services and food. The service is cheap because the drivers live in low-standard housing, and women provide cheap domestic services. Without such services, only a few middle- or upper-class people could afford the lifestyles they enjoy.

Informal mechanisms are neither limited to the poor, nor to the "global south." As well documented by Eugenie Birch (2005), even in the legalistic USA, planning incorporates both formal mechanisms such as regulations, public hearings, mandated checklists, and informal mechanisms such as lobbying, advocacy reports, and recourse to the media. Without these, the formal system of planning is bound to fail.

Formal processes not only depend on informal processes but also enable the latter. These are inseparable in Gangtok, Galle, Colombo, and Tashkent. Formal–informal is, therefore, a false opposition. They are interlinked; they compete, interact, complement, overlap, and coexist.

In short, abstract spaces are incomplete and have cracks, gaps, fissures, and fuzzy margins. They do not stand alone but depend on the subjects' compliant occupation for success. This is paradoxical as creators' intentions for the spaces have to fail for the (compliant) occupation to succeed. It causes an endemic incongruence between how abstract spaces are conceived and occupied, an incongruence authorities are unable to resolve. Abstract spaces continually fail, but they depend on lived spaces and informal practices for survival and their logic is a science of muddling through (see Lindblom 1959). The "success" and "dominance" of abstract spaces are more discursive than "material."

People's Negotiation of Provided and/or Imposed Spaces

Resisting, Coping, Contesting

The crisis of abstract spaces is much deeper when observed from subjects' vantage points. Almost no one totally accepts provided and/or imposed spaces and subjectivities. The immediate reaction to the imposition of subjectivities and space is resistance, trying to keep it at bay. An immediate reaction in Galle was to protest against the designation of Galle Fort as a World Heritage site. In Dharavi the Slum Federation first opted to resist the idea of redevelopment. Once the project begins, and the power balance favors the authority, the first reaction of inhabitants is to cope with imposed subjectivities, conditions, and spaces. In Tashkent, Galle, and Jaffna, the subjects hardly had another choice at the beginning. Thus, they coped with the predicament.

Coping, too, transforms abstract spaces. In coping with the stagnant housing stock in Tashkent, the youth and the owners of apartments transformed kitchens into bedrooms and loggias into kitchens. In so doing, they transformed apartments, neighborhoods, and the city, laying conditions for a new housing market, and resorting to traditional methods (also modernized in the process).

In this way, the subjects also address the same gap (i.e., the incongruence between abstract and lived spaces). They do so from their side, using their own perspectives, tools, and tactics, with the intention of improving the quality of their lives. While, for authorities and creators, the mismatch is created by the subjects, for subjects, it is between the daily activities and cultural practices they need and wish to perform and the constraints imposed by available spaces. This is precisely what the youth in Tashkent, the inhabitants of Galle, and the people in Jaffna try to resolve from their side. Observing this negotiation of space requires the use of appropriate focus, framework, and vantage point.

As evident in late nineteenth-century Colombo, becoming a subject itself opens up room to create or negotiate abstract space. People hardly ever stop their reaction to abstract spaces at the level of accepting subjectivity, even if that was their initial objective.

The endemic gap and conflict between abstract and lived spaces is accentuated when the same physical space is endowed with different meanings, particularly by the authorities/providers and subjects/recipients. In a setting of multiple meanings, the power—whether the government in Gangtok or an NGO in a post-tsunami area—attempts to impose its own meaning over others. As brilliantly demonstrated by Yeoh (1996), subjects of colonial Singapore contested the meanings from public arcades and private dwellings to municipal practices. In late nineteenth-century Ceylon, when the colonial authorities drove a railway line to Jaffna, establishing Colombo's authority over northern Ceylon, northerners rode (back) to Colombo and created a Tamil migrant neighborhood in Wellawatta (Perera 1998).

Possible negotiations depend on the power balance. It is hard to gain much through protests if powerful actors possess the power to implement the projects and are determined to carry out. People usually avoid the heavy hand of the authorities and find ways to resist without being too overt. Most studies of history and politics focus on the privileged minority of leaders and their wars. This type of thinking implies that the weaker social agents are a political nullity unless organized and led by outsiders, particularly the middle class (see Scott 1985). Even peasant rebellions, let alone revolutions, writes Scott (1985), are few and far between. Even when a revolution happens, its outcomes are mixed, diverse, and uneven. The outcomes of revolutions are also negotiated after the event.

The ordinary people featured in the studies prefer to let the powerful interventions continue and then nibble into the structures those interventions impose. Once a project is implemented, as in Galle, the subjects hardly try to totally eradicate or replace the project, but try instead to make it work for them within their own worldviews and accepted constraints. In Galle, as the residents try to make a profit at their individual scale, the fort is turning into a tourist environment from which people can benefit. In this sense, after authorities' interventions, the "products" of people's processes include some components and aspects of the "official plan." The interventions are displaced, familiarized, and incorporated into people's spaces. People's spaces are thus in dialogue with impositions, interventions, and constraints. The conception of people's spaces somewhat relies on the past, nostalgia, outside impositions, and familiar spaces, but it is largely directed at building a present with some sense of future.

Familiarizing and Negotiating

For people, familiarizing space is key to living. In addition to holding different meanings of space, people find different ways to practice those meanings, bringing their spatial conceptions into conflict with those of the authorities and/or providers. People, in the words of Goh Beng-Lan (2002: 202), "always struggle within their own immediate contexts of constraints and opportunities to produce a meaningful life with their own particular values and goals." They provincialize and transform select material and ideas that come their way into something familiar and useful for them within their immediate context and constraints (Appadurai 1996; Goh 2002; Perera 2009; Vidyarthi 2015).

As evident in the chapters, people are hardly passive recipients of external initiatives. According to Hamdi (2004: xxiv), people want to achieve their purposes, however small or local, and make gains in novel and transformative ways. When spaces and plans disrupt their lives, people hardly stop at the point of simply coping or even resisting the impositions. First they see gaps, cracks, and interstices in abstract spaces, and opportunities for changing their circumstances. They widen these openings and negotiate spaces for their needs and aspirations, both accommodating and contesting the larger system, in a context of constraints and opportunities. There is always the possibility of using state power, as evident in Galle and Gangtok; then, the result is a compromise. Yet nothing can completely prevent ordinary people from transforming abstract (and absolute) space into livable space or carving out the latter from the former.

The subjects see various ways to interpret external impositions and pressures, in terms of strengths and weaknesses of the authorities and their own capacities, and ways in which to expand their areas of social and spatial control. As the studies highlight, people displace, reshape, provincialize, and recontextualize hegemonic spatial narratives, thus constructing the best possible livelihood for themselves. In Galle Fort, people develop their own tourist environment: This follows the government's intention, but not its intended result. The way the inhabitants of Gangtok and Galle Fort build through the ordered abstract spaces, government rules, and the World Heritage designation well illustrates how people make use of potential gaps and opportunities.

In familiarizing space, among other adjustments, the subjects both adapt themselves to extant and assigned subject positions and spaces and adjust space to accommodate their daily activities and cultural practices. The possible amount of adjustment that can be made without causing confrontations, or the room for maneuvering, depends on the power relations and the creativity and ability of the community and/or individuals. The people we studied transformed apartments, neighborhoods, cities, and regions. As they familiarize space, they also adapt their daily activities and cultural practices within the context they produce. As they could not afford traditional houses, some inhabitants of Tashkent conducted their traditional activities in the dining space. Yet others bought *hovlis*, constructing a redefined "traditional" life in a redefined "traditional" *mahalla*.

The subject formation is a threshold. Being a subject opens up the possibility for a person to intervene into the social and spatial structure and grants more room for maneuvering. In Kalametiya, the government, aid agencies, and the NGOs used their imaginations to help tsunami victims recover from the disaster. Making use of this aid, the survivors drove their lives in directions of their choice, but within constraints. The NGOs and individuals provided the necessities such as houses. People used these as raw materials for the construction of their own lives. They accepted the houses with thanks, but transformed these by adding kitchens, changing toilet doors, incorporating verandahs into living rooms, and building extensions. Such familiarization not only limits the intrusion of formal and/or external norms into subjects' lives and territories, but also enables the subjects to develop more room for their activities. While the providers of these spaces expect the subject to change, the latter have a way of familiarizing imposed and provided spaces.

Familiarization is driven more by immediate needs, concerns, aspirations, and passions, and less by larger goals, in a formal sense. The youth in Tashkent simply wanted a place to live, the Kalametiyans wanted a place to cook, and the people in Jaffna wanted to survive. They do not see the huge housing issue that politicians and professionals see by means of abstracting the existing conditions within their frameworks and experiences. People operate at local and individual scales, but their actions impact larger scales of space.

Their actions are also short term with some larger idea. People do not see the significance of plans unless they are convinced. Unlike well-thought-out long-term programs of professionals, ordinary people use immediate strategies, causing and building upon their incremental effects, and employ more discreet tactics than the overt use of power. The weaker subjects begin to produce their spaces in the cracks and the margins of what we see as the formal society by developing protective enclaves and interstices, as in the case of women in Colombo (Chapter 2), in the form of ephemeral and kinetic spaces. This was precisely the process of building kitchens by tsunami survivors, the owner-builders of Gangtok, and the person who began his jackfruit business at Moratumulla Handiya.

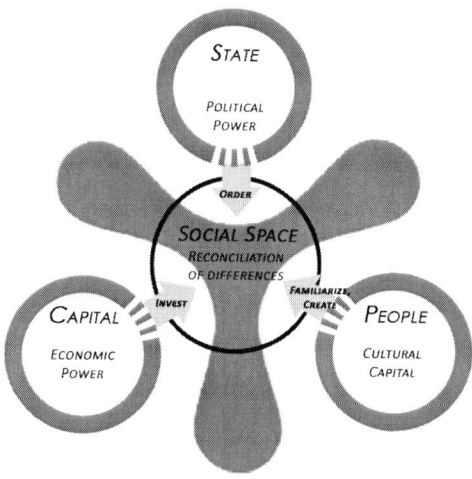

FIGURE 11.2 Production of Social Space (Schematic) (credit: Nirmani Liyanage).

Lived spaces are developed out of local experiences, current circumstances, and outside influences and are constituted by various interplays between social and physical realities and imaginations (Figure 11.2). People's imaginations are not fantasies (Appadurai 1996; Vidyarthi 2015). They employ their own cultures and worldviews as interpretive lenses to relate to their environments; they view spaces from their own backgrounds, including community, history, and memory (Umemoto 2005). The quality and character of cultural practices and the social spaces these entail are developed within people's own worldviews, which provide them with a picture of the way things are and a concept of nature, self, time, and society (Geertz 1973).

In Kalametiya, Gangtok, and Daanchi, the subjects pursued their desires to be global, modern, and/or normal, but within their own perceptions. They perceived the influences and conceived their own modernities, globalities, and normalities in relation to both external "demands" and the potential and constraints in their immediate social and spatial environments. In Prakash's (2010: 2) words: "Urban dwellers experience their globally situated and connected urban space as decidedly local life-worlds, thick with specific experiences, practices, imaginations, and memories." Sundar Poudel's wife pressed her husband to build a "modern house" to make sure their daughter could marry an urban boy. Seeing familiarizations such as these in Galle Fort, Tashkent, and Gangtok requires paying attention to infrapolitics—small-scale informal politics of space.

In infrapolitics, subjects' reactions are not clearly evident to the dominant. In Dharavi the dominant can neither read the environment, nor the spatial processes. The illusive consent, apparent in all above cases, "provides a convenient cover for subordinate groups to create a space for resistance and the development of alternative world views" (Scott in Holtzman and Hughes 2010: np). As Scott (1985: 26) asserts, those with power are not in total control of the stage:

> They may write the basic script for the play but, within its confines, truculent or disaffected actors find sufficient room for maneuver to suggest subtly their disdain for the proceedings. The necessary lines may be spoken, the gesture made, but it is clear that many of the actors are just going through the motions and do not have their hearts in the performance.... [They convey] the impression of compliance without substance.

We see the same in all the cases in this volume. Infrapolitics of space exposes us to a different aspect of the conflict between abstract and lived spaces, the creators and imposers of space, and their occupants and users. In the process of accommodation and familiarization, the subjects question, resist, displace, provincialize, recontextualize, and reshape hegemonic spaces and spatial practices, and also build new ones off these. The subjects in Galle, Colombo, and Gangtok opted to subvert the designs of their authorities under the guise of conforming to them.

This type of "resistance" is different than direct confrontations such as anti-colonial or proletariat struggles, which are organized to overthrow a regime in power. Ashish Nandy's (1994: 113) observation in regard to India is most telling in this regard:

> Aztec priests after their last act of courage die and leave the stage free for those who kill them and sing their praise; the unheroic Indian response ensures that part of the stage always remains occupied by the "cowardly" and the "compromising" who may at some opportune moment assert their presence.

Small struggles are not dramatic, certainly not for the mainstream media, professional, and scholar. Nor is the study of these lucrative. These processes of space-making are confined to the backstages of (formal) social life. The Galle Heritage Foundation and the Green Movement have little knowledge of how "their subjects" transform the houses and the environment they provided. They view some of the practices as illegitimate, but not important enough to intervene. Together these undramatic acts practiced behind the backs of the authorities form the hidden transcript of these ordinary people.

Lived spaces—and their hidden transcripts—which grow through resistance, contestation, familiarization, and the simple creation of space are themselves an achievement of people's processes. They affect the overall structures—including abstract spaces—in varying scales. In Gangtok, people build the city. In Mayfair Mei-Hui Yang's (2004) examination of the rise of sacred spaces in Chinese cities, an interviewee in Wenzhou highlights that it is best for common people not to speak too much lest they lose out. As evident, Dharavi's protection lies in its illegibility (Chapter 7). Although these commonplace forms of resistance do not overthrow governments, they chip away at the structures and policies and pave the way for larger struggles. Scott (1985: xvi) details this:

In place of land invasion, they prefer piecemeal squatting; in place of mutiny, they prefer desertion; in place of attacks on public or private grain stores, they prefer pilfering. When such stratagems are abandoned in favor of more quixotic action, it is usually a sign of great desperation.

The mismatch between abstract and lived spaces is far greater than the gap between transcripts. It highlights a crucial conceptual failure: Abstract spaces target bodies, but the reaction comes from selves. Built upon abstracted information such as statistics, maps, land uses, and populations, the authorities and providers of space distribute and organize bodies in space. The product is a well-defined object, physical space, over which the creators and the authorities have clear power. As evident in women crossing the colonial divides, it is not bodies, but the selves with agency, that react to extant controls and the environment.

Hence, people's (re)actions—including occupation—do not fall within the logic of abstract space; people neither use Enlightenment-based rationality, nor mathematical relationships, or body types. From a people's standpoint, the gap between abstract and lived spaces is caused by the differences in worldviews, thinking processes, and approaches. These differences make the responses to abstract space and the creation of lived spaces incalculable and unmappable within the rationality of abstract space.

People have a power and rationality that power and formal knowledge cannot read. As evident in Dharavi, it is impossible even for activist Sheela Patel to bridge this gap. Although knowing the "exact" number of residents and dwellings in Dharavi—as she wishes—may help the resistance, a proper count is inadequate to dispense social justice. As evident in Dharavi and Galle, selves defy their identification as bodies and their objectification through classification. This is a crucial basis of the production of lived spaces and their difference with abstract spaces.

Although the authorities may establish some control over bodies, it is impossible to maintain a spatial order that depends on organizing bodies in space. The subjects with less power usually do not fully subvert imposed identities and spaces, but, as evident in Colombo and Galle, they provincialize and displace, to construct their identities in the room they so create or negotiate.

As authorities do not seek the consent of the subjects, the latter, too, react to authorities' actions off the government's "radar." People, too, check how far they can enhance their living conditions by pushing the boundaries. Even the 60 families who volunteered their houses to Galle Heritage Foundation, allowing the construction of the sought-after image of World Heritage, also wanted the organization to improve their houses.

Bypassing and Subverting

Going beyond negotiating abstract space, people also bypass the regulations when the gatekeepers are asleep or are too busy to notice. The residents of Galle surreptitiously built at night, avoiding the eyes of the security and their neighbors. Rather than following organized plans of action, as authorities and planners do, people used tactics such as anticipation and timing (see de Certeau 1984; Simone 2010). Place-making tactics remain ad hoc, disjointed, and with limited linkages to other practices (Kamel 2014). In the present-day environment, which is largely com-modified and managed by state agencies and capital, people's spaces are influenced by and influence the spaces of power and capital. Regardless of the presence of state agencies and laws, most cities and urban neighborhoods in the global south are produced the same way as Gangtok.

The transformative capacity of the subjects is key to the production of lived spaces. Here, I refer to subjects' capacity to transform what is given and found to something useful in addressing their needs and aspirations. As evident in indigeniz-ing and feminizing Colombo, marginality is an enormous source of creative energy (see Ashcroft *et al.*, 2002).

Imagination and creativity are central to the subjects' ability to go beyond the imposed conditions and futures. Patsy Healey (1997: 270) sees the capacity of ordinary people to recognize cracks and interstices in the social structure, oppor-tunities for "doing things differently," and "to widen a crack into a potential for change." The values, intentions, and purposes that condition the actions, symbols, norms, and ideological forms people create constitute the indispensable background to this exercising of agency (see Yeoh, 1996; Perera, 1998; Kusno, 2000; Hosagra-har, 2005; Allen 2012).

The success of such negotiations hinges on the subjects' capacity to observe, time, and transform extant subjectivities and spaces. People in this volume hardly pushed at the authorities at the latters' strongest place and time; instead they used weaker places—cracks and margins—to penetrate the structure. This is precisely how they build in Gangtok through the state's system but from outside of it.

In this, the informal relies on the formal and feeds on it. The small space-making processes of small people are not separate from stronger power structures and pro-cesses; yet, small space-making is not structurally determined by the power struc-tures. To think the opposite is to privilege and reproduce the power centers. People do not see abstract spaces as total systems. Instead of trying to defeat formal systems and abstract spaces, all actors in this volume have fed off of their energy and used aspects of these as resources.

As the powerful institutions use temporary and informal buildings, or kinetic elements (Mehrotra 2008), ordinary people also use high-end formal environments for various functions. The mall, which evolved with expanding consumerism in the West, has been imported to almost every country. Sasanka Perera (2005) observes that air-conditioned malls in Colombo are used by the youth and lower-income populations as: (1) a respite from the tropical heat, sun, and shelter from rain; (2) toilets in a city with almost no public toilets; (3) a meeting place to sit, listen to music, and exchange ideas, particularly by younger people and lovers; (4) a space to consume images from what is displayed and from other mall-walkers; and (5) a place in which to be seen by others and to exhibit current fashions.

As evident, the processes of reacting to abstract space bring about long-term large-scale changes as well. In nineteenth-century Colombo, as discussed, the indigenizing process subverted the structure of the colonial city. It brought a power institution to the side of the Black City. Although unintended, such mega impacts are not limited to nineteenth-century Colombo. Through daily building, the citizens of Gangtok are also shaping the city which the authorities represent through a few formal spaces like the town hall and the market.

In short, it is ignorant to define social space only around what the authorities and capital create. People do not live or carry out their activities in abstract spaces; it is impossible. Almost all subjects negotiate space for their daily activities and cultural practices, thus creating lived spaces. The subjects are affected by the context of constraints imposed by absolute and abstract spaces, but their responses range from accepting subjectivity to radically transforming extant and provided spaces. The subjects appropriate formal spaces like malls and build cities like Gangtok. In so doing, they use abstract spaces, traditions, and vernacular practices as raw materials and social capital.

Lefebvre (1991: 54) stresses that a "revolution that does not produce new space has not realized its full potential." Boggs and Kurashige (2012) and Gustavo Esteva (2005) stress that revolutions are ongoing and we need to recognize them. Small space-making efforts of small people add up to huge transformations that far surpass any production of formal spaces. Some spatial processes, as in nineteenth-century Colombo and Gangtok, continue to subvert the formal spatial structures.

Creating and Protecting Their Own Spaces

At the other end of the spectrum are Dharavi (India), Daanchi (Nepal), and *handiya* (Sri Lanka), which expose us to a totally different process and structure in which people create lived spaces and the authorities try to find accommodation (Chapters 7, 8, and 10). In slightly different Gangtok, people try to build the way they did before regulations, and the state tries to find accommodation (Chapter 9). A large proportion of lived spaces, such as self-established settlements, owner-built spaces, and *handiya*s, is more directly produced by the inhabitants with very little inter-vention from outside.[1] It is the authorities who intervene in these to infuse their order.

People created Gangtok long before the state introduced building regulations. After regulations were introduced, people tried to find accommodation within these for their building processes. Yet, from another perspective, people continue to build the way they did and the state is trying to get the people to accommodate its system, As people find ways to overcome impediments posed by state regulations, the local government is trying to incorporate the building process that falls outside of the regulatory system by applying exceptions such as allowing the formalization of buildings after they are built and charging a nominal fine for violations.

Self-builders and those who adapt housing—as in Tashkent and Galle—create most housing, thus producing and reproducing the urban. In Dharavi, the inhabit-ants have created an efficient proportion of land uses (from an urban planning perspective), an employment base, and a huge industrial and recycling complex that subsidizes middle-class living. While all self-built settlements do not have such high performance standards as Dharavi, many such as the Smokey Mountains in Manila do. While the people's spaces in Tashkent and Galle were made in response to authorities, Dharavi was built by people. Despite the privileging of the central business districts, used by a few, housing is the core of urbanization, and the low-income groups create the majority. Ordinary people are the biggest builders (Neuwirth 2005); they create urbanism and urbanity, especially for the majority of citizens (see Prakash 2010a).

Handiya is a people's space par excellence. When used as the threshold to look out from, the whole spatial structure in Sri Lanka is very different to what the mainstream projects. *Handiya* is the organizer of local space, the network that provides the spatial structure for urban and rural areas across Sri Lanka. These are created by the inhabitants, not by any power agency, with very little friction from power institutions and related subjectivities.

Like Dharavi, *handiya* finds its protection from the authorities and powerful actors in its illegibility. Neither *handiya*s nor the self-established settlements have been reconceptualized or incorporated by professionals or academics into mainstream thinking.[2] This is precisely why the authorities are unable to read *handiya*s and self-established settlements like Dharavi. This is further evident in the failure of attempts to replicate *handiya*s in places like Radampola.

The lack of understanding of people's spaces and processes is due to the intellectual poverty of mainstream scholarship caused largely by the statist and Western-scientific (or natural science) orientation of research. Dharavi fulfills most planning norms, but it is illegible to authorities, planners, and scholars. Sri Lanka's social space at all scales is organized around *handiya*s, but there is not a single academic paper on this. It is easy even for the advocates of people's spaces to get lost: The engagement with the state and power—although from oppositional standpoints—makes them follow the paths drawn by these power agencies. Most of the time, the people's production of space has very little to do with the abstract spaces of the authorities and professionals or the low-end highlighted in scholarly work (see Perera and Tang 2013). Scholars see abstract spaces as dominant mainly because we see space from the statist and scientific vantage points and conceptual frameworks. The privileged position these outside-in perspective hold within this discourse, i.e., above-ground conditions, is due to what Said (2004) calls the positional superiority.

Dharavi, Gangtok, and Moratumulla Handiya demonstrate the people's production of space for themselves, from their own standpoints, using available resources, within extant contexts, constraints, and potentialities. *Handiya*s have a strong sense of place, belonging, and ownership. As soon as new spatial changes are introduced from outside, whether three-wheel taxi parks or chain grocery stores, the *handiya*-based structures localize these. In fact, people familiarize the strange, employing structures, processes, and activities based on the *handiya*, self-built settlements, and similar structures. In this process, *handiya* also gets "modernized." Yet the change is gradual (and local): It neither displaces inhabitants as in gentrification nor disrupts the identity and sense of place.

People's Spaces

People's spaces and spatial processes are diverse; they operate in myriad ways across various cultural contexts in which different attitudes toward space are expressed and practiced by the subjects. Spaces that people produce are like parallel life-worlds. No real (absolute) city, neighborhood, village, or space can be grasped in its totality by any single person, certainly not within mainstream, abstract knowledge systems. Well evident in the above chapters, migrants, women, Buddhists, Muslims, youth, owner-builders, and disaster victims see and know the same (physical) neighborhood in different ways. They perceive extant space, conceive new possibilities, and then transform space to accommodate and enhance their daily activities and cultural practices in their own ways within the extant context.

The processes through which spaces change and acquire new meanings are neither linear, nor mathematical, or Western-scientific, but social. People do not use pure categories and opposites to conceive space either, nor do they produce third spaces that depend on dualities. The negotiations progress like "event cascades": "action sequences which gather momentum, reverse course, change direction, stall, and resume anew" (see Roseneau 1990). As illustrated in the above studies, various spatial histories and streams of thought cross each other's paths and influence each other at different points, generating new streams of perceptions, conceptions, and practices.

These processes highlight the incongruence between society and space. Although connected, the transformation of society and space is neither isotemporal, nor isomorphic. Although the spatial transformations in colonial Colombo took place in the 1860s–1880s, the pivotal political turning point was the 1848 rebellion. Transformation of space is a process through which the changes in society and space affect and influence each other.

The changing points of spatial transformations are not clean, and the spaces so produced are transtemporal and translocal. Space cannot be purely defined within a compartmentalized time zone, but the time of the place is made up of a combination of contemporary, residual, and emergent spaces. Galle Fort is Dutch, British, Muslim, Sinhala, colonial, postcolonial, and neoliberal all at the same time. In the spaces we observed, it is important to scrupulously and insistently distinguish between the "oppositional" and the "alternative" (see Raymond Williams 1980 in Spivak 1999).

The changes are not determined by external factors: The external pressures are first conceived by the subjects within their worldviews and actions and then adapted within the potential and constraints in the locale. As Huyssen (2008: 3) highlights: "the city dwellers imagine their own city as the place of everyday life, the site of inspiring traditions and continuities as well as the scene of histories of destruction, crime, and conflicts of all kinds." People of Daanchi transform physical spaces in "traditional" houses by infusing "modern" elements into these, and incorporate "traditional" elements, symbols, and spaces such as *puja* (worship) rooms to fulfill their needs but within their own notions of modernity.

People's spaces are not territorially confined, but connected, influenced by, and influencing to other places across states, cites, and regions. By translocality, Appadurai (1996) refers broadly to the geographical imagination associated with the everyday life experience of migrant workers—such as the Filipinas—who adapt their "original" visions of the home country and cultural practices as part of living in a new place such as Hong Kong. New Kalametiya was built by foreign NGOs with the help of foreign donors and consultants. The recipients of disaster aid used the external aid, ideas, and connections as raw materials to develop their own (trans)locality connected to various places across nations and regions the way these can work for them. In Daanchi and Kalametiya, too, influences come from faraway places, but the inhabitants create their own globality, in turn influencing faraway places.

When people are involved in the negotiation of space, culture acts as a third regulator (or a major factor of influence) besides the state (polity) and the market (economy) (Figure 11.2). People are not always selfish, as economics might suggest, nor are the negotiations one-sided or even bilateral. Once we go beyond the government–people (or civil society) binary, people are influenced by a multitude of factors including history and the neighbors, in addition to capital. Cities are also "densities of stories, passions, hurts, revenge, aspiration, avoidance, deflection, and complicity," asserts Simone (2008: 103).

As evident in the previous chapters, people are more inclined to adhere to social norms than laws because the former are local in nature, fathomable, and are based on the interests of a particular community. Laws are also better followed when they become accepted social norms, or part of the culture. As all studies illustrate, rules are not rigid in most places; most of the time if a particular action does not negatively affect the community, the rules can be negotiated between neighbors or altered with the consent of an elder member of the community. Hence, social norms have a better standing among people. Kamal (in Gangtok) did not find it necessary to follow the sanctioned drawing, but he met his neighbor's request and built the common wall without obstructing the neighbor's window. In this, social concern took care of what justice was supposed to, but law was incapable of doing. Conversely, people tend to see what others have as entitlements, which the law may not support. Where Kamal and Dorji live, the shops directly open to the street. Their buildings disregard the law that requires a deeper setback, but respect customary spatial practices and adhere to the former setback. Evidently, along with the state and the market, culture acts as a primary regulator of society.

Culture is the source of diversity, especially of distinct built environments. The dense and seemingly haphazard environments of Dharavi and Gangtok serve both the material and psychological needs of the people (see Turner and Fichter 1972; Lang 1994). In comparison to formal, designed environments that have often lost their human appeal in the pursuit of abstract spaces and monumentality, environments built piece by piece by individuals and communities are human in scale, feel, and function. The residential communities in Gangtok are lively, dynamic, and animated, and the people who live and work in these environments inject life into these. Such people's spaces have a sense of place and belonging. Even the terraces of the buildings become meeting places where men and women come to bask in the sun, dry clothes, read a book, or play a guitar.

In sum, the state and capital are not the sole producers of space: The creation, definition, adaptation, restructuring, interpretation, and transformation of space are also carried out by the large majority of ordinary individuals, small groups, and community organizations operating at various scales—including neighborhood, urban, and regional scales—and for a multitude of reasons. The failure of the formal system of space (i.e., abstract space, which is a perception of the powerful, the privileged, and the professionals) is complemented, bypassed, and subverted by people. People actively perceive, adopt, occupy, manage, resist, and transform formal spaces and spatial orders of the authorities, regulators, and the elite into tangible, comprehensible, and associable spaces that can support the adapted daily activities and socio-cultural practices of the subjects through individual and small-scale spatial processes. They begin this process in the margins, cracks, and interstices of the formal society, carving lived spaces out of abstract spaces.

Social space is largely defined by this conflict between imposed and/or provided spaces and the spaces people need and desire to carry out their (adapted) daily activities and cultural practices, and the struggle by the providers and subjects to reconcile this difference (Figures 11.1, 11.2). There is never a balance, but a seesaw, constantly tipping to one side or the other, making the disadvantaged party respond and reproduce the seeming balance. Hence the production of social space, or lived space, is never complete, and is thus an ongoing process.

As evident in Dharavi, Gangtok and, especially, *handiya*, people produce most of their spaces with little interference from the authorities and the powerful, below their radar. In these, we see the reversal of the spatial conflict in which space is produced by people, later negotiated by the authorities and dominant actors. This is not new; it is an older and more widespread practice than the production of abstract space. There are many more dimensions to people's spaces, but those remain for study another day. Nonetheless, ordinary people do produce more variety and quantity of spaces than the authorities even when they are subject to abstract spaces. It is important for us to acknowledge, engage, and critique these spaces and spatial processes.

Notes

1 See also Munasignhe's (2013) work on small towns in Sri Lanka.
2 An attempt to address this issue is found in Roy (2004) and Roy and AlSayad (2004).

References

Allen, J.R. (2012) *Taipei: City of displacements*, Seattle and London: University of Washington Press.

Appadurai, A. (1996) *Modernity at Large: Cultural dimensions of globalization*, Minneapolis, MN: University of Minnesota Press.

Ashcroft, B., Griffiths, G., and Tiffin, T. (2002 [1989]) *The Empire Writes Back: Theory and practice in post-colonial literatures*, New York: Routledge.

Bhabha, H.K. (1994) *The Location of Culture*, London and New York: Routledge.

Birch, E. (2005) "U.S. Planning Culture Under Pressure: Major elements endure and flourish in the face of crisis" in B. Sanyal (ed.) *Comparative Planning Cultures*, New York: Routledge, 331–58.

Boggs, G.L. and Kurashige, S. (2012 [2011]) *The Next American Revolution: Sustainable activism for the twenty-first century*, Berkeley, CA: University of California Press.

Chatterjee, P. (2006) *The Politics of the Governed: Reflections on popular politics in most of the world*, New York: Columbia University Press.

Chatterjee, P. (2007) "Towards a Postcolonial Modernity: AsiaSource interview with Partha Chatterjee—2007," *Asia Source: A resource of the Asia Society*. Online. Available: www.asiasource.org/news/special_reports/chatterjee.cfm (accessed January 10, 2015).

de Certeau, M. (1984) *The Practice of Everyday Life*, Trans. S.F. Rendell, Berkeley, CA: University of California Press.

Esteva, G. (2005) "The Revolution of the New Commons." Online. Available: www.inmotionmagazine.com/global/gest_int_4.html (accessed March 3, 2015).

Foucault, M. (1980) *Power/Knowledge: Selected Interviews and Other Writings 1972–1977*, edited by Collin Gordon, New York: Pantheon Books.

Geertz, C. (1973) *The Interpretation of Culture*, New York: Basic Books.

Goh, B.L. (2002) *Modern Dreams: An inquiry into power, cultural production, and the cityscape in contemporary urban Penang, Malaysia*, Ithaca, NY: Cornell University Press.

Hamdi, N. (2004) *Small Change: About the art of practice and the limits of planning in cities*, Sterling, VA: Earthscan.

Healey, P. (1997) *Collaborative Planning: Shaping places in fragmented societies*, Vancouver: UBC Press.

Holtzman, B. and Hughes, C. (2010) "Points of Resistance and Departure: An interview with James C. Scott," *Upping the Anti* 11. Online. Available: http://uppingtheanti.org/journal/article/11-points-of-resistance-and-departure-an-interview-with-james-c.-scott (accessed February 2, 2015).

Hosagrahar, J. (2005) *Indigenous Modernities: Negotiating architecture and urbanism*, London: Routledge.

Huyssen, A. (2008) "Introduction: World cultures, world cities" in A. Huyssen (ed.) *Other Cities, Other Worlds: Urban imagineries in a globalizing age*, Durham, NC: Duke University Press, 1–26.

Kamel, N. (2014) "Learning from the Margin: Placemaking tactics" in V. Mukhija and A. Loukaitou-Sideris (eds.) *The Informal American City: Beyond Taco trucks and day labor*, Cambridge, MA: MIT Press, 119–36.

Kusno, A. (2000) *Behind the Postcolonial: Architecture, urban space and political culture in Indonesia*, London and New York: Routledge.

Lang, J. (1994) *Urban Design: The American experience*, New York: Van Nostrand Reinhold.

Lefebvre, H. (1991 [1974]) *The Production of Space*, trans. D. Nicholson-Smith, Cornwall: Blackwell Publishing.

Lindblom, C.E. (1959) "The Science of "Muddling Through," *Public Administration Review*, 19: 79–88.

Mehrotra, R. (2008) "Negotiating the Static and Kinetic Cities: The emergent urbanism of Mumbai" in A. Huyssen (ed.) *Other Cities, Other Worlds: Urban imagineries in a globalizing age*, Durham, NC: Duke University Press, 205–18.

Munasinghe, J. (2013) "Planning and Self-Organizing: The case of small towns in Sri Lanka" in N. Perera and W.S. Tang (eds.) *The Transforming Asian City: Spatial practices, knowledge, and emergence*, New York: Routledge, 207–21.

Nandy, A. (1994 [1983]) *The Intimate Enemy: Loss and recovery of self under colonialism* (8th edn.), New Delhi: Oxford University Press.

Neuwirth, R. (2005) *Shadow Cities: A billion squatters, a new urban world*, New York: Routledge.

Perera, N. (1998) *Society and Space: Colonialism, nationalism, and postcolonial identity in Sri Lanka*, Boulder, CO: Westview Press.

Perera, N. (2005) "Importing Problems: The impact of a housing ordinance on Colombo," *Arab World Geographer* 8, 1–2: 61–76.

Perera, N. (2009) "People's Spaces: Familiarization, subject formation, and emergent spaces in Colombo," *Planning Theory* 8, 3: 50–74

Perera, N. and Tang, W.S. (2013) *Transforming Asian Cities: Intellectual impasse, Asianizing space, and emerging translocalities*, New York: Routledge.

Perera, S. (2005) *Alternate Space: Trivial writings of an academic*, Colombo: Yellow House Publications.

Prakash, G. (2010) *Mumbai Fables*, Noida: Harper Collins.

Roseneau, J.N. (1990) *Turbulence in World Politics: A theory of change and continuity*, Princeton, NJ: Princeton University Press.

Roy, A. (2004) "Transnational Trespassings: The Geopolitics of Urban Informality" in A. Roy and N. Alsayyad (eds.) *Urban Informality: Transnational Perspectives from the Middle East, Latin America, and South Asia*, Lanham, MD: Lexington Books, 289–317.

Roy, A. (2005) "Urban Informality: Toward an epistemology of planning," *Journal of the American Planning Association* 71, 2: 147–58.

Roy, A. and AlSayad, N. (eds.) (2004) *Urban Informality: Transnational perspectives from the Middle East, Latin America and South Asia*, Lanham, MD and London: Lexington Books.

Said, E.W. (2004 [1978]) *Orientalism*, New York: Vintage Books.

Scott, J.C. (1985) *Weapons of the Weak: Everyday forms of peasant resistance*, New Haven, CT: Yale University Press.

Scott, J.C. (1990) *Domination and the Arts of Resistance: Hidden transcripts*, New Haven, CT: Yale University Press.

Scott, J.C. (1998) *Seeing Like a State: How certain schemes to improve the human condition have failed*, New Haven, CT: Yale University Press.

Simone, A. (2008) "The Last Shall be First" in A. Huyssen (ed.) *Other Cities, Other Worlds: Urban imagineries in a globalizing age*, Durham, NC: Duke University Press, 119.

Simone, A. (2010) *City Life from Jakarta to Dakar: Movements at the crossroads*, New York: Routledge.

Spivak, G.C. (1999) *A Critique of Postcolonial Reason: Toward a history of the vanishing present*, Cambridge, MA: Harvard University Press.

Turner, J.F.C and Fichter, R. (1972) *Freedom to Build: Dweller control of the housing process*, New York: Macmillan.

Umemoto, K. (2005) "Walking in Another's Shoes: Epistemological challenges in participatory planning" in I.B. Stiftel and V. Watson (eds.) *Dialogues in Urban and Regional Planning*, London: Routledge, 180–208.

Verma, G.D. (2002) *Slumming India: A chronicle of slums and their saviours*, New Delhi: Penguin Books.

Vidyarthi, S. (2015) *One Idea, Many Plans: An American city design concept in independent India*, New York and London: Routledge.

Wang, D. (2003) *Street Culture in Chengdu: Public space, urban commoners, and local politics, 1870–1930*, Stanford, CA: Stanford University Press.

Yang, M.M.H. (2004) "Spatial Struggles: Postcolonial complex, state disenchantment, and the popular reappropriation of space in rural Southeast China," *Journal of Asian Studies* 63, 3: 719–55.

Yeoh, B. (1996) *Contesting Space: Power relations and the urban built environment in colonial Singapore*, Kuala Lumpur: Oxford University Press.

INDEX

Page numbers in *italics* denote tables, those in **bold** denote figures.